AF861745

CONFISCATION IN PRIVATE INTERNATIONAL LAW

VRIJE UNIVERSITEIT TE AMSTERDAM

CONFISCATION IN PRIVATE INTERNATIONAL LAW

ACADEMISCH PROEFSCHRIFT

TER VERKRIJGING VAN DE GRAAD VAN DOCTOR IN DE FACULTEIT DER RECHTSGELEERDHEID OP GEZAG VAN DE RECTOR MAGNIFICUS DR. D. NAUTA, HOOGLERAAR IN DE FACULTEIT DER GODGELEERDHEID, IN HET OPENBAAR TE VERDEDIGEN OP VRIJDAG 27 APRIL 1956, DES NAMIDDAGS TE 13.30 UUR, IN HET MINERVAPAVILJOEN, ALBERT HAHNPLANTSOEN 2 TE AMSTERDAM

DOOR

PIETER ADRIAANSE
GEBOREN TE MAASSLUIS

Springer-Science+Business Media, B.V.

ISBN 978-94-011-8240-9 ISBN 978-94-011-8915-6 (eBook)
DOI 10.1007/978-94-011-8915-6

Promotor
PROF. MR P. J. VERDAM

TO MY WIFE

CONTENTS

ABBREVIATIONS

A.C.	Appeal Cases Reports
A.G.	Amtsgericht
A.J.I.L.	American Journal of International Law
All E.R.	All England Law Reports
A.L.R.	American Law Reports
Ann. Dig.	Annual Digest and Reports of Public International Law Cases
Annuaire	Annuaire de l'Institut de Droit International
Belg. Jud.	La Belgique Judiciaire
Brit. Yearb.	British Year Book of International Law
Bruns Z.	Zeitschrift für ausländisches öffentliches Recht und Völkerrecht
Bulletin	Bulletin de l'Institut Juridique International
Cass.	Cour de Cassation
Ch.	Chancery Division Reports
Chicago L.R.	Chicago Law Review
Clunet	Journal de droit international
Cmd.	Command Papers
Col. L.R.	Columbia Law Review
Conf. Int. Law Ass.	Conference International Law Association
D.	Recueil Dalloz de doctrine, de jurisprudence et de législation (hebdomadaire)
Dept. of State Bull.	Department of State Bulletin
D.J.Z.	Deutsche Juristenzeitung
Le Droit Mar. Fr.	Le Droit Maritime Français
Entsch. Rg.	Entscheidungen des Reichsgerichts
Gaz. des Trib.	Gazette des Tribunaux
Gaz. du Palais	Gazette du Palais
Harvard L.J.	Harvard Law Journal
Hudson	M. O. Hudson, Cases and other Materials on International Law (St. Paul, Minn., 1951)

Hudson, International Legislation	M. O. Hudson, International Legislation (1919–1941)
I.C.L.Q.	The International and Comparative Law Quarterly
I.L.Q.	The International Law Quarterly
J.Bl.	Juristische Blätter
J. des Trib.	Journal des Tribunaux
J.W.	Juristische Wochenschrift
K.B.	King's Bench Reports
L.G.	Landesgericht
Ll.L.L.R.	Lloyd's List Law Reports
L.Q.R.	The Law Quarterly Review
L.T.R.	Law Times Reports
Martens, Nouveau Rec.	G. F. de Martens, Nouveau Recueil Général de Traités et autres actes relatifs aux rapports de droit international
Mich.L.R.	Michigan Law Review
Modern L.R.	Modern Law Review
Neth. Int. L.R.	Nederlands Tijdschrift voor Internationaal Recht (Netherlands International Law Review)
N.J.	Nederlandse Jurisprudentie
N.J.B.	Nederlands Juristenblad
N.J.W.	Neue Juristische Wochenschrift
Nouvelle Revue de dr. i. pr.	Nouvelle Revue de droit international privé
Ö.J.Z.	Österreichische Juristen-Zeitung
O.G.H.	Oberster Gerichtshof (Austria)
O.L.G.	Oberlandesgericht
P.	Probate, Divorce and Admiralty Division Reports
Pitt Cobbett	Pitt Cobbett, Cases on International Law (London, I, 1947, II, 1937)
Q.B.	Queens Bench Reports
R.C.D.I.P.	Revue Critique de droit international privé
Rec. des Cours	Recueil des Cours de l'Académie de Droit International (La Haye)
R.M. Themis	Rechtsgeleerd Magazijn Themis

R.O.	Arrêts du Tribunal Fédéral Suisse, Recueil Officiel
Répertoire	Répertoire de droit international, fondé par A. Darras
Revue Darras	Revue de droit international privé (et de droit pénal international)
Revue dr. int.	Revue de droit international
Revue de dr. int. et de dr. c.	Revue de droit international et de droit comparé
Revue de dr. int. et de lég. comp.	Revue de droit international et de législation comparée
Revue int. de dr. comp.	Revue internationale de droit comparée
S.	Recueil général des lois et des arrêts, fondé par J.-B. Sirey
Schweiz. Jahrb. für intern. R.	Schweizerisches Jahrbuch für internationales Recht
Scott, Cases	J. B. Scott, Cases on International Law (St Paul, 1937)
Seidl-Hohenveldern	Ignaz Seidl-Hohenveldern, Internationales Konfiskations- und Enteignungsrecht (Berlin-Tübingen, 1952)
T.L.R.	Times Law Reports
Transactions	Transactions of the Grotius Society
Travaux	Travaux du Comité Français de Droit International Privé
Trib.	Tribunal
Trib. comm.	Tribunal de commerce
W.	Weekblad van het Recht
Yale L.J.	Yale Law Journal
Z.A.I.P.	Zeitschrift für ausländisches und internationales Privatrecht (Rabel's Zeitschrift)
Z. f. intern. R.	Zeitschrift für internationales Recht (Niemeyer's Zeitschrift)
Z.f.O.	Zeitschrift für Ostrecht
Z.f.öff.R.	Zeitschrift für öffentliches Recht
Z.f.Osteur. Recht	Zeitschrift für osteuropäisches Recht

CHAPTER I

THE PROBLEM

I. INTRODUCTION

"*La propriété étant un droit inviolable et sacré, nul ne peut en être privé, si ce n'est lorsque la nécessité publique, légalement constatée, l'exige évidemment, et sous la condition d'une juste et préalable indemnité.*" These classic words from the *Déclaration des droits de l'homme et du citoyen* mark an important stage in the development of the conceptions of the inviolability of private property. Apart from the political and philosophic background of the *Déclaration* and despite the fact that it was preceded by extensive expropriations without compensation in the course of the French revolution [1], it can hardly be denied that the idea thus formulated and subsequently adopted in the French Constitution of 1791, in the *Code Civil* [2] and in the legislation of many countries outside France, has given a directive to the law of expropriation in what is commonly called the Western world. At the same time this idea was crystallized in the Fifth Amendment to the U.S. Constitution: "... nor (shall any person) be deprived of life, liberty or property, without due process of law; nor shall private property be taken for public use, without just compensation." Up to the present time the principle of the inviolability of private property is still acknowledged [3] and defended

---

[1] Cf. Friedman, 14.

[2] *Code civil*, section 545: "*Nul ne peut être contraint de céder sa propriété, si ce n'est pour cause d'utilité publique, et moyennant une juste et préalable indemnité.*" Here and elsewhere public necessity was replaced by public utility.

[3] Unfortunately a glance at the constitutions of various countries is sometimes misleading. The vast majority of constitutions (see, for instance, Mirkine-Guetzevitch, *Les Constitutions Européennes*, Paris, 1951 and for America Russell H. Fitzgibbon, *The Constitutions of the Americas*, Chicago, 1948; also A. J. Peaslee, *Constitutions of Nations*, Concord N.H., 1950) contain a provision equivalent to the passage quoted from the *Déclaration des droits de l'homme et du citoyen*. Still history shows that this in no way means an unconditional application of the principle.

bij many States. Admittedly, the *Déclaration* leaves room for expropriation in case of public necessity which soon changed into expropriation for public utility. Such expropriation, however, was to be invested with proper guarantees for just compensation and due process of law.

However, the twentieth century in particular has seen a development undermining this principle at an ever increasing pace. The gradual extension of what was held to come within the field of public affairs led to an increase in expropriations. The considerable enlargement of the principle of public utility, the undermining of the *equilibrium* between compensation and the goods expropriated and the abandonment of the principle of prompt compensation often tended to transform expropriations for the sake of public utility into a caricature of the *Déclaration des droits de l'homme et du citoyen.*

This determined undermining of the foundations of expropriations for the public good led to a form of expropriation which is synonymous with confiscation.

Obviously this development caused repercussions in many quarters. The economic consequences were often of far-reaching effect, as may be seen from the situation in Russia after the revolution, in Mexico after the oil expropriation and in Iran after recent events. In the legal domain not only domestic but also international issues were raised. In the latter case they were matters of public international law, but besides questions of private international law had to be faced as well. Public international law can boast of a prolific literature [1], but the same cannot be said as regards private international law [2]. In the last few years however private international law has come into the limelight. In 1950 it figured on the programme of the 3rd International Congress of Comparative Law in London [3]; in 1952 it

---

[1] See, for instance, the bibliography, which is by no means exhaustive, in Friedman's recent work, a study otherwise rather superficial and somewhat tendentious.

[2] Apart from various periodical articles we chiefly point to the work of Edward D. Re, *Foreign Confiscations in Anglo-American Law*, New York, 1951, which covers only part of the subject and the study of Ignaz Seidl-Hohenveldern, *Internationales Konfiskations- und Enteignungsrecht*, Berlin-Tübingen, 1952, both excellent monographs.

[3] *Revue Internationale de Droit Comparé* 1950, 530; *Z.A.I.P.* 1951, 535; *Revue Hellénique de Droit International* 1950, 285.

was discussed by the *Institut de Droit International* at Siena [1] and recently, in 1954, it was the principal item of the meeting of the Netherlands Branch of the International Law Association [2].

This study aims at contributing to the not too extensive literature on the subject.

II. BACKGROUND

One cannot consider law and justice without considering at the same time the people whom they concern. And people again cannot be imagined without feelings, political and social views, and economic interests. The law could not exist without such a background. The history of various acts of confiscation in the twentieth century proves the enormous importance of the background underlying these problems. Russian confiscations are only becoming intelligible in the light of the Bolshevist doctrine of revolution; the *Mexicanization* of the oil industry is in keeping with Mexican social development preceding it; the confiscations which took place in Germany under the Nazi regime must be understood as the outcome of a certain ideology; unfortunately confiscations due to operations in time of war are self-explanatory. A single school of thought governs each one alike: rights of individuals are considered of less and less importance. It was not by chance that the infringement of private property, notably in the great political upheavals, often went hand in hand with a declining interest in the protection of the individual freedom. Where the state infringes the proprietary rights of individuals, it will even more readily do the same as regards personal freedom. One might explain this by saying that this is a conflict between collectivism and individualism but these mere terms are far from exhaustive connotation. Firmly established traditions have broken adrift and changed ideas about the relationship between the state and individual freedom are gaining ground. No one knows exactly where all this will lead us. In this respect the phrase "iron curtain" has some significance which however may

[1] *Annuaire de l' Institut de Droit International* 1950 (Bath) I, 42 (report of A. De La Pradelle) and 1952 (Siena) II, 251.

[2] *Mededelingen van de Nederlandse Vereniging voor Internationaal Recht* 1954, 1 (Reports of Mr L. Erades and Mr K. Jansma; these reports of the Netherlands Branch of the International Law Association are only available in the Dutch language).

be less pregnant than might be believed at first sight. Even on the Western side of the curtain there is a tendency pointing towards expropriation without adequate compensation. It speaks volumes that at the meeting of the *Institut de Droit International* at Siena no resolution could be reached [1]. It is equally significant that the Universal Declaration of Human Rights has weakened the strict wording of the *Déclaration des droits de l'homme et du citoyen* to: "No one shall be arbitrarily deprived of his property" (section 17) [2]; that also the Protocol of Paris (20-3-1952) [3] to the Convention for the protection of human rights and fundamental freedoms (Rome, 4–11-1950) [4] did not get any further than: "No one shall be deprived of his possessions except in the public interest and subject to the conditions provided for by law and by the general principles of international law" (section 1). Despite the fact that the jurisprudence of private international law shows a certain unanimity, one can hardly dismiss the thought that opinions on confiscation are afloat and that we may well be drifting into currents which will become a testing ground of strength. A study of confiscation in private international law can do little more than give a critical historical survey mainly confined to the 20th century and particularly to the present day situation. It is hard to make any forecast about future developments. A discussion of the *ius constituendum* becomes likewise a precarious matter, the more so since taking a definite standpoint involves the risk of being denounced either as a collectivist or an individualist. Our time does not tend any more towards the acceptance of a well-balanced relationship between individual freedom and state authority and readily affixes labels. Moreover, a study like the present becomes so easily the subject matter of politics. We have endeavoured to avoid this and have tried to confine ourselves to the legal aspects.

In this chapter the nature of our subject is indicated, the outlines are drawn, some directions are given as to our arguments and further some observations are made regarding important confiscatory acts. The next chapter will attempt to elucidate some general points. Thus we shall examine whether recognition

[1] *Annuaire* 1952 (Siena) II, 322.
[2] *Cmd.* 7662; text also to be found, e.g., in Drost's work, 258.
[3] *Cmd.* 9221; cf. *Brit. Yearb.* 1951, 360.
[4] *Cmd.* 8969; *A.J.I.L.* 1951, Suppl. 24.

of the confiscating state or government should be decisive in determining the legality of the confiscatory measure. The role of jurisdictional immunity often invoked by states and governments will also be examined. These doctrines will often be conclusive as such, and no considerations will be given to the merits of each case. Chapter II will further contain some observations on *situs* problems since our study will show the importance of the *situs* of goods confiscated or to be confiscated. Chapter III and IV will examine a number of cases which could be termed territorial and extra-territorial confiscations. In a concluding Chapter V the *rationes decidendi* will be considered, different points of view will be examined and we shall put forward our own views.

III. NATURE OF CONFISCATION

History shows that confiscation [1] preceded expropriation with compensation for public utility. Nevertheless it is not difficult to understand what is meant by confiscation by proceeding from the notion of expropriation for public utility. The wording of the *Déclaration des droits de l'homme et du citoyen* which has served many a constitution as a model comes to our aid. Expropriation for public utility, an idea typically pertaining to public law, includes various elements.

The term expropriation indicates any deprivation of property. In connection with public utility it gradually has gained a specific meaning and is now ordinarily used to indicate expropriation by public authorities and for public utility, to which the principle of adequate compensation is attached [2]. The term expropriation refers to expropriation for public utility with compensation and not to confiscation, although the latter is also a sort of expropriation.

Another feature of expropriation is the necessity of government action. [3]. If not authorized by or on behalf of a government, any seizure would amount to robbery or theft, in stead of expropria-

---

[1] For a summary see C. J. Friedrich, *Confiscation*, in Encyclopaedia of the Social Sciences IV, 183.

[2] Some authors as e.g. Friedman, use the terms expropriation and confiscation indiscriminately, which sometimes leads to confusions; others as e.g. Seidl-Hohenveldern and Wolff, (*Private International Law*, 534) distinguish between the two.

[3] Cf. Re, 141.

tion for public utility. The question whether a certain body should be credited with governmental character often depends in large measure on its recognition. This matter will be considered later [1].

The action of the government must further be "for public utility". This phrase is to be found in nearly all regulations of the law of expropriation. Indeed it is a rather vague and elastic one, its tenor to a considerable extent being determined by the expropriating government. However, with Parliament exercising a decisive influence abuse is not very likely to occur.

A last element is the compensation which not only must be just (i.e. complete or full), but also granted or at least secured before the expropriation has taken place. Regarding this a great unanimity reigned during the first decades of this century, but certain symptoms tended and are tending to show that here, too, views are changing.

If the above elements are considered essential to expropriation, it is evident that any deviation will bring about something different from expropriation for public utility. Thus, for instance, a seizure not executed by or on behalf of the government amounts to forced exchange, theft or robbery; if the element of public utility happens to be lacking, a *détournement de pouvoir* with a discriminating effect may present itself.

Now, similarly confiscation begins where compensation becomes uncertain. Confiscation may be regarded as an overstepping of the boundaries set for expropriation, as the collapse of its strongest foundations. Therefore expropriation without compensation is called confiscation, regardless of the fact whether or not the requirement of public utility is met [2]. Whereas the term confiscation indeed presumes an action by the government, it is deemed immaterial whether public utility is involved.

The question may be raised whether one can still speak of confiscation where compensation granted is inadequate. And where, in such a case, must the line be drawn? If compensation is utterly disproportionate to the real value, it is safe to speak of confiscation; this, for instance, was commonly done in the so-

---

[1] *Infra*, 27 ff.
[2] Cf. Re, 141.

called Hungarian Optants case [1]. But can we speak of expropriation if compensation does not correspond to the total value of the property, but only amounts to half of it? Or can we speak of expropriation if no payment is made at once, but extends over a number of years, or is made in securities hardly or not at all convertible? And what about the problem of value itself? The dispute as regards subjective and objective values will never be settled. It is difficult to give satisfactory answers to all these questions. Still it is of importance to include in our study not only cases of pure confiscations, but also cases of expropriations in which compensation has been tampered with. This fits in with common parlance, which in general is inclined to regard expropriation with a confiscatory tendency as confiscation. Hence this study will not only deal with definite confiscations, as e.g. those executed in Soviet Russia after the revolution, but also with some debatable confiscations, as e.g. the Mexicanization of the oil industry in Mexico.

Confiscations may occur in various forms and will often be hidden by a subtle veil. They may take place as isolated cases, though, as practice shows, various examples prove that confiscation may manifest itself as part of a more comprehensive action. This was, for instance, the case with respect to the liquidation of the congregations in France [2], which contained a confiscatory element; the like may occur in cases of nationalization [3]. It *may* occur, because nationalization, unlike expropriation, is in itself a neutral term; as often as not it may be accompanied by compensation. Only the latter form is included in our observations, in view of the confiscatory element.

Nationalization means that a business becomes state-owned property; it becomes a "nation affair". This is, as practice shows, more than mere confiscation, for in nationalization as a rule different phases can be distinghuished, although they often coin-

[1] See for some literature on the subject Friedman, 81; literature is very extensive.

[2] Cf. *infra*, 13 ff.

[3] This is often called socialization. The two terms are sometimes used indiscriminately. The practical difference can hardly be defined; mostly the difference may be seen in the *animus* underlying the act. Cf. W. A. Robson *c.s.*, *Problems of Nationalized Industry*, London, 1952, 347: "The infusion of the public corporations by a genuine spirit of democracy is what people have in mind when they speak of the conversion of nationalization to socialization." "A socialist industry ... is one in which the social implications of public ownership and operation have been substantially realized." Cf. also A. Zeegers, *Socialisatie*, Amsterdam, 1948.

cide. Nationalization of a corporation as a rule involves its dissolution; private enterprise disappears as such and is either continued as an independent public body, or merged with other public enterprises, or entirely liquidated. Besides the dissolution comes the confiscatory element: confiscation of the property and cancellation of debts. Different acts may contain confiscatory elements: the German measures against the Jews before and during World War II are also an example of an action by a government with a confiscatory element.

Summarizing it may be said that by confiscation is understood any governmental action by which private property is seized without compensation, no matter in what form or under what name. The term expropriation, although a general one, from now on will be used, in accordance with common parlance, to indicate expropriation for public utility against just compensation. In this way a terminology is employed which makes it clear what is meant. The tendency to use the term expropriation both for expropriation with and without compensation (cf. Friedman [1]) leads to confusions. De La Pradelle's [2] distinction between "expropriations" as seizures in isolated cases, which ought to be accompanied by a just compensation, and "nationalizations" as seizures which form part of structural reforms (e.g. agrarian reforms), which may be performed without just compensation is also confusing. We should further prefer not to use the term nationalization [3] for every confiscation or expropriation, but only for confiscation or expropriation of enterprises [4].

The literal definition of confiscation encompasses also the levying of taxes but the own nature of tax-levy distinguishes it from confiscation [5]. The aim of tax-levy is to make it financially possible for the government duly to accomplish its task. Levying of taxes affects all the residents or subjects of a state or at least certain categories of them; it is nearly always a levy in money and naturally has no penal character. Confiscation will very often be

---

[1] Friedman, *op cit.*; Wortley, *Transactions* 1947, 25.

[2] *Annuaire* 1950 (Bath) I, 61; this distinction runs parallel to the one used by Friedman between individual and general expropriation (Friedman, 7).

[3] In the Reports by Erades and Jansma the term expropriation has practically been replaced by the term nationalization; Cheshire, 134, is using the notion nationalization as accompanied by compensation.

[4] Cf. Re, 15.

[5] Cf. Foster, 462.

directed against definite individuals, thus producing a discriminatory effect; it aims mostly at certain property and often has a penal character. For the rest attention may be drawn to what might be called borderline cases; a suggestion in this direction was made by Lord Justice Scrutton in *Luther* v. *Sagor* [1]. Neither pure taxation measures, nor the exercise of "police power", as found in criminal law proper, fall within our scope.

IV. SCOPE OF THE PROBLEM

Whereas the concept confiscation itself already limits this study, a further restriction is imposed by the fact that this topic in the main will only be discussed from the point of view of private international law. Thus attention will be focused on case law and statute law, insofar as they touch upon private international law. Up to now this has not been the case on a large scale. It is true that the Soviet Russian confiscations have been made the object of some literature, published for the greater part in periodicals, but not until recently has the problem as a whole received its deserved attention. So Beitzke [2] could rightly state: "*Internationalrechtliche Enteignungsproblemen werden meist unter völkerrechtlichen Gesichtspunkten betrachtet. Das genügt aber nicht zur Klarung der zivilrechtlichen Folgen von Enteignungen*". The *Legatum Visserianum* at Leyden called attention to the aspect of private international law by organizing an international essay prize-contest in 1948; the excellent monograph by Seidl-Hohenveldern is the fruit of this contest; so is the present study [3].

Confiscation has been constantly considered from the point of view of public international law. The literature is quite overwhelming; moreover, the subjects which are of importance to the law of nations outnumber those which are of interest to private international law. Various *causes célèbres* pertaining to the law of nations therefore fall outside the scope of our study [4]. And in the remaining cases, which are to be discussed in the present study, the aspect of public international law has often

[1] [1921] 3 K.B. 532.
[2] Beitzke, 93.
[3] The embryo of this study was awarded an honourable mention.
[4] Cf. Friedman, chapter 3.

been most closely considered, e.g. in the case of the expropriation of the oil business in Mexico [1].

In public international law the question culminates in whether or not confiscation of goods belonging to aliens is allowed by the law of nations. On this issue opinions clash very strongly [2]. The authors who state that public international law does not permit confiscation of goods of aliens as being contrary to the law of nations, often advance this opinion in the form of a defence [3] or with uncertainty [4]. Here, if anywhere in international law, it is extremely difficult to establish what is the settled law. The answer to this question falls outside our scope and for the sake of limitation an indication of the nature of this aspect will suffice.

While public international law concerns the legality of the confiscation of foreign-owned property and possible compensation, private international law concerns the private legal effects of confiscations as to the title of property seen outside the territory of the confiscating state. Questions arising in the field of private international law within the territory of the confiscating state are solved very simply, e.g. by prohibiting litigation on these questions, as regulated by section 2 of the Russian Civil Code.

Meanwhile it is remarkable to observe that elements of public law still play a part here. This is due to the very phenomenon of confiscation. Confiscation in itself belongs typically to the domain of public law; since, however, it interferes with existing relations of ownership, it also has consequences in the field of private law. Within the frontiers of the confiscating state an act of confiscation of course will mainly be regarded as belonging to public law. But as soon as the act is laid before a foreign court, things become different, since the foreign court will decide on the case independently. The views of these courts may vary considerably, depending on whether the confiscatory measure is considered a rule simply pertaining to the law of property of the confiscating

---

[1] Cf. Kunz, *The Mexican Expropriations*, with further literature.

[2] Cf. opinions expressed at the Sessions of the *Institut de Droit International* at Bath and Siena (*Annuaire* 1950 and 1952).

[3] E.g. Fachiri, *Brit. Yearb.* 1929, 32.

[4] E.g. François I, 210; Scelle, 693, "*La doctrine s' est divisée ...*" "*Il semble bien, en effet, qu'il existe une règle ...*"

state, or whether the emphasis is placed on the aspect of state interference which the measure presents. If the latter aspect is considered the more important, there is sometimes a tendency to abandon the term private international law in favour of what is called by the Germans *Internationales Verwaltungsrecht*[1]. For the very reason that confiscation is a phenomenon both pertaining to public law and yet unmistakably linked with the law of property, it may not be objectionable to see the subject "the effect of foreign confiscations" in the domain of private international law, provided the particular character of the phenomenon confiscation is always clearly recognized[2].

V. TERRITORIALITY

In public international law nationality is an important feature in matters of confiscation, while in private international law a prominent part is assigned to territoriality. Case law with respect to our subject affords a certain unanimity: confiscations of goods in the territory of the confiscating state at the time of the confiscation are considered differently from confiscations purporting to affect property outside the territory of the confiscating state; courts generally take quite another point of view depending upon which case is at issue. Consequently confiscations may be denoted as either territorial (domestic) or extra-territorial. Whether the rather unanimous views of the courts are justified must be considered more closely. Meanwhile it seems justified to deal with the cases according to this distinction, since this is closely co-ordinate with practice. Two examples illustrate this.

A parcel of goods is confiscated in Soviet Russia[3]; the Soviet Russian government considers itself to be the owner of the goods. This government sells the goods which afterwards find their way abroad (say in state X). The original owner who has escaped after the revolution, now lodges a claim with a court of state X, alleging that he and not the person who has bought the goods from the Soviet-Russian government is the owner. Here two persons are involved in an action which in the last resort goes

[1] Cf. Seidl-Hohenveldern, 2,3.

[2] Ficker, 61, constantly speaks of "*Ineinander und Übereinandergreifen*" of "*Kollisionsprivatrecht*" and "*Kollisionsverwaltungsrecht.*"

[3] Cf. *Luther* v. *Sagor* [1921] 1 K.B. 456 and [1921] 3 K.B. 532.

to the question of the title to property and accordingly lies within the scope of private international law. Yet elements of public law also play a part here, because as a rule the question is raised whether it is open to the court to sit in judgment upon the acts of sovereign governments. So here a typical issue of territorial confiscation is at stake, the confiscation itself having been entirely effected on Soviet Russian territory.

A business-man in a certain country Y has a balance in his favour elsewhere[1]. A confiscatory measure with regard to his business is taken in Y. Does this measure also affect the balance elesewhere? If it does, the extra-territorial claim is recognized; otherwise, this claim is rejected.

Here territoriality clearly plays a part, as will also appear when we consider the actual cases. Whether this part is a desirable one is another matter. We shall refer to this later. It may be said now that there is a substantial difference between territorial confiscations on the one hand and extra-territorial confiscations on the other[2].

A territorial confiscation, which has for its object property within the territory of the confiscating state, is an act that can be performed and accomplished completely by the state-organs involved. Such a confiscation need not come within the scope of private international law. If it does, when the question of title to property is raised abroad, it is for the foreign court, if so minded, to decline to give effect to an act which already has unmistakably taken place.

It is different with extra-territorial confiscations. Here the confiscating state can never effectuate the measure through the medium of its own normal organs; it cannot but confine itself to proclaiming that it has acquired certain properties. In order to dispose of these properties the co-operation of the foreign country, mostly the foreign court, is indispensible. Thus the extra-

---

[1] Cf. *Frankfurther* v. *Exner* [1947] 1 Ch. 629.

[2] Cf. Re, 49; Erades, 2, distinguishes between three types of cases. Besides those cases which can generally be indicated as territorial or extra-territorial confiscations, he thinks he may see as the third type cases of the following nature: a life insurance company established in state A has a branch in state B. This branch is nationalized by state B. The policyholders who have contracted with the branch sue the company in state A. We fail to see why this should be a separate type of cases. Complications, indeed, arise here, notably as to the *situs* of the debt and also because the company as such continues to exist.

territorial confiscation, if it is not to be a mere sham, will always come within the scope of private international law, and the foreign *forum* is, in fact, invited to take part in the confiscatory measure itself.

So there are differences indeed [1]. Whereas generally speaking public law cannot be said to have a scope strictly limited to its domestic territory, compulsion inherent in public law does have such limitations. This compulsion cannot be exercised by a state with its organs outside its territory.

VI. SOME CONFISCATIONS OF THE TWENTIETH CENTURY

The twentieth century has produced a surprising number of actions in connection with confiscations. The Soviet-Russian confiscations, for example, produced a stream of actions and the same may be said of other confiscations. For a proper understanding of the matters at issue, a few remarks will first be made as to the background of certain confiscations.

1. The Carthusian Monks

First of all we would refer to the case of the Carthusian monks.

The suspicion of religious congregations which arose in France after the Revolution, was crystallized in the well-known Act of July 1, 1901 [2]. By this Act the continuance of the congregations was made conditional upon governmental authorization, in the absence of which the congregation would be dissolved. For a proper understanding of the situation it may be worthwile to recall its history. Under the Act of 1817 [3] any legal status of a congregation had to be approved; in practice such approval was never granted [4]. Congregations operating without legal status were nevertheless tolerated [5]. This spirit of tolerance was discontinued by the Act of 1901. The principles laid down in

[1] Cf. Ficker, 71.

[2] Text in Sirey, *Recueil des Lois, Table Décennale* 1901–1910.

[3] This Act was applicable to men's congregations; to women an Act of 1825 was applicable.

[4] *Répertoire*, V. 2.

[5] Loubers rightly speaks of a "*régime de tolerance*", *Répertoire*, V, 2.

1817, were now carried out rigidly; in the absence of authorization dissolution was to follow. A system of a stone-hard mentality; the more so since not a single authorization was granted [1]. From this it may be evident that the legislation in question had a political purpose. The goods of the congregations fell a prey to liquidation, and the latter was arranged in such a way that confiscation seems the only proper word for it [2].

Application of the Act soon followed and with regard to the Carthusian Congregation this application had consequences that are of importance to our study. In France the *Pères Chartreux* had a large settlement in the monastery *la Grande Chartreuse,* in the immediate vicinity of the little town of Fourvoirie where the famous liqueur was made. The monks had made a large business out of the manufacture of this liqueur and it could justly be claimed in various decisions that the liqueur enjoyed world fame. This very fame was what brought the matter before foreign courts: whereas several other congregations were liquidated without any international legal consequences, the Carthusian case entailed international repercussions. The famous liqueur was put on the market under certain trade-marks, which had been registered not only in France, but also in many other countries. It was on account of these trade-marks that the conflict arose, the course of which has been recorded especially by Pillet [3]. His commentaries and opinion have given this question the publicity it undoubtedly deserves.

As noted, the Act of 1901 required special authorization for the continuance of the congregation, in the absence of which liquidation was to follow. The authorization, though applied for, was not given; instead of it a liquidator, M. Lecouturier, was appointed by the District Court of Grenoble [4]. On April 23, 1904 [5] he obtained from this court a decision that the trade-mark was part of the *fonds de commerce,* a finding upheld by the Court of Appeal of Grenoble on July 19, 1905 [6], the Court of Cassation

---

[1] *Répertoire,* V, 2.

[2] Pillet, *Des Personnes Morales* . . ., 388.

[3] A. Pillet, *Des Personnes Morales en Droit International Privé,* Paris, 1914; A. Pillet, *Le Régime International de la Propriété Industrielle,* Paris, 1911; *Mélanges Antoine Pillet,* II, Paris, 1929; note in S. 1908.4.9.

[4] On March 31, 1903, *Revue Darras* 1907, 284.

[5] *Revue Darras* 1907, 284; *Gaz. des Trib.,* May 8, 1904.

[6] *Revue Darras* 1907, 284.

dismissing an appeal [1]. This did not, however, pave the way for the trade-marks registered abroad and consequently Lecouturier requested the court to interpret the decision of July 19, 1905, in such a way that the decision would also extend to the trade-marks registered abroad. The court, however, holding that the considerations of parties would not permit the decision being upset, did not go into the matter [2]; the appeal was dismissed [3]. Apart from this it may be remarked that, had the court interpreted its decision according to Lecouturier's wish, it would have been of no consequence with respect to foreign countries. Then as well as now foreign courts would have considered the matter independently. Meanwhile the Carthusian congregation, whose continuance as such was prohibited in France, had left the country and re-established the business in Tarragona. The manufacture of liqueur was there continued and was not only dispatched to the old customers abroad, but also imported into France. The manufacture in Tarragona was undertaken through the medium of a company named Union Agricola and soon Lecouturier took legal proceedings against this company. The result however, was not so favourable for the liquidator, for the District Court of Grenoble [4] took the stand that the Carthusian congregation could not be denied the right to use its name in the trade-mark. It is true that a trade-mark and bottle different from the one formerly used in France had to be adopted, but the name, the proper indication of the liqueur, was allowed to be continued, even in France.

Afterward the liquidator sold the mark tot M. Cusenier who continued to use it. A great confusion resulted; now three kinds of *Chartreuse* had come to exist: the "real" old one manufactured before the liquidation, the liqueur manufactured in Tarragona which, thanks to the monks' exclusive knowledge of the secret formula possessed the same qualities as the old one and finally the liqueur put on the market by Cusenier, which according to the connoisseurs had only the name and colour in common with *Chartreuse*.

With the seizure of the trade-mark in France the liquidator

[1] *Revue Darras* 1907, 284, S. 1908.1.185; decision of July 31, 1906.

[2] Decision of March 27, 1906, S. 1908.2.95, *Revue Darras* 1907, 285.

[3] *Revue Darras* 1907, 285.

[4] Decision of May 18, 1905, S. 1908.2.117, *Revue Darras* 1907, 286.

and, naturally, also his assignee Cusenier, were not content and consequently several law suits ensued abroad, in nearly all of which the congregation was successful.

2. *Soviet Russia*

For a study of confiscation as seen from the point of view of private international law the measures taken in this respect in Soviet Russia during and after the revolution of 1917 present a mirror in which the problem is almost completely reflected. In the field of private international law the consequences of the nationalizations have been considerable, due mainly to the fact that much foreign capital had been invested in Russian business before Wold War I.

Our study is focused on confiscation, including nationalization with a confiscatory element. The history of the Russian measures is so notorious that for convenience we beg to refer to the very extensive literature on the subject; reference may for instance be made to the work of Bunyan and Fisher. For the greater part these measures bear on nationalization of corporations and less on mere confiscations. In the latter we are interested only insofar as they have had consequences in the field of private international law. Confiscations themselves have of course been very extensive in Russia. We only recall the confiscation of land over which, naturally, cases outside Russia were hardly fought.

Only few decisions of isolated cases of confiscations are known, although some of them are very important [1]. More frequently various measures of nationalization are at stake [2].

What is especially striking when studying the text of the

[1] Thus, for instance, the case *Luther* v. *Sagor* [1921] 1 K.B.456 and [1921] 3 K.B 532.

[2] In search of the various texts, a student who has no command of the Russian language and consequently has no access to the official collections of Soviet Russian decrees, will only find translations of decrees which caused the greatest stir abroad. A good source is Raoul Labry's collection, *Une Législation Communiste*, Paris, 1920, which gives the French translation of many decrees. Further mention must be made of the work by W. Hahn and A. von Lilienfeld-Toal, *Regelung des Handels und Verkehr in Ruszland*, Jena, 1921, in which several decrees are republished in German translation. In the book by J. Bunyan and H. H. Fisher, *The Bolshevik Revolution*, Stanford University Calif., 1934, some texts in English translation are inserted; the measures specially concerning the nationalization of the banks have been published in German by P. Wohl in *Ostrecht* 1925, 113, as far as we could ascertain in full. Moreover, the decrees concerning the nationalization of the banks can also be found elsewhere, e.g. in *Histoire des Soviets*, ed. Henri de Weindel, Paris, 1922, 64. Also in several decisions themselves large parts of decrees are often quoted, e.g. *Russian Commercial and Industrial Bank* v. *Comptoir d'Escompte de Mulhouse and others* [1923] 2 K.B. 630.

decrees is the comparative carelessness with which they are composed. This in itself is not to be wondered at. In Russia from of old the technique of legislation has been a weak point and since moreover a section of the population that included a comparatively large percentage of skilled lawyers had been eliminated, it is understandable that both legal form and substance of several regulations bore an unsatisfactory character. Little homogeniety is to be found in the various documents. Strict interpretation of the texts of the decrees concerning banks may lead to a conclusion as arrived at by an English court [1], which is in sharp contrast to the real intention of the decrees. Whether this conclusion was right is a matter we shall discuss later. A warning may be given here against too formalistic an interpretation of the Russian decrees, because they cannot be measured by common Western standards. Moreover, the slipshod style of the decrees is mainly caused by framing them in great haste. After all the revolution had been advanced with the slogan "rob the robbers". Once the aim had been attained this slogan had to be realized. Thus it was believed that control of the banks would secure the financial power of the country. Hence banking was among the first branches of trade and industry to be nationalized. In this connection it is a disputed point, whether the banks have also formally lost their legal personality. This is not expressly stated in any decree and, as a consequence, their continuance as such might be assumed [2]. However, the matter is not as simple as that.

The measures we encounter time and again are first of all those concerning the nationalization of the banks. As remarked, a comprehensive survey of these measures was given by Wohl [3].

Next we meet with the nationalization of the Russian merchant fleet [4]. Decrees concerning the nationalization of the insurance business are of frequent occurrence as well [5]. Also at issue now

[1] Thus the decision *Russian Commercial and Industrial Bank* v. *Comptoir d'Escompte de Mulhouse and others* [1925] A.C. 112.

[2] Decision Berlin 31-3-1925, *Clunet* 1925, 1057, *J.W.* vol. 54, 1300, *re Ginsberg* g. *Deutsche Bank*. See, however, final decision 25-10-1927, *Z.f.O.* 1928, 1583.

[3] *Ostrecht* 1925, 113.

[4] Labry, 371; Hahn und Von Lilienfeld-Toal, 106; Bunyan and Fisher, 611.

[5] Labry mentions a decree of 1-12-1918 declaring the entire insurance business (fire, transport, life etc.) a state monopoly and directing the immediate liquidation of the companies. A decree of 18-11-1919 refers to life insurance in particular, *Ostrecht* 1926, 206.

and then is the decree of November 19, 1920, providing for the property of all movables of Russians emigrated or fled to pass to the state. Finally there are various measures, which are referred to only once or twice.

A great deal of subject-matter is accounted for by France. From of old France was bound to Russia with many ties, both cultural — in aristocratic Russian circles a great deal of French was spoken — and financial. Several large banks in Russia had branches in France; a great many French people were financially interested in Russian corporations. Hence a veritable fload of decisions arose in France, not only in our field but also with regard to the law of persons, the family law and the law of succession.

A survey of the numerous suits brought in France presents a sharp *caesura* caused by the recognition of the Soviet Russian government. France is not singular in this; in England, too, as in some other countries, the question of this recognition, to which we shall refer later, came much to the foreground. The question at issue was always whether or not the legislation of an unrecognized government had to be ignored.

In Germany matters were different yet; there the Rapallo Treaty played a great part. In the U.S.A. these matters came to be governed by the interpretation of the so-called Litvinov Assignment.

Though the courts' attitude in these countries is affected by various considerations, practical conclusions as a rule do not diverge very much.

In the Baltic countries [1] and in other Eastern-European countries [2] extensive measures after the pattern of the Soviet Russian confiscations have been taken. Private international case-law in this respect is still coming into being.

3. Oil in Mexico

The sensational expropriation of the private oil concerns in Mexico by the Mexican government had different aspects. In

[1] Cf. H. W. Briggs, *Non-recognition in the courts: The Ships of the Baltic Republics*, A.J.I.L. 1943, 585.

[2] Cf. the articles by Doman, Drucker, Fawcett, Gutteridge and Rado on the subject; see our bibliography.

addition to the important economic side of the matter, the legal aspect was of the greatest importance. The companies involved in this expropriation for the major part represented foreign interests. Various questions came to be treated on a diplomatic level. In these discussions the international legality of the expropriation was considered as well as the previous question whether the expropriation bore a confiscatory character. Unlike in the case of the Russian expropriations, it was a point in dispute whether the seizure had to be seen as a confiscation or as an expropriation for public utility with compensation. In some countries cases followed in connection with the expropriation. Although these cases are not always of a nature peculiar to private international law, yet it is of importance to discuss them, because the point at issue was often the very issue of power to review from the private international legal aspect. At this place some remarks may be made about the previous history and the further course of the expropriation.

An extensive literature has come into existence as regards the procedure of the expropriation, the causes leading up to it, the way in which and the conditions under which diplomatic contact was carried on.The following short survey is derived especially from the excellent summarizing work by Joseph L. Kunz: "The Mexican Expropriations", which, being written in 1940 does not relate the closing act of the oil conflict.

Kunz points out, and this becomes also clear from other literature, that the expropriations are to be regarded especially against the background of the revolution started in Mexico about 1910, and since ever rolling on, "one and the same revolution. It is a social, collectivistic movement against the background of an intense nationalism — an Indian nationalism" [1]. This movement mainly aimed at two objects: agrarian reform and "Mexicanization of Industry", which is another term for nationalization. The problem of expropriation is linked up with both of them and pertains to the law of nations so far as property of aliens is concerned. Consequently, the literature on the subject is almost exclusively devoted to the aspect of public international law [2].

---

[1] Kunz, 2.

[2] We mention a.o. A. Garcia Robles in *Revue de droit international* 1939, 514; Kunz in *The Mexican Expropriations*, New York, 1940, and in *The Hungarian Quarterly* 1939, 42; L. H. Woolsey in *A.J.I.L.* 1938, 519 and C. C. Hyde in *A.J.I.L.* 1938, 759.

Expropriation in Mexico was not confined to oil concerns. In line with the social revolution expropriations were also effected with regard to land, which gave rise to a controversy, especially with the U.S.A., because many American citizens owned land in Mexico. This, however, is a separate question and, barring within Mexico, has no consequences in the field of private international law.

The oil conflict in question was caused directly by the Expropriation Act of 1936. This act was a basic one, under which by further decree of the President expropriations could be effected. Early in 1937 an organization for the control of national oil was called into existence. Meanwhile in the oil concerns a serious social conflict had arisen; the labourers demanded higher wages, but their request was refused. Feelings ran so high that a strike broke out, which was declared legal by the Federal Labour Board. The matter assumed more and more threatening proportions, the trade unions pushed on and all this resulted in President Cardenas signing a decree on March 18, 1938 [1], providing for the expropriation of 17 oil concerns. In consequence of the fact that those interested in these concerns were for the major part foreigners (American, British and Dutch companies, chiefly representing Standard- and Shell-interests) there were serious international repercussions. Unlike Great Britain which after a brief spar of exchanging notes broke off diplomatic relations [2], the U.S.A. particularly, and also the Netherlands [3] made representations through diplomatic channels. The U.S.A. added strength to her representations by reducing her purchases of silver in the Mexican market. The companies themselves objected as well. Before the Mexican courts they argued that the expropriation decree was against the constitution, but this argument was dismissed in every instance. Meanwhile the U.S.A. had not contained herself to representations only, but had also started negotiations. The fundamental problem pertaining to the law nations: is the confiscation of the property belonging to aliens legal? was fairly

[1] See text in *Bulletin*, vol. 39, 150.

[2] *Cmd.* 5758 (1938), also printed in *Mexico: Expropriation of Foreign-owned Oil Properties*, ed. Huasteca Petr. Cy., 1938, in which also the American-Mexican notes are stated.

[3] See *Annuaire Grotius* 1938, 110 and H. E. Scheffer in *De Volkenbond* 1938–1939, 10.

soon solved. Both the U.S.A. and Mexico took the view that such an act is not permitted and again both took it for granted that expropriation for public utility provided there is due compensation, is indeed legal. In addition, however, the U.S.A. with an appeal to the law of nations laid claim to an "adequate, effective and prompt compensation". This claim was opposed by Mexico with the argument that the international rule only requires payment, but not prompt payment. In the present case a compensation had been promised, but this did not need to be paid until 10 years had elapsed; moreover, no preparation for any payment had been made as yet. Whether or not one could speak of confiscation in this case could not be ascertained as yet, since the answer to this question actually depended on whether and to what extent payment, i.e. real payment would be made. Consequently this difficulty played an important part in the courts' considerations. Eventually, after lengthy negotiations, the problem has been settled in a way not altogether unsatisfactory from a practical point of view. But at the time of the courts' adjucating upon the cases which we are now going to discuss, a practical arrangement had not yet been arrived at.

Besides denying that „prompt payment" was prescribed by the law of nations, Mexico refused arbitration as proposed by the U.S.A., because in her opinion the affair was a purely national one. This stand was not quite fair. The Mexican legislation had required the companies that wanted to carry on the oil business in Mexico to possess Mexican nationality. The large American, British and Dutch oil concerns therefore had vested interests in subsidiary companies, established in accordance with Mexican law, but this did not alter the fact that the interests themselves remained American, British and Dutch as before.

Nevertheless, negotiations were carried on and eventually the U.S.A. was the first to come to an agreement on November 19, 1941 [1], providing that experts should fix the amount of compensation. This led to an agreement between the experts of the two governments embodied in an exchange of notes of September 29, 1943 [2]. The agreement covered a scheme of payment and from that time on payment has been effected regularly. So even-

[1] *Dept. of State Bull.* 1941, II, 399.
[2] *Dept. of State Bull.* 1943, II, 230.

tually the U.S.A., perforce, yielded to payment in instalments.

Great Britain and the Netherlands went the same way; they, too, had at first made representations, Great Britain, as remarked, even broke off diplomatic relations, but here, too, negotiations were held though they did not lead to an agreement[1] until later. A uniform agreement was concluded since British and Dutch oil interests ran parallel to each other; experts were again appointed who were to fix the amount of compensation; the Netherlands and Great Britain jointly appointed an expert. For the rest the British and Dutch agreements were similar to the American one.

A *note gaie* which, in conclusion, should not be left unmentioned, is that after this affair, Mexico, in 1949, started negotiations with the U.S.A. about the subject: American aid in the development of the Mexican oil industry[2]!

4. *The Spanish Tragedy*

In the cases arising out of the requisitions and expropriations in the Spanish Civil War, the international "curtain" of jurisdictional immunity has mostly been a bar to decisions in respect of title to property.

So the question may arise whether treatment of the above subject fits within the scheme of this study. We take the affirmative view, since in this connection the borderlines may also be shown — this may be useful with a view of limitating the lines — and since some courts did examine the validity of requisition or expropriation.

The concept of requisition is connected with the law of war and so matters are a little different from e.g. the Soviet Russian measures. Moreover in the laws of war a right to compensation is generally sequent to requisition so that in itself it remains to be seen whether the latter may be called confiscation. Like in the Mexican case it depends on the extent to which a foreign court has confidence in such compensation. But there is yet another thing. From the cases of requisition of ships which we shall discuss, it appears that these ships were to be placed at the

---

[1] For the Netherlands, *Staatsblad* G 158 (1946), for Great Britain, *Cmd.* 6768. The exchanges of notes of the two countries happened on February 7, 1946. See also *The Petroleum Times* 1947, 887 and 1000.

[2] See *Dept. of State Bull.* 1949, I, 466 and II, 153.

disposal of the Spanish government, which did not mean that such expropriation would be definite. Here the problem has a distinctive character and Preuss [1] rightly remarks: "While the decisions follow in general those (viz. consequences) laid down in similar cases growing out of the Soviet decrees of nationalization, the Spanisch Civil War cases contain sufficient elements of novelty to justify their careful study" [2].

In studying this subject mainly two kinds of measures appear to be involved: in the first place requisition of ships, which produced a good many cases and secondly a few other expropriation measures.

So far as ships were concerned the question of jurisdictional immunity nearly always arose, owing to which the decision was given on grounds derived from international law. That is why the question of ownership mostly could not be answered and according to many courts it was not allowed to be answered. "Whether that possession was rightful according to Spanish, English or international law", Preuss remarks, while speaking about some English decisions, "was not inquired into. They left entirely undecided the question whether a foreign government's decree purporting to requisition ships outside territory under its control would be recognized in England as giving to that government a right to possession or control of the ships" [3].

Certainly the situation was somewhat complicated. After the revolt had broken out in 1936, Italy and Germany recognized as early as November 1936 General Franco as the head of the Nationalist Government at Burgos. The other big powers did not recognize Franco. Only when the situation became clear after the fall of Barcelona on January 31, 1939, did recognition by Great Britain and France follow. Before that two governments, the Republican and the Nationalist ones pretended to be the legitimate government of Spain [4].

---

[1] L. Preuss, *State immunity and the requisition of ships during the Spanish Civil war*, A.J.I.L. 1941, 263 and 1942, 37.

[2] *A.J.I.L.* 1941, 263.

[3] *A.J.I.L.* 1941, 276.

[4] A great deal of literature has grown out of the history of the Spanish tragedy; the book by Patricia A.M. van der Esch, *Prelude to War*, The Hague, 1951, gives a fascinating survey. The arising legal problems are well elucidated by N. J. Padelford, *International Law and Diplomacy in the Spanish Civil Strife*, New York, 1939.

5. *World War I and World War II*

The various measures taken by the belligerent powers during World War I [1] can certainly not be considered mere confiscations. These measures did decidedly not intend such an effect. In the first instance — and this meant something new — it was a question of sequestration, of attachment till after the war [2]. In all the belligerent countries the necessity was manifest to *freeze* the property of enemies [3]. This in itself did not at all mean expropriation, let alone confiscation. However, the possibility of confiscation was there. Such was likewise the case with the various decrees concerning the prohibition of trading with the enemy. This also bore a temporary character and could not be considered a specifically confiscatory measure. However, as soon as the *freezing* passed into *liquidation* (after the economic conference of the Allied Powers in Paris in June 1916 [4]) these regulations naturally rather tended to confiscation. Everything would now depend on how this affair would turn out, but certainly these measures came close to debatable confiscations, which would be regarded by the courts with as much suspicion as confiscations proper. For the time being compensation was out of the question, while prompt compensation was not considered at all. This matter was eventually settled by the Peace Treaties. In the Treaty of Versailles, section 297 (and the corresponding sections of the other treaties) it was stipulated that the Allies were allowed to liquidate the property seized, that Germany would be credited with the counter-value on the balance sheet of reparation payments and that eventually Germany was to make good the value of the expropriated property to the individuals dispossessed. By doing so the matter was really construed in such a way that, in order to be able to redeem her reparation payments, Germany expropriated the property against compensation; confiscation therefore did not come into the question. This may be a matter of opinion since compensation did not

---

[1] A clear survey of this is offered by e.g. J. A. Gathings, *International Law and American Treatment of alien enemy property*, Washington, 1940; also J. W. Garner, *International Law and the World War*, London, 1920.

[2] See Gathings, 46.

[3] See Gathings and Garner for the regulations in various countries.

[4] See on this Gathings, 50.

amount to very much, but before the peace treaties were concluded it was positively a question of debatable confiscation. Otherwise, in the field of private international law only sporadic controversy was carried on on this point [1].

The measures taken by Germany were, of course, redressed by the peace treaties.

Although World War II did not break out until 1939, its shadows plainly showed years ahead. The policy of the *Dritte Reich* involved various measures aimed at the Jews and other "enemies" of the German *Reich*. Each time Germany occupied fresh territories these measures were declared applicable to a wider field, until at last after the outbreak of the war almost all Europe suffered under the German occupation and with it under the legislation modeled in German style. During the war, of course, in Germany and the occupied territories, measures similar to those in the other belligerent countries were taken in respect to enemy property.

As observed, before the outbreak of the war the struggle was aimed particularly at the Jews and "enemies of the people". This struggle was waged among other things through the so-called racial legislation (marriage regulations, sterilization etc.) but also in the economic field by means of restrictions and prohibitive measures with regard to the following of certain occupations and trades, the holding of offices, the imposition of fines; in fact, it was made almost impossible for Jews and those who were placed in the same position to participate in the country's economic life, not to speak of other measures such as concentration camps. Insofar as these measures were aimed at strangling the Jews economically, numerous cases in the field of private international law have arisen in several countries; notably concerning the German legislation regarding the appointment of *Verwalter* (the anti-Jewish measures were using the term *Verwalter*, whereas the measures on enemy property generally were speaking of *Treuhand*). Although in the statutory provisions no mention was made of mere confiscation, they paralysed the rights of the owners of untertakings; also the course of action of the *Verwalter* was such

[1] G. Sauser-Hall, *L'occupation de guerre et les droits privés*, Schweiz. Jahrb. für intern. R. I (1944), 113: "*La jurisprudence au sujet de ces problèmes n'est pas abondante.*"

that only naive judges could regard these measures as non-confiscatory. Such naive judges, as far as we could ascertain, were *mirabile dictu* found only in the Netherlands, though the major part of Dutch decisions on the subject took another stand.

In World War II as well measures were taken similar to those in World War I.

Measures of a different kind, however, also came into being.

During the last war a good deal of cases arose out of certain expropriatory decrees of the governments- in-exile [1]. The fact is that these governments had to face the necessity of having to prevent the property of their subjects from falling into German hands. Thus on May 24, 1940 the Netherlands Government issued the well-known A I Decree, providing that the property of Dutchmen (and legal persons) resident in occupied territory should pass into the hands of the Dutch government. The Norwegian Government, too, enacted a similar order. About both decrees legal proceedings were carried on. Certainly no confiscation was at stake here, because the sting of non-payment of compensation was missing. Yet the A I Decree was not a question of expropriation for public utility either, but rather a sequestration with the deliberate obligation of *restitutio in integrum*. Because of the related character the cases wich arose out of them will also be discussed.

Among the many effects of World War II is also Germany's present status. The confiscations in Eastern-Germany [2] and the reactions in Western-Germany caused difficult problems due to the existence of this dual Germany. Questions arising here may be considered as belonging to the field of private interlocal law rather than of private international law. Naturally they come close to questions of private international law [3].

---

[1] Cf. a.o. the observations of Flory, Lourie and Meyer, Marks and Ulrich; see our bibliography.

[2] Cf. Raape, 431.

[3] Cf. the monographs by Beuck and Ficker.

CHAPTER II

PRELIMINARY TOPICS

I. THE PROBLEM OF RECOGNITION

1. The Dogmatic Point of View

The recognition of a state or government belongs to the sphere of public international law and a detailed study thereof [1] is therefore outside the scope of this monograph. We must, however, examine its impact on private international law.

There appear to be two main views. The first is the old, dogmatic one, which proceeds from the principle that legislative and other acts of an unrecognized government are to be ignored. The other one does not allow non-recognition as such to influence the legality of the acts of such an unrecognized government. As a rule the former view is connected with the idea that recognition has a constitutive character. This opinion is most strictly adhered to in English and French case law and can also be found in Belgium, Rumania and Italy. Lauterpacht illustrates this view clearly, by stating: "The correct and reasonable rule is that both the unrecognized government and its acts are a nullity" [2], and although aware of the difficulties inherent in this view, he sticks to it consistently [3].

English case law, which is a good example of this point of view, was developed gradually. *City of Berne* v. *Bank of Eng-*

---

[1] From the voluminous literature in this field we mention the recent studies of H. Lauterpacht, *Recognition in International Law*, Cambridge, 1947, and Ti-Chiang Chen, *The International Law of Recognition*, New York, 1951; for a comprehensive review, see B. Landheer and J. L. F. van Essen, *Recognition in International Law*, Selective Bibliographies of the Library of the Peace Palace, II, Leyden, 1954.

[2] Lauterpacht, *op. cit.*, 147.

[3] Lauterpacht, *op. cit.*, 147.

land (1804) [1] which decision might be taken as one of the earliest cases on this point is of considerable importance. This case decided that the recognition of a foreign state or government is the exclusive privilege of the government [2]. Consequently the acts of unrecognized governments are to be ignored: "It is extremely difficult to say that a judicial court can take notice of a government not recognized by the government of the country in which that court sits". (Lord Eldon) [3]. This precedent was followed in several similar decisions [4]. Dissenting opinions can be found [5], but the Eldon doctrine was followed in *Mighell* v. *Sultan of Johore* [6].

An illustration of the so-called dogmatic conception can be found in *A. M. Luther* v. *James Sagor & Co* [7]. The point in issue was the original owners title to a load of timber confiscated in Soviet Russia and exported to England. The defendant produced a letter from the Secretary of State for Foreign Affairs, dated October 5th, 1920, to establish that the United Kingdom had recognized Soviet Russia by having granted a limited immunity to the trade delegation conducted by Krassin. The defendant relied on the following sentence: "His majesty's Government assent to the claim of the Delegation to represent in this country a state government of Russia". The plaintiff, however, produced

[1] Scott, *Cases*, 57.

[2] As in the U.S.A. this line of conduct led to the rule that as to matters of recognition enquiries are made with the Executive; concerning England this is shown from *Mighell* v. *Sultan of Johore* [1894] Q.B. 149, *Luther* v. *Sagor* [1921] 1 K.B. 456, 3 K.B. 532; as for the U.S.A.: *Salimoff* v. *Standard Oil Co of New York* and *Salimoff* v. *Vacuum Oil Co*, 89 A.L.R. 345 and *Ann. Dig.* 1933–1934, 22. Cf. Ti-Chiang Chen, 230, n. 41.

[3] Some decisions present a less clear picture. In *Wright* v. *Nutt* (1788) 1 H.Bl. 136, cit. Ti-Chiang Chen, 158 and *Folliott* v. *Ogden* (1789) 1 H.Bl. 123, cit. Ti-Chiang Chen, 138, the fact that the acts of an unrecognized government were allowed to stand may also be explained by retroactivity. In *Ogden* v. *Folliott* (1790) 3 Term Rep. 726, cit. Ti-Chiang Chen, 158, and *Dudley* v. *Folliott* (1790) 3 Term Rep. 584, cit. Ti-Chiang Chen, 158, the decision was in accordance with the subsequent case *City of Berne* v. *Bank of England*. It should be borne in mind, however, that these were cases from the American War of Independence which by no means may serve automatically as a yard-stick for other situations.

[4] E.g. *The Lomonosoff* [1921] P. 97, equalizing with help against piracy or mutiny the assistance in pilfering a ship from the bolsheviks in Murmansk, where there was "no established government at all."

[5] *Yrissari* v. *Clement* (1826), Scott, *Cases*, 19 ("The existence of unacknowledged states must be proved by evidence," Lord Chief Justice Best) and *The Charkieh* (1873) L.R. 4 Adm. & Eccl. 59, Pitt Cobett, I, 25 (Sir Robert Phillimore).

[6] [1894] 1 Q.B. 149.

[7] [1921] 1 K.B. 456.

another letter, also from the Secretary of State for Foreign Affairs, dated November 27th, 1920, stating that Krassin to some extent was "exempt from the process of the courts" and entitled "to represent the state government of Russia" (which by no means implied a solution for special legal questions). The letter stated explicitly: "I am to add that His Majesty's Government have never officially recognized the Soviet government in any way". This decided the case. In answer to further enquiries by the court the Foreign Office stated that nothing was to be added to this letter. The court giving judgment said: "If a foreign government is recognized by the government of this country, the subjects and courts of this country may, and must, recognize the sovereignty of that foreign government and the validity of its acts. If a foreign government or its sovereignty is not recognized by the government of this country a judicial court either cannot, or at least need not, or ought not to, take notice of, or recognize such foreign government or its sovereignty". Judgment was given for the original owner, whose counsel had called the confiscation a "seizure by bandits". It is clear from this case that both an unrecognized government and its acts are considered a mere nullity by the courts.

The same opinion was expressed in *The Annette and The Dora* [1], in which case the court refused to recognize a requisition of ships by the Provisional Government of Northern Russia, i.e. the ships were returned to the original owners.

In the case *Héritiers A. Bouniatian c. Société Optorg* [2] the French court, turning down an appeal to the validity of confiscation, reasoned that non-recognition of the Soviet Union implied an ignoring of Soviet Russian law. The goods at stake in this lawsuit were on Russian territory while being confiscated and were transported to France afterwards. The position was comparable with the case *Luther* v. *Sagor*. Although the court's *ratio decidendi* was that there was no *bona fide* possession (the rule *en fait de meubles possession vaut titre* only applies to a *bona fide* possessor) it stressed that the point in case was *"l'enlèvement par violence de la chose au cours d'opérations exécutées sur l'ordre d'une groupe*

---

[1] [1919] P. 105.

[2] *Trib. civil de la Seine* 12–12–1923, *Clunet* 1924, 133.

de force, qui, au moment ou elles ont lieu, n'a point été l'objet d'une reconnaissance diplomatique en qualité de gouvernement régulier". The other French cases in the period prior to the recognition were decided similarly [1]. Belgian [2], Italian [3] and Rumanian [4] courts found to the same effect [5], [6].

2. *The U.S.A.: a Medium Point of View*

The American school of thought, in a way, might be called a medium point of view. At first it was wholly based on the dogmatic standpoint. In *Rose* v. *Himely* (1808) [7], which is regarded as the American pendant of *City of Berne* v. *Bank of England* [8], Chief Justice Marshall stated: "It is for the governments to decide whether they will consider St. Domingo as an independent nation and until such decision shall be made ... courts of justice must consider the ancient state of things as remaining unaltered ...." *Clark* v. *United States* (1811) [9] and *Gelston* v. *Hoyt* (1818) [10] also

---

[1] *Affaire du Kolang, Cour d'Appel* of Algiers 23–1–1923, *Clunet* 1924, 1046 and several decisions related to the nationalization of corporations.

[2] *Jelinkova* c. *de Serbouloff*, Brussels 5–6–1925, *Pasicrisie Belge* 1926, III, 131 (divorce).

[3] *Di Polloni et Svoroni* c. *Fédération des Travailleurs de la mer et Soc. Coop. Garibaldi*, Court of Genoa 7–3–1930, *Clunet* 1931, 761; *Katsikis* c. *Soc. Fati Svoroni di Pallone*, Court of Genoa 19–5–1923, *Clunet* 1923, 1021 (not regarding confiscation).

[4] *Banque russe pour le commerce étranger* v. *Association d'emprunt et de dépôt de Cetatea-Alba*, Rumanian Court of Cassation 4–11–1921, *Clunet* 1925, 1125; Court of Cassation 13–2–1929, *Z.f.O.* 1930, 673; 5–12–1932, *Clunet* 1935, 718.

[5] In a few Dutch decisions (*De Nederlanden van 1845* v. *Helvetia*, The Hague District Court, 9–3–1933, *N.J.* 1933, 1662, *Ann.Dig.* 1933–1934, 80 and The Hague Court of Appeal 3–6–1937, *N.J.* 1937, 1675, *Ann.Dig.* 1935–1937, 204), the possibility of ignoring was suggested on that ground. The Irish decision *The Ramava, Ann.Dig.* 1941–1942, 91, completely takes the dogmatic point of view.

[6] This standpoint elicits the question which law, then, does apply. In France the csarist law was still considered binding with regard to the Soviet confiscations, cf. J. Delehelle, *La Situation juridique des Russes en France*, Lille, 1926, 45. In the most difficult cases the *force majeure* notion was resorted to, though French law was also applied: *Héritiers A. Bouniatian* c. *Soc. Optorg, Trib. civil de la Seine* 12–12–1923, *Clunet* 1924, 133 and *Affaire du Kolang, Cour d'Appel* of Algiers 23–1–1923, *Clunet* 1924, 1046; the Egyptian decision *Gross* v. *Gretchenko*, Court of Alexandria 30–4–1924, *Clunet* 1924, 1112, likewise assumed the continuance of the old law; in the opinion of an Italian court, however, csarist law was no longer applicable; remarking that this law was a *cadavre législatif*, it had recourse to *les principes généraux de droit* (Court of Genoa 19–5–1923, *Clunet* 1923, 1021).

[7] 4 Cranch 240, cit. Ti-Chiang Chen, 240.

[8] Scott, *Cases*, 57.

[9] 3 Wash. C.C. 101, cit. Ti-Chiang Chen, 230.

[10] 3 Wheat. 246, cit. Ti-Chiang Chen, 230.

took this line. The same opinion was held in several subsequent decisions [1], [2].

A symptom of changing views [3] can be seen in the case *O'Neill* v. *Central Leather Co.* [4], which laid down, that the Villa faction (though unrecognized as the Mexican government) in Mexico had the right to confiscate property and pass valid title to purchasers [5]. The same trend was evident in *Boris N. Sokoloff* v. *National City Bank of New York* [6]. In this case Judge Cardozo cited some cases [7] relating to the Civil War; on the analogy of those cases he felt entitled to tone down somewhat the strictly dogmatic rule: "It would be hazardous... to say that a rule so comprehensive and so drastic is not subject to exceptions under pressure of some insistent claim of policy or justice". Mentioning the desirability of applying "self-imposed limitations of common sense and fairness" he drew the conclusion that an unrecognized state or government "may gain for its acts and decrees a validity quasi-governmental, if violence to fundamental principles of justice or to our own public policy might otherwise be done". The appeal of Cardozo to the said precedents was not wholly justified [8]; the decisions referred to the War of Secession, with the courts deciding matters which, after all, were domestic affairs. The point at issue in the present case, however, was the validity of the measures of a foreign state. Nevertheless Cardozo's views resulted in a more satisfactory and realistic approach to the arising problems. Without doubt the fact that the U.S.A. for a

[1] *The Nueva Anna* (1821), 6 Wheaton 193, 37 A.L.R. 750; *The Ambrose Light* (1885), 25 F. 408, Hudson, 132; *The Rogdai, Ann.Dig.* 1919–1922, 51; *The Penza, Ann. Dig.* 1919–1922, 53; *The Tobolsk, Ann.Dig.* 1919–1922, 53. It appears from *Russian Government* v. *Lehigh Valley Railroad Co., Ann.Dig.* 1923–1924, 48 and *Lehigh Valley Railroad Co* v. *State of Russia, Ann.Dig.* 1927–1928, 58, that the Kerenski-regime was regarded as the official Russian government as long as the opposite was not expressly proved.

[2] Only exception: *Consul of Spain* v. *La Conception* (1819) Fed. Cas. No. 3137, 2 Wheel. Cr. Case (1819), 597, cit. Ti-Chiang Chen, 244; Johnson J. considered it possible " ... to deduce the fact of national independence from history, evidence or public notoriety where there has been no formal public recognition."

[3] Already announcing themselves in *Underhill* v. *Hernandez*, 168 U.S. 250 (1897); cf. *infra*, 64.

[4] 87 N.J.L. 552, 94 Atl. 789 (1915), cit. Re, 87.

[5] Likewise *Molina* v. *Commision Reguladora Del Mercado de Henequen*, 92 N.J.L. 38, 104 Atl. 450 (1918), cit. Re, 167.

[6] *Clunet* 1925, 443, 446, *Ann.Dig.* 1923–1924, 44 and 37 A.L.R. 712.

[7] *Williams* v. *Bruffy*, 96 U.S. 176 (1877); *Baldy* v. *Hunter*, 171 U.S. 388 (1897); cf. Lauterpacht, *Recognition*, 146.

[8] Cf. Noël-Henry, 103-104.

long time withheld recognition of the Soviet Government played its part.

It is difficult to say whether or not American case law has reached a settled opinion regarding this point. In many cases [1] the rule laid down by Judge Cardozo was applied or its application was made possible. Some decisions even took the more realistic view. More recent cases however were decided on the lines of the old dogmatic conception [2].

3. The Realistic Approach

Squarely opposed to the strictly dogmatic point of view is the realistic approach. This school of thought might also be denoted as the legal reality point of view, a standpoint strongly upheld especially by Dickinson. Swiss case law represents the purest example of it. Dutch case law too — after some hesitations — is based on this view. It proceeds from the idea that recognition should be left where it belongs, i.e. in the sphere of the law of nations governing the mutual relations between states and administrations. The law of an unrecognized government should be recognized as such by the judiciary as soon as that government can be considered effective. So it is effectiveness that counts.

In the first instance of *Banque Internationale de Commerce de Pétrograd* v. *Hausner* [3] it was decided that according to the conflict rules Russian law was applicable in principle, but not in practice, since Soviet Russia was not recognized by Switzerland. The Swiss Federal Court, however, considered the non-recognition as only implying that the Soviet government in international affairs did not represent Russia as far as Switzerland was concerned. This did not prevent Soviet law from being

---

[1] E.g. *Salimoff* v. *Standard Oil Co. of New York* and *Salimoff* v. *Vacuum Oil Co.*, *Ann.Dig.* 1933–1934, 22; *Fred. S. James & Co.* v. *Second Russian Insurance Cy.*, *Ann. Dig.* 1925–1926, 57; *Russian Reinsurance Co. and Paul Rasor* v. *Francis R. Stoddard and the Bankers Trust Co.*, *Clunet* 1925, 451, 1070, *Ann.Dig.* 1925–1926, 54; *Banque de France* v. *Equitable Trust Co. of New York* and *Banque de France* v. *Chase National Bank*, *Ann. Dig.* 1929–1930, 43 (The latter two decisions, however, reckon with the danger of double payment too); *The Denny*, *Ann.Dig.* 1941–1942, 80.

[2] *The Kotkas*, *Ann. Dig.* 1941–1942, 70; *The Regent*, *Ann. Dig.* 1941–1942, 73; *The Signe*, *Ann. Dig.* 1941–1942, 74, 86; *The Maret*, *Ann. Dig.* 1943–1945, 29; *Latvian State Cargo and Passenger S. S. Line* v. *Clark*, *Ann.Dig.* 1948, 45, *A.J.I.L.* 1949, 380; *A. S. Merilaid & Co.* v. *Chase National Bank*, *Ann. Dig.* 1947, 15, *A.J.I.L.* 1948, 231.

[3] *R.O.* 50 II 507 (1924), decision of 10–12–1924.

in existence and having consequences: "*Le Tribunal fédéral ne peut que s'incliner devant le fait accompli et en enregistrer le résultat* [1]"

In the Netherlands at first there was some hesitation. The Dordrecht District Court [2] as early as 1927 assumed a certain impact of Soviet law ("paralysis of the corporations"), but the Hague District Court (1933) [3] and the Hague Court of Appeal (1937) [4] put the question — without answering it — whether Soviet legislation should be recognized as such. The Amsterdam District Court, however, in 1935 passed judgment to the contrary [5] and afterwards the Amsterdam District Court and Court of Appeal [6] also completely accepted the view laid down in the *Hausner* case.

We prefer the realistic view to the dogmatic one [7]. Undoubtedly the dogmatic view can be applied in court very simply, but the results are most unsatisfactory. This is indicated *expressis verbis* by Lauterpacht. In addition to that it proceeds from false premises. Recognition is an act on diplomatic level, having its main effects in the field of international law. In recent times recognition was given a character far more political than is desirable and non-recognition often is a weapon in international affairs. As a result a state will most certainly not recognize a given state or government for the sole reason that its effectiveness is undeniable. Effectiveness and recognition are two separate notions. The drawback of the indistinct notion of the difference between the effectiveness of a government (the existence *de*

---

[1] In *Schinz* c. *Bächli*, *R.O.* 52 I 218 (1926), *Clunet* 1928, 219, most curiously, a certain hesitation became apparent. The case was described as a *question controversée*. *Tcherniak* c. *Tcherniak*, however, *R.O.* 54 II 225 (1928), *Clunet* 1928, 208 (no confiscation) was decided in line with the *Hausner*-case; likewise *Wilbuschewitz* c. *Autorité tutélaire de la Ville de Zürich et Dép. t. de justice du canton de Zürich*, *R.O.* 51 II 259 (1925), *Clunet* 1926, 1110 and *Erben Prochorow* c. *Obergericht Zürich*, *R.O.* 55 I 289 (1929).

[2] *Vseobtchaia Stroitelnaia Kompania* v. *Smit*, 12-1-1927, *N. J.* 1927, 447, *Ann. Dig.* 1927–1928, 71.

[3] *De Nederlanden van 1845* v. *Helvetia*, 9-3-1933, N.J. 1933, 1662, *Ann. Dig.* 1933–1934, 80.

[4] *De Nederlanden van 1845* v. *Helvetia*, 3-6-1937, *N.J.* 1937, 1675, *Ann. Dig.* 1935–1937, 204.

[5] *Exportchleb* v. *Goudeket*. *N.J.* 1935, 1058, *Ann. Dig.* 1935–1937, 117.

[6] *Herani* v. *Wladikawkaz Railway Co*, *N.J.* 1940, No. 1095 and 1943, No. 496, *Ann. Dig. Suppl. Vol.*, 21.

[7] To the same effect a great number of authors, e.g.: Dickinson, *Mich. L.R.* 1923; Borchard, *A.J.I.L.* 1932, 261; François, I, 183-184; Van der Molen, *De Rechtsgedingen* ..., 20; Schnitzer, I, 188; Freund, *Clunet* 1924, 51; Melchior, 83; Wohl, *Ostrecht* 1925, 26; Spiropoulos, 156; Stierlin, 99; Stille, 48; Seidl-Hohenveldern, 20.

facto) on the one side and the diplomatic recognition *de facto* or *de iure* on the other hand comes to light when maintaining the typically dogmatic view (i.e. acts of an unrecognized government lack legal character). The intrinsic weakness of this dogmatic point of view is demonstrated very plainly by Lauterpacht in his assertion: "The correct and reasonable rule is that both the unrecognized government and its acts are a nullity. That rule, it must be admitted, would cease to be reasonable if it became customary to refuse recognition to governments not on the ground that they are not effective but for such reasons as that they are 'unworthy of a place in the Society of Nations'. Had any such practice become a permanent feature of the policy of recognition, there would be room for reconsideration of a well-established and sound principle of law" [1]. It is incomprehensible, then, that while writing (in 1947!): "The principles ... are sound and inescapable — so long as recognition is not withheld arbitrarily for political reasons. They become artificial and productive of hardship, when the test of effectiveness ... is abandoned ..." [2] he yet maintains the dogmatic view. Consequently Ti-Chiang Chen [3] is perfectly right in advocating a more "realistic approach", in which the effectiveness plays a decisive part. Recognition is an act of international law and as such it can in no way prejudice the legal character of the legislative acts of a state-subject. This legal character is present as soon as the government at issue is regarded as an exponent of sovereignty. To ascertain this is a factual task to be left to the courts. There is no question of the *forum* interfering with its governments foreign policy as the courts are not the organ to decide foreign policy. This is the function of the Executive.

4. *Difference between de facto and de iure Recognition?*

It may be wondered whether in countries where such a preponderant place is accorded by the judiciary to the fact of recognition, a distinction is drawn between recognition *de facto* and *de iure*. It is generally assumed, that this distinction is all but irrelevant

---

[1] Lauterpacht, *Recognition*, 147.
[2] Lauterpacht, *Recognition*, 154.
[3] Ti-Chiang Chen, 166.

to private international law [1]. As regards public international law the distinction is also of little importance [2]. It is nevertheless important to keep a clear notion of the terms used in this field and their meaning. Much misunderstanding is bound to arise when the difference between recognition of an existing situation, i.e. the finding as a fact that a certain entity wields power *de facto* and the recognition *de facto* or *de iure* is disregarded [3].

5. *Retroactivity*

The intrinsic weakness of the dogmatic view (ignoring the acts of an unrecognized government) becomes evident if due attention is paid to the way in which English [4], American [5] and French [6] case law resorts to the retroactivity of recognition. That proves

---

[1] *Luther* v. *Sagor* [1921] 3 K.B. 532, L. J. Bankes citing *Williams* v. *Bruffy*, 96 U.S. 176 (1877) and *Underhill* v. *Hernandez*, 168 U.S. 250 (1897) (see Re, 132-133); the decision in the first instance *A/S. Tallina Leavauhisus* v. *Tallina Shipping Co and Estonian S.S. Line* (1946) 79 Ll. L.L.R. 245, *Brit. Yearb.* 1946, 384, did distinguish; on appeal, however, this argument was dismissed, *A/S Tallina Laevauhisus* v. *Estonian State S.S. Line* (1947) 80 Ll.L.L.R. 99, *Brit. Yearb.* 1947, 416. In *Banco de Bilbao* v. *Rey*, *Banco de Bilbao* v. *Sanchez*, *Clunet* 1938, 602, a decree of the Bask-government not recognized by Great Britain, was held a nullity; on appeal a certain distinction was made between *de iure* and *de facto* recognition ([1938] 2 K.B. 176); a decree of the *de iure* recognized Republican government was not applied, this government no longer wielding actual power over Bilbao, where the head office of the bank was established. Further it appears from *Bank of Ethiopia* v. *National Bank of Egypt and Liguori* [1937] 1 Ch. 513, that a *de facto* recognized government exercising actual authority is preferred over the *de iure* government. For the rest *Haile Selassie* v. *Cable and Wireless Ltd* (*no 2*) [1939] Ch. 182, did not make a certain distinction between *de iure* and *de facto* recognition; however, the point in this case was not confiscation but the question whether Italy was to be looked upon as the legal successor of the Ethiopian sovereign as regards a sum of money, recoverable in England; here a recognition *de iure* was demanded. In the Dutch decision *The Sendeja*, President Haarlem District Court, 24-7-1937, *N.J.* 1937 No. 863, *Ann. Dig.* 1935–1937, 203, the *de facto* power played a part, apart from questions of *de iure* and *de facto* recognition; cf. *infra* 53 ff., 83.

[2] Ti-Chiang Chen, 270; Lauterpacht, *op. cit.* 336.

[3] A clear exposition is given by Ti-Chiang Chen in Chapter 18 of his study.

[4] E.g., *Luther* v. *Sagor* [1921] 3 K.B. 536; *Princess Paley Olga* v. *Weisz* [1929] 1 K.B. 718; *Lazard Bros. and Co* v. *Banque Industrielle de Moscou*, *Lazard Bros. and Co* v. *Midland Bank Ltd.* [1932] 1 K.B. 617, [1933] A.C. 289. The older cases were divided, cf. Ti-Chiang Chen, 172-173. In *Luther* v. *Sagor* the cases *Williams* v. *Bruffy*, 96 U.S. 176 (1877), *Underhill* v. *Hernandez*, 168 U.S. 250 (1897), *Oetjen* v. *Central Leather Co.*, 246 U.S. 297 (1918) and *Ricaud* v. *American Metal Co.*, 246 U.S. 304 (1918), were cited as "weighty expressions of opinion."

[5] E.g., *Williams* v. *Bruffy*, *Underhill* v. *Hernandez*, *Oetjen* v. *Central Leather Co.* and *Ricaud* v. *American Metal Co.*, *supra* n. 4; cf. Ti-Chiang Chen, 175.

[6] Clear examples in *Cie Nord de Moscou* c. *La Union et Phénix Espagnol*, *Cour d'Appel* of Paris 13-6-1928, *Clunet* 1929, 119; *Marchak* v. *Rabinerson*, *Cour d'Appel* of Paris 15-2-1933, *Clunet* 1933, 959.

the failure of the dogmatic view, expressed characteristically by Ti-Chiang Chen: "The doctrine (of retroactivity) is a fiction created to rectify the errors of another fiction, namely the fiction that a power does not exist where it does in fact exist" [1].

In the meantime it may be said that by retroactivity the most unsatisfactory consequences of the dogmatic doctrine are removed, although it involves an element of legal insecurity [2].

II. JURISDICTIONAL IMMUNITY

In a study of the question how far a confiscation by a certain state is considered valid elsewhere, one encounters a number of cases where the basic issue often remains undecided. In those cases the confiscating state invokes its jurisdictional immunity, which may happen both when a claim is filed directly against a state or government (e.g. for compensation) and when a claim of recovery of goods in its possession is made. In the last few years the problem of immunity holds the center of the stage. It was discussed by the International Law Association [3]. In England a committee (the Somervell-committee) is charged with studying the question whether or not the English point of view on immunity is desirable [4]. That so much attention is paid to this subject is not surprising. In many countries changing views regarding the tasks of the state have precipitated an acute phase and this has already produced a convention [5] on an important point. The number of states, however, which have entered into this convention is limited [6], [7]. A trend towards abandoning at least the

[1] Ti-Chiang Chen, 186. In the same sense Stille, 105-106.

[2] Incidentally the recognition of Soviet Russia by the United Kingdom came after the decision in the first instance but before the appeal case in *Luther* v. *Sagor* [1921] 1 K.B. 456 and [1921] 3 K.B. 532.

[3] *Report* 44th Conf. Int. Law Ass. 1950, 204 and *Report* 45th Conf. Int. Law Ass. 1952, 210.

[4] Committee set up by the Lord Chancellor, under the chairmanship of Lord Justice Sommervell (*Report* 44th Conf. Int. Law Ass. 1950, 207).

[5] Convention for the Unification of certain Rules relating to the Immunity of State-owned vessels. Signed at Brussels April 10, 1926 (Hudson, *International Legislation* III, 1837).

[6] A number of continental and South-American states.

[7] For the rest, the convention only regulates the exploitation and transport, not the question of ownership. Cf. *The Garbi*, President of the Middelburg District Court 22-10-1938, *N.J.* 1939, No. 96, *Ann. Dig. Suppl. Vol.* 155, where immunity was granted as no exploitation or transport was involved.

system of absolute immunity is clearly discernable [1]. As a rule a substitution of the absolute immunity by a limited one is advocated, while the well-known distinction of acts *iure imperii* (the state acting as such) as contrasted with acts *iure gestionis* (the state taking part in e.g. trade and industry on an equal footing with its subjects) serves as a yard-stick in deciding whether the exception of immunity should be granted.

It may be said, that only English case law still advocates the doctrine of absolute immunity [2], which means that the question whether the action is taken *iure imperii* or *iure gestionis* is not investigated. Meanwhile even in England, the stronghold of absolute immunity, a turning of the tide is discernable. The setting up of the Somervell- committee was evidently prompted by the opinions of Lord Macmillan, Lord Thankerton and Maughan in the *Cristina*-case. There are as yet no decisions expressing those changed views.

In the U.S.A. a remarkable difference of opinion between the Executive and the courts may be found. The Executive clearly maintains that it is desirable to differentiate between cases involving acts *iure imperii* and those involving acts *iure gestionis* [3]; immunity should only be granted in the former case. The Judiciary however still insists that such distinctions do not matter and that immunity should be granted anyway [4], provided that the property involved is *de facto* possession of the defending state [5].

A number of states do practice the distinction between acts performed by a foreign state acting *iure imperii* and *iure gestionis*. In the former case jurisdictional immunity is granted to such a foreign state; in the latter immunity cannot be invoked.

---

[1] Cf. as for this and the subject as a whole: Lauterpacht, *The Problem of Jurisdictional Immunities of Foreign States*, Brit. Yearb. 1951, 220.

[2] E.g., *The Parlement Belge* (1880), 5 P.D. 197, Pitt Cobbett, I, 283; *The Porto Alexandre* [1920] P. 30; *The Cristina* [1938] A.C. 485; *Krajina* v. *Tass Agency* [1949] 2 All E.R. 274.

[3] Letters of The Acting Legal Adviser of the Department of State to the Acting Attorney General dated 13–4–1949 (*Dept. of State Bull.* 1949, 592) and dated 19-5-1952 (*Dept. of State Bull.* 1952, 984); cf. W. W. Bishop, *New United States policy limiting sovereign immunity*, A.J.I.L. 1953, 93.

[4] *The Schooner Exchange* v. *Mc Faddon*, 7 Cranch 116, (1812), Hudson, 306; *The Pesaro*, 271 U.S. 562 (1926), *Ann. Dig.* 1925–1926, 186; *The Navemar*, 303 U.S. 68 (1938), *Ann. Dig.* 1938–1940, 176.

[5] *Republic of Mexico* v. *Hoffman*, 324 U.S. 31 (1945), *Ann. Dig.* 1943–1945, 143.

Italy and Belgium held this view of old, as did Austria and Switzerland. Ireland rendered some similar decisions. France earlier advocated the absolute immunity, but later abandoned it. In the Netherlands the same opinion is held, although some exceptions occur. In Germany a turning of the tide is noticeable in a trend to accept a distinction [1].

The distinction between acts *iure imperii* and acts *iure gestionis* which distinction is one of the most important facets of the problem of immunity, appears to play a part much less preponderant in the cases connected with confiscation measures and similar actions. This is largely because the cases mostly involved actions to be described as *iure imperii*. For that reason the distinction was often not explicitly made. Neither can the distinction be applied when a claim for compensation is filed against the confiscating state, for in such a case the very act of confiscation must be appreciated and there is no denying that confiscation as such must always be considered an act *iure imperii*. Only a sole dissenting decision may be cited [2]. The position is somewhat different if the claim is directed against a confiscating state in possession of the property. Then the question whether the state, using that property, is acting *iure imperii* or *iure gestionis* does make sense [3].

Several decisions are to be mentioned here, mainly regarding the requisition of ships. It is not always clear, however, whether the point is confiscation or expropriation for public utility.

---

[1] A good review of the cases in various countries is to be found in Lauterpacht, *Brit. Yearb.* 1951, 250.

[2] A claim for compensation for confiscation was dismissed owing to the immunity of the state or government in question in *Hertzfeld* c. *U.S.S.R.*, *Cour d'Appel* of Paris 14-4-1938, *Clunet* 1938, 1034, *Ann. Dig.* 1938–1940, 243; Swedish Supreme Court 5-5-1934, *Bruns Z.* 1935, 681; *Poortensdijk* v. *Soviet Republic of Latvia*, Amsterdam District Court 14-1-1941, *N.J.* 1941, No. 338, Amsterdam Court of Appeal 3-12-1942, *N.J.* 1943, No. 340, *Ann. Dig. Suppl. Vol.* 142; to the same effect *De Froe* v. *U.S.S.R.*, Amsterdam District Court 11-1-1932, *W.* 12453, Netherlands Supreme Court 2-12-1932, *N.J.* 1933, 980, *Ann. Dig.* 1931–1932, 170, relating to the non-payment of Russian Bonds by the U.S.S.R.. Differently: the judgment *Trib. civil de la Seine* 12-1-1940, *Ann. Dig.* 1938–1940, 245, *re Réprésentation comm. de l'U.R.S.S.* c. *Soc. Franç. industr. et comm. des Pétroles* (*groupe Malapolska*), where a claim for compensation for confiscation, executed in Poland, was recognized. However, here the issue was that an act of sovereignty was not at stake, but rather an infringement of property on occupied territory in violation of international law. On formal grounds this judgment was reversed on appeal, *Cour d'Appel* of Paris 12-2-1941, *Ann. Dig. Suppl. Vol.* 145.

[3] *Infra*, 42 ff.

Different distinctions may be made in this connection. Some countries regard the recognition of the foreign government as a *conditio sine qua non* for the granting of immunity. In *The Annette and The Dora* [1] an English court decided that immunity could not be pleaded since no recognition was given to the Russian Provisional Government. The Irish decision *The Ramava* [2] also took this view. The French case *Rousse et Maber* c. *Banque d'Espagne e.a.* acted upon the same principle [3].

There are also countries, where the granting of immunity is not influenced by recognition. In the U.S.A. this is evident in *Wulfsohn* v. *R.S.F.S.R.* [4] and *Nankivel* v. *Omsk All Russian Government* [5], in the Netherlands in *De Froe* v. *U.S.S.R.* [6] and *Weber* v. *U.S.S.R.* [7], [8].

When the action against the foreign state or government relates to tangibles, immunity is only granted if such state or government has actual possession of the goods. Meanwhile, in some exceptional cases a state having lost possession of the confiscated goods successfully pleaded immunity and recovered the goods, e.g. in the Austrian decision *re Oesterreich-Ungarische Bank* [9] and the Belgian case *Saez Murua* v. *Pinillos and Garcia* [10]. However, studying those cases more closely the conclusion can be drawn that judgment could be given for the plaintiff even without

---

[1] [1919] P. 105, *Ann. Dig.* 1919–1922, 43; cf. *The Gagara* [1919] P. 95, *Ann. Dig.* 1919–1922, 45, where immunity was granted in view of the Foreign Office statement that Britain had "recognized the Esthonian National Council as a *de facto* independent body."

[2] *Ann. Dig.* 1941–1942, 91.

[3] *Cour d' Appel* of Poitiers 26-7-1937, *Ann. Dig.* 1935–1937, 189.

[4] *Ann. Dig.* 1923–1924, 39.

[5] *Ann. Dig.* 1923–1924, 134.

[6] Supreme Court 2-12-1932, *N.J.* 1933, 980, *Ann. Dig.* 1931–1932, 170.

[7] Amsterdam Court of Appeal 30-4-1942, *N.J.* 1942, No. 757, *Ann. Dig. Suppl. Vol*, 140.

[8] However in the U.S.A. the right to sue is not granted to an unrecognized government: *R.S.F.S.R.* v. *Cibrario, Ann. Dig.* 1923–1924, 41; *The Penza, Ann. Dig.* 1919–1922, 53; *The Rogdai, Ann. Dig.* 1919–1922, 51; *The Tobolsk, Ann. Dig.* 1919–1922, 53. Recent Dutch decisions indicate the contrary; there the effectiveness plays the leading part: *Republik Maluku Selatan* v. *Kon. Paketvaart Mij*, President Amsterdam District Court 2-11-1950, *N.J.* 1950, No. 804; appeal case Amsterdam Court of Appeal 8-2-1951, *N.J.* 1951, No. 129; *Republik Maluku Selatan* v. *Nieuw Guinea*, President The Hague District Court 10-2-1954, *N.J.* 1954, No. 549; *Republik Maluku Selatan* v. *Nieuw Guinea*, Court of Justice New Guinea 7-3-1952, *N.J.* 1953, No. 100.

[9] *O.G.H.* 27-8-1919, *Z.f. intern. R.* 1920, 505, *Modern L.R.* 1950, 70.

[10] *Cour d'Appel* of Brussels 17-1-1938, *Cour de Cassation* 23-11-1939, *Ann. Dig.* 1938–1940, 289.

a plea of immunity [1]. Applying the principle of secondary immunity would have produced identical results [2]. In addition to this, the sole claim to certain properties especially without possession will not provide immunity [3].

If actual possession is the condition, this still may be explained two ways: as a *maximum* or as a *minimum*. Construing the condition as a *maximum* means that a closer investigation is unnecessary, if only there is actual possession [4]; in that case actual possession settles the dispute. This view is held in the U.S.A. in e.g. *The Janko* [5] and *Ervin* v. *Quintanilla* [6]. On that basis *The Navemar* [7] makes no exception; no actual possession being assumed, an investigation could be made as to title and right to possession. For the rest the District Court stated that possession acquired in America by force cannot form the basis for immunity. In contrast to this opinion is the case of *Ervin* v. *Quintanilla* [8], where the ship (the San Ricardo) was seized peaceably and not by force.

The same point of view is seen in England, where the question at issue was dealt with in several decisions. There, too, possession will suffice [9], except when gained by forcible seizure on British territory [10], [11].

---

[1] So invoking immunity was superfluous. Cf. Seidl-Hohenveldern, 10-11.

[2] *Infra*, 129 ff.

[3] Lord Maughan in *The Cristina*: "There is no authority for the view, that if he wrongfully obtained possession ... and it was in the hand of a third person, he could claim to stay proceedings ... merely by stating that he claimed it"; ditto *Haile Selassie* v. *Cable and Wireless Ltd.* (*no 1*) [1938] Ch. 839: a sum of money is not awarded on the sole ground that a claim has been made: the title to the money must be proved.

[4] Factual or physical possession is another term.

[5] (*The Norsktank*), *Ann. Dig.* 1943–1945, 107.

[6] *Ann. Dig.* 1938–1940, 219; here the tanker San Ricardo was seized by the Mexican authorities in the port of Mobile, Alabama. Cf. Re, 117.

[7] *Ann. Dig.* 1938–1940, 176; the same: *The Motomar, Bulletin* vol. 41, 270.

[8] *Ann. Dig.* 1938–1940, 219; the same; *Fields* v. *Predionica I. Tkanica, Ann. Dig.* 1941–1942, 204 and 208, dealing with a "protective" requisition, executed in Brazilian territorial waters.

[9] *The Jupiter* (*No 1*) [1924] P. 236; *The Arantzazu Mendi* [1938] P. 233, [1939] P. 37, [1939] A. C. 256; *The Cristina* [1938] A.C. 485; *The Cristobal Colon, Ann. Dig. Suppl. Vol.*, 156; *El Neptuno* (1938) 62 Ll.L.L.R. 7; *The Rita Garcia* (1937) 59 Ll.L.L.R. 140; *The Arraiz* (1938) 61 Ll.L.L.R. 39; *The Kabalo* (1940) 67 Ll.L.L.R. 572; *Dollfus Mieg et Cie* v. *Bank of England* [1950] Ch. 333; *U.S. of America* v. *Dollfus Mieg et Cie and Bank of England* [1952] A.C. 582 (immunity to the Allied States in the possession of gold bars stolen by Germany).

[10] *The Abodi Mendi* [1939] P. 178; besides the ship in question was in the custody of the Admiralty Marshal.

[11] *The Cristina* [1938] A.C. 485; *El Condado* (1937) 59 Ll.L.L.R. 119; a somewhat allied situation was presented in the case *Civil Air Transport Inc.* v. *Central Air*

The French decisions *Agusquiza* c. *Société Sota y Aznar (The Arno-Mendi)* [1], *Société Cementos Rezola* c. *Larrasquitu et Etat Espagnol (The Itxas-Zurri)* [2] and *Lafuente* c. *Llaguno y Duranona (The Saturno)* [3] take the same view as regards expropriation: here it was pointed out explicitly, that the point in case was not confiscation [4].

Construing on the contrary the condition of possession as a *minimum*, means that immunity is not granted if there is only actual possession, but that there remains room for some enquiry; in that case actual possession is a *conditio sine qua non*, though other factors for granting immunity may also arise. Thus it is assumed in several decisions, that in no case can immunity be granted, if the confiscation involved aims at extraterritorial validity. Some Austrian decisions [5] take this standpoint and the French case *U.R.S.S.* c. *Chaliapine* [6] also proceeds from it, although it is difficult to presume actual possession in cases of trade-marks or copyrights.

The same opinion was held by the Swedish Supreme Court *re The Rigmor* [7] and *The Solgry* [8]. Here the question at issue was an expropriation by a Norwegian Order in Council providing tor compensation. At the time when the order was put into effect the ships were in Swedish territorial waters. The British government, which bought the ships, successfully invoked immunity, which was not deemed inconsistent with the fundamental principles

---

Transport Corp. [1953] A.C. 70 (cf. *I.L.Q.* 1950, 418 and 1951, 159). In this case some aircraft was sold by the Chinese Nationalist Government, the aiicraft now being in Hong-Kong. The employees holding the aircraft sympathized with the Chinese Communist Government and refused to pass the aircraft to the purchaser. The employees stated that they represented the government. Although this Communist government was recognized *de iure* by Great Britain, it was held that such recognition was "not to invalidate acts of the previous *de iure* government."

[1] *Cour d' Appel* of Bordeaux 28-3-1938, *Nouvelle Revue de dr.i.pr.* 1938, 332, *Ann. Dig.* 1935–1937, 195.

[2] *Cour d' Appel* of Poitiers 20-12-1937, *Clunet* 1938, 287, *Ann. Dig.* 1935–1937, 196.

[3] *Lafuente* c. *Llaguno y Duranona* (*Saturno*), *Cour d'Appel* of Bordeaux 28-3-1938, *Ann. Dig.* 1938–1940, 152.

[4] In a similar case, *Navires Arabara et Napartara, Trib. civil* of Bayonne 18-11-1937, *Le Droit Mar. Fr.* 1938, 473, however, immunity was refused in view of the circumstance, that the home port of the ships was not under the factual authority of the intervening Spanish government.

[5] *Handelsgericht* Vienna 21-6-1948, *Z.A.I.P.* 1949–1950, 479; *Hoffmann* v. *Dralle*, *Clunet* 1950, 748.

[6] *Cour de Cassation* 15-12-1936, S. 1937.1.104, D. 1937.1.63.

[7] *Ann. Dig.* 1941–1942, 240.

[8] *Ann. Dig. Suppl. Vol.*, 153.

of Swedish law. The latter point was of great importance. The Swedish Supreme Court, adjudicating upon a purely confiscatory nationalization, which involved an Esthonian ship (the Toomas which sailed when the nationalization decree was enacted) stated explicitly, that such a confiscation could not have extra-territorial effect. The ownership therefore could not rest with the Soviet Government, although she was the actual possessor of the ship [1]. Nevertheless execution against the ship was frustrated by the immunity of the Soviet Union [2]. Therefore, the *minimum* view was actually replaced by the *maximum* view since at first mere possession was held not to justify a title to immunity; afterwards such possession was considered to be sufficient.

Occasionally it is examined whether the property involved is used *iure imperii* or *iure gestionis*. Such is the case in *Hoffmann* g. *Dralle* [3] and in *U.R.S.S.* c. *Chaliapine* [4]. As mentioned above, the nature of most of the issues was such, that in the decisions the distinction is hardly discernable [5].

Of course there are also decisions which take no clear stand on all these issues [6].

It may easily be gathered that there is no unanimity as to how far immunity should go. Besides a strong tendency to limit the immunity to cases of acts purely *iure imperii*, there is also a

---

[1] *Russian Trade Delegation and others* v. *Carlbom* (I), *Ann. Dig.* 1943–1945, 61.

[2] *Russian Trade Delegation and others* v. *Carlbom* (II), *Ann. Dig.* 1943–1945, 112.

[3] *O.G.H.* 10-5-1950, *Clunet* 1950, 748; the same Munich 16-5-1950, *Brunz Z.* 1951–52, 254.

[4] *Cour de Cassation* 15-12-1936, S. 1937.1.104, D. 1937.1.63. This became also apparent from *The Ramava*, *Ann. Dig.* 1941–1942, 91; immunity, it is stated, only goes for vessels, which are *publicis usibus destinatae*. In *Nederlandse Bank* v. *Arktigugol*, Amsterdam Court of Appeal 29-4-1943, *N.J.* 1943, No. 600, it was assumed that the nationalized corporation *in casu* was no state organ.

[5] *Supra*,38.

[6] Immunity granted if there was possession: *Urrutia and Amollobieta* v. *Martiarena*, Brussels *Cour d'Appel* 7-7-1937, *Ann. Dig.* 1935–1937, 237; *The Ibai*, Supreme Court Argentina, *Ann. Dig.* 1935–1937, 247, *Ann. Dig.* 1938–1940, 293; *The Garbi*, President Middelburg District Court 22-10-1938, *N. J.* 1939, No. 96, *Ann. Dig. Suppl. Vol. 155*; *The Baurdo*, President Rotterdam District Court 2-8-1937, *N.J.* 1937, No. 912, *Ann. Dig.* 1935–1937, 200; *The Guernica*, Supreme Court Norway, *Ann. Dig. Suppl. Vol.*, 139; *The Maliakos* (U.S.A. decision), *Ann. Dig.* 1941–1942, 217; *The Johannis P. Goulandris* (U.S.A. decision), *Ann. Dig.* 1941–1942, 224; *Etat Espagnol et Banque d'Espagne* c. *Banco de Bilbao* (*Mydol*), *Cour d'Appel* of Rouen 7-12-1937, *Ann. Dig.* 1935–1937, 229; the assumption of the court that the subject dealt with was no confiscation but a protective requisition may have been of influence.

Immunity refused for lack of actual possession: *The Sendeja*, President Haarlem District Court, 24-7-1937, *N.J.* 1937, No. 863, *Ann. Dig.* 1935–1937, 203; *The Katingo Hadjipatera* (U.S.A. decision), *Ann. Dig.* 1941–1942, 221.

demand for further limitations: the condition *gained peaceably* is significant. A latent unwillingness to grant immunity in cases glaringly contrary to one's own principles of law becomes evident. It is beyond our scope to consider this matter further; suffice it to say that limitation of the immunity is desirable generally, both from the commercial point of view — since a full-fledged application of immunity would place private trade in an unfavourable position compared with state trade — and from the viewpoint that a given legal order must be entitled to remove the cloak of immunity, if it covers flagrant injustice, especially when that injustice has been accomplished on its own territory. It is self-evident that it is extremely difficult to draw the lines here. Case law gives a good illustration of this difficulty. That immunity in itself may cover injustice too, is demonstrated in the *El Condado*-cases: the Spanish ship El Condado was requisitioned as she was lying in the Scottish harbour Greenock. The Spanish consul seized her and being sued by the original owners pleaded immunity, for he had now gained actual possession. The Scottish court [1] decided in his favour. However, a subsequent action changed the situation completely. The Spanish government claimed damages and now the immunity did not arise. The court now said that the Spanish government, waiving its immunity, had to prove its title. This it was unable to do since the ship was in a Scottish port at the time of the requisition and therefore within Scottish jurisdiction; the claim therefore was dismissed [2]. On appeal, this judgment was upheld [3]. In deciding the question whether immunity should be granted, the court cited the *Cristina*-case. There the Spanish government appeared as defendant, and could as such invoke immunity. Here it submitted voluntarily to the tribunal, for "... the Spanish government, so far from pleading its immunity from legal process, has by the action expressly invoked the jurisdiction of the Court". If immunity would be granted now "it would mean immunity when the jurisdiction is declined and immunity when the jurisdiction is invoked". The results were: no immunity and no requisition of a ship, which was in Scotland, because "such (i.e. confiscatory) legislation will not

[1] (1937) 59 Ll.L.L.R. 119.
[2] (1939) 63 Ll.L.L.R. 83.
[3] (1939) 63 Ll.L.L.R. 331.

be held to affect property in this country or without the territory administered by such government".

In granting immunity in the first *El Condado*-case the court drew the distinction between "gained peaceably" and "gained by forcibly seizure". Yet the immunity covered an extra-territorial confiscation. The Swedish Supreme Court would not go that far [1], but yet shrunk from the consequences [2].

A heavy responsibility rests on the courts: doing justice here is extremely difficult.

III. SITUS PROBLEMS

1. Intangibles

It is clear from the cases that the *situs* of a certain object is most important when questions of confiscation are involved. The courts generally decide differently, if the property in question is situated within or outside the territory of the confiscating state, although exceptions do occur. The *situs* problem will therefore always be a preliminary issue when the court bases its judgment thereupon.

As to tangibles the question is not difficult. Here one has to ascertain where the property involved was situated at the time when the confiscatory measure came into force. The usual difficulties concerning the *situs* of e.g. *res in transitu* need not arise here.

Regarding intangibles and ships the problem is more complicated.

Concerning intangibles a *situs* notion is often operated with indeed — although there is no agreement as to the question where that *situs* is to be located — but such an approach has something artificial. Evidently this proceeds from the analogy of the *situs* of tangibles. It should also be borne in mind, that the *situs* of tangibles can be ascertained physically, without any relevance to the legal field. The *situs* of a chose in action, however, is always defined with respect to a given legal relation and may even differ according to this. The present situation of the *situs* problem in private international law, therefore, is most

[1] *Russian Trade Delegation and others* v. *Carlbom* (I), *Ann. Dig.* 1943–1945, 61.
[2] *Russian Trade Delegation and others* v. *Carlbom* (II), *Ann. Dig.* 1943–1945, 112.

unsatisfactory. The artificial character of the matter is evident [1].

It may be useful to review some cases that have come before the courts. There are, for instance, several decisions concerning industrial and artistic property.

The decisions re the Carthusian liqueur are well-known [2]. The claims at issue were those of the French liquidator of the Congregation of the *Pères Chartreux* for the trade-marks registered abroad [3]. The use of the *situs* notion in this connection is bound to produce some distorted reasonings. The trade-mark at issue was registered in different countries. If it was assumed that there was only one *situs*, this undoubtedly had to be located in France, giving the liquidator a chance of winning his case; such an assumption, however, would misjudge the fact that the trade-mark might be valued differently according to the countries involved. If a court wished to dismiss the claims, a multiple *situs* had to be construed. Consequently the odd figure of an intangible with a

---

[1] Most modern authors in the field of private international law discern the disadvantages of the artificial *situs* notion, but they nevertheless operate with it, e.g., Dicey, 309, Cheshire, 427, 450, Rabel III, 392.

[2] Cf. *supra*, 13 ff.

[3] All these claims were rejected:

Argentina: *Lecouturier* v. *Rey*, Court of Buenos Ayres 23-12-1905, *Revue Darras* 1907, 612.

Belgium: *Rey c.s.* c. *Lecouturier*, *Trib. Comm.* of Brussels 13-2-1907, *Revue Darras* 1907, 446; *Rey c.s* c. *Fouyer*, *Trib. Comm.* of Brussels 13-2-1907, *Revue Darras* 1907, 273; *Cour d'Appel* of Brussels 20-5-1910, *Revue Darras* 1911, 732.

Brazil: *Rey* v. *Lecouturier*, Supreme Court 10-5-1907, *Clunet* 1907, 1171; *Rey* v. *la Junte commerciale de Rio*, Court of Appeal of Rio de Janeiro 14–5–1907, *Clunet* 1908, 579.

England: *Lecouturier* v. *Rey*, decision in the first instance 19-10-1907, *Revue Darras* 1908, 270; this judgment, unfavourable for the monks, was reversed: [1908] 2 Ch. 715, *Revue Darras* 1908, 270, [1910] A.C. 262, *Revue Darras* 1910, 914.

Germany: *Rey and Dr Levy* v. *Lecouturier*, Hamburg District Court 4-5-1905, *Revue Darras* 1907, 950 (unfavourable for the monks); Hamburg District Court 23-2-1906, *Revue Darras* 1907, 415 (truce); Hamburg Court of Appeal 5-11-1907, *Revue Darras* 1907, 949 (liquidator's claim dismissed); Supreme Court of Leipzig 29-5-1908, *Entsch. Rg.* 69, 1, *Revue Darras* 1908, 815 (affirmation of the previous decision); Hamburg District Court 11-12-1908, *Revue Darras* 1909, 314.

Netherlands: *Rey* v. *Lecouturier*, The Hague District Court 1-3-1907, *Revue Darras* 1907, 458; The Hague Court of Appeal 28-10-1907, *W.* 8615, *Revue Darras* 1908, 313; *Lecouturier* v. *Rey*, Supreme Court 5-3-1908, *W.* 8691, *Revue Darras* 1908, 843.

Switzerland: *Rey* c. *Jaccard*, Supreme Court 13-2-1906, *R.O.* 32 I 148, *Revue Darras* 1907, 282; *Compagnie Fermière de la Grande Chartreuse* c. *Rey*, Supreme Court 11-7-1913, *R.O.* 39 III 640.

U.S.A.: *Baglin* v. *Cusenier*, Circuit Court of New York 18-11-1907, *Revue Darras* 1907, 972; Supreme Court, 221 U.S. 580 (1911).

Only in Tunis, decision of 11-5-1907 *Rey* c. *Lecouturier*, S. 1908.2.115, was judgment given in favour of the liquidator.

diversified *situs* arose. The Austrian Supreme Court decided a comparable case in the same way [1].

Establishing the *situs* of debts leads to may questions. According to current opinion the *situs* may even vary according to the legal relations. Those who, as regards confiscation, maintain that the *situs* must be established, unevitably fall prey to distorted arguments. Seidl-Hohenveldern who seeks a solution mainly on the ground of equitable considerations [2] believes that determination of the *situs* is necessary and shows the lack of unanimity by summing up the different opinions. A glance at the cases shows that the courts often wrestle with this problem. Satisfactory solutions are reached indeed; in such cases a *situs* is construed afterwards, as demanded by *communis opinio*. For the rest, the choice of a *situs* is sometimes avoided and an argument is set up closely approaching the view to be developed by us.

In French case law the *situs* question is of little importance in view of the tendency, dominant in France, not to attribute significance to the distinction between territorial and extra-territorial confiscation. This is obvious from the case *Crédit National Industriel* c. *Crédit Lyonnais* [3]. In this case the Crédit National Industriel had a claim against the Pétrograd branch of the Crédit Lyonnais. Judgment was given in favour of the plaintiff on the ground that the confiscation was contrary to public policy. A similar decision was given by the Paris Court of Appeal in *Yosselevitch* c. *Terestchenko* [4]. In these cases the *situs* question did not arise. Several other decisions demonstrate that the *situs* question becomes often complicated when a nationalized corporation is in question [5]. Then the issue is often decided without the *situs* playing a part; the matter in issue may be, for

---

[1] *Hoffmann* v. *Dralle*, *O.G.H.* 10-5-1950, *Clunet* 1950, 748.

[2] *Op. cit.*, 102.

[3] *Trib. comm. de la Seine* 25-5-1925, *Clunet* 1926, 376; *Cour d'Appel* of Paris 18-2-1926, *Clunet* 1927, 1061; owing to the depreciation of the ruble this decision did not mean anything to the claimant. In the same sense *Bauchon* c. *Crédit Lyonnais*, *Trib. civil de la Seine* 28-10-1925 and *Cour d'Appel* of Paris 17-6-1927, *Clunet* 1927, 1061.

[4] *Cour d'Appel* of Paris 23-4-1931, *Clunet* 1931, 1117.

[5] *Karagoulian* c. *Banque russe pour le commerce et l'industrie*, *Cour d'Appel* of Paris 17-5-1927, *Clunet* 1928, 131: the summoning in France depends on the status of the French branch of the Russian company; ditto *Dame Krivitzky* c. *Banque russe pour le commerce étranger*, *Trib. comm. de la Seine* 19-11-1927, *Clunet* 1928, 132; *Rabinovitch* c. *Banque russe pour le commerce étranger*, *Trib. comm. de la Seine* 15-5-1925, *Clunet* 1927, 354.

instance, whether an action can be brought and in such cases the *situs* question is often left undecided.

As regards English case-law it is of importance to trace the significance of the *situs*, though it plays a secondary part. This is illustrated by two cases concerning life insurance.

In the first place we refer to *Bürger* v. *New York Life Insurance Cy* [1] concerning policies issued by the Russian branch of an American company. There was no divergence of opinion as to which law was applicable according to the conflict rules; the proper law in this case was the Russian law. The point was exactly what that law was supposed to provide. In first instance [2] the court decided, that under Russian law all insurances had been annulled, so that no benefit was due. On appeal the decision was reversed. Lord Justice Bankes considered the relevant Russian law very carefully and then cited the Decree of December 1st, 1918 [3] (insurance is a state monopoly, all companies are to become state organizations; a liquidation is ordered to take effect immediately and to be concluded on April 1st, 1919 at the latest), the Decree of February 8th, 1919 (extension of the first decree to foreign companies operating in Russia), the Decree of November 18th, 1919 [4] (all life-insurances annulled, all premiums confiscated), and finally section 2 of the Russian Civil Code (prohibiting the courts to adjudicate upon cases originating before November 7th, 1917). In contrast he cited a circular of the People's Commissariat of Justice of October 16th, 1924 [5], interpreting the decrees in such a way as to make them inapplicable to insurances contracted by non-Russian companies. He held this interpretation to be binding [6] and concluded that the assurer had to pay. Lord Justice Atkin concurred, but Lord Justice Scrutton delivered a dissenting judgment that the decrees were couched in general terms and that the interpretation of the circular was an *excès de pouvoirs*, lacking binding force. Although the *situs* of the life assurance was not specifically examined, the question might be raised whether the court intended to indicate the *situs* of the

[1] 43 T.L.R. 601.
[2] The decision in the first instance was not published.
[3] Labry, 269.
[4] *Ostrecht* 1926, 206.
[5] *Ostrecht* 1926, 209.
[6] Under a decree of February 1, 1923.

debt to be located in Russia. This was certainly not the case. The court disregarding the *situs* question altogether, only ascertained whether the insurance had in fact been confiscated. The same conclusion can be drawn from *Perry* v. *Equitable Life Assurance Society of the U.S.A.* [1]. Here it was also beyond doubt that Russian law was applicable in principle. Contrary to the Court of Appeals decision in the *Bürger*-case, but in accordance with the judgment in the first instance, it was assumed that the contract at issue was nullified on the grounds mentioned above.

It is to be noted that the insurance was held to be unaffected by confiscation in the first case and to be affected in the second one. It is remarkable that in the former case it was assumed that the claim could be realized in England, because judgment was given for the plaintiff on the ground that in principle the claim would also have been justified in Russia! There is no denying that this judgment is intrinsically weak. The contrast between both decisions is obvious especially because they concern cases of the same nature. This may be explained by the rule of having experts prove the foreign law as a matter of fact to be decided by the court. There was uncontradicted evidence in the *Bürger*-case, though not so in the *Perry*-case.

First Russian Insurance Cy v. *London & Lancashire Insurance Cy* [2] also concerned insurance. Here the point was which law should be applied to a contract of re-insurance. The court decided that English law was applicable since the forms were issued and signed by the London branch of the plaintiff company. The court also pointed out that the Russian insurance decrees lacked binding force outside Russia ("For the decree has no extra-territorial effect". "I come therefore to the conclusion that the effect of the decree was to deprive the plaintiff of the power of carrying on an insurance business within Soviet territory, but that it did not affect their power of carrying on that business abroad".) Evidently a *situs* outside the Soviet Union was assumed. The case was the same *In re Russian Bank for Foreign Trade* [3] and *In re Russo-Asiatic Bank* [4]; here the subject was a debt "locally situated" in England, which meant a choice of *situs*.

[1] 45 T.L.R. 468.
[2] [1928] 1 Ch. 922.
[3] [1933] 1 Ch. 745.
[4] [1934] Ch. 720.

American courts also introduced a *situs* notion in some cases concerning insurance. In *Kleve* v. *Basler Lebensversicherungs-Gesellschaft* [1] it is clearly pointed out that "... assets of the parties in Germany" are in issue. The same view had been held before in *Dougherty* v. *Equitable Life Assurance Society* [2] and was affirmed in *Bloch* v. *Basler Lebensversicherungs-Gesellschaft* [3].

2. *Ships*

Although a ship may actually be called a tangible physical object, there is no agreement on the question, whether the territorial boundaries of a confiscating state coincide with the boundaries between territorial and extra-territorial confiscation. This is not surprising. A ship is an object, a thing, but has a name, she is christened, she has a nationality. Marriages, births, deaths aboard ship, are attributed to the Mothercountry. It is a well-known adage that *ship is territory,* a ship is a floating portion of the flag-state. This adage has a certain significance though subject to limitations. On the one hand the ship is considered *territory* in certain legal relations, on the other hand she is purely an object. In general the latter view prevails as soon as the ship is berthed in a foreign port, the former when she sails on the high seas. The character of the ship as an object becomes evident in foreign ports where she is liable to arrest.

Regarding the confiscation of ships it will be wise to bear in mind the function of the ship. It goes without saying that here the object of the confiscation is in view. The property desired, representing an economic, political or military value plays a leading part. The character of the ship as an object with its own soul, as a territory where people work, marry, are born and die, falls into the background. Thus far it is not different from other physical tangible objects. There is only the high sea and this sometimes complicates the affair.

The territorial notion of confiscation is generally interpreted by the courts in a restricted sense, so that a ship on the *neutral* high seas and certainly in a foreign port is presumed to be out-

---

[1] *Ann. Dig.* 1943–1945, 4.
[2] *Ann. Dig.* 1933–1934, 67.
[3] 73 N.Y.S. (2d) 523, extract in *A.J.I.L.* 1948, 502.

side the territory of the confiscating state. Consequently the rule that the ship is a floating portion of the flagstate is usually left out of consideration.

This view is evident in several decisions of English case law, e.g. *The Jupiter (No 3)*. The history of the said case is interesting [1]. The Jupiter was a ship belonging to the Ropit company [2]. After the nationalization of the Russian merchant fleet [3] she left Odessa, took refuge in Marseilles and finally arrived at Dartmouth. The master, Lepine, an enthousiastic supporter of the Soviet state, surrendered his ship and papers to the Russian trade representative in England; subsequently the Ropit claimed ownership to the ship. The Soviet Government however, invoked immunity [4] and the court accepted this plea. The Soviet government therefore remained in possession of the Jupiter. But it sold the ship to an Italian shipping-company (Cantiere Olivo) and now the Ropit tried again to acquire the ship (*The Jupiter (No 2)*). The Italian Company pleaded that without the defendant's consent the court lacked jurisdiction since this was a dispute between foreigners (the court cited *The Annette* [5], stating that it had jurisdiction, the ship being in British territorial waters). The company argued that the claim was indirectly directed against the Soviet government as the legal predecessor of the defendant, attempting to circumvent state immunity in this way. The court dismissed this argument, allowing the Ropit to continue the action. In the third *Jupiter*-case the ownership itself came up for discussion. The court put the case as follows: Captain Lepine, by handing over the ship, acted contrary to good faith; so judgment had to be given in favour of the Ropit unless the defendant proved that the Soviet government (his predecessor in title) had a better title. The defendant tried to adduce evidence to this effect by means of a statement made by the Russian *chargé d'affairs* in Italy, stating that the ship was Russian state property. The court refused to accept this: such a

[1] *The Jupiter (No. 1)* [1924] P. 236; *The Jupiter (No. 2)* [1925] P. 69; *The Jupiter (No. 3)* [1927] P. 122, [1927] P. 250.

[2] Cf. the Ropit lawsuits in France, *infra* 59 ff.

[3] Decree, see Labry, 371; Hahn and Von Lilienfeld-Toal, 106; Bunyan & Fisher, 611.

[4] Cf. Noël-Henry's note to the extract, published in French translation in *Clunet* 1927, 1139.

[5] [1919] P. 105.

statement would only hold good if the question of immunity played a part. Since this was not the case, judgment was given for the Ropit. In addition the nationalization decrees could only have a strictly territorial effect: it was assumed that Odessa (where the Jupiter berthed) was not yet a part of Soviet territory at the time of the confiscation [1]. The Court of appeal upheld this decision [2]. The finding that the decrees have a strictly territorial effect was mainly based on the consideration that this was the intention of the Soviet government itself. But Noël-Henry [3] rightly remarks in the light of this that the attitude of the Soviet government gives rise to some doubt. Be that as it may, it was assumed that a ship outside the presumed Soviet Russian orbit could not be regarded as Russian territory.

The same is shown by the *Tallina*-cases [4]. After Soviet forces occupied Esthonia on June 21st, 1940, a new government was established which proclaimed the Esthonian Soviet Republic and made preparation for large-scale nationalization after the Russian example of the years 1917–1919. On August 6th, 1940 the country was absorbed by the Soviet Union and on August 25th the new constitution was made public. Section 6 of this constitution among other things declared all means of transport to be state property. A further decree mentioned the nationalization of the shipping companies including all their assets where-ever situated, as well as balances with banks at home and abroad and claims to insurance benefits.

Since English courts maintain that extra-territorial confiscation is unacceptable, the *situs* question was paramount. In the cases mentioned above a certain sum was claimed for the destruction of the insured ship, the Vapper, on July 6th, 1940. If the ship was held to be *extra territorium*, the confiscating state or its legal successor would not have the requisite interest in the sum insured. Apart from other arguments the decision stated that the decree was *ultra vires* as section 6 of the constitution was supposed to aim at territorial effect. Underlying this argument is the fact

[1] Herzfeld, 2, calls it a "borderline case."

[2] [1927] P. 250.

[3] *Clunet* 1927, 1146.

[4] *A/S Tallina Laevauhisus* v. *Tallina Shipping Co and Estonian S.S. Line* (1946) 79 Ll.L.L.R. 245, *Brit. Yearb.* 1946, 384; *A/S Tallina Laevauhisus* v. *Estonian State S.S. Line* (1947) 80 Ll.L.L.R. 99, *Brit. Yearb.* 1947, 416.

that the Vapper was not inside the territory of the confiscating state at the time of the confiscation. The same trend is shown in *The Olev and other Esthonian vessels* [1].

The Scottish decision *The El Condado* [2] takes the same view: requisition by the Spanish government of a Spanish ship in Scotland is ineffectual, for "such (i.e. confiscatory) legislation will not be held to affect property situated in this country or without the territory administered by such government".

The Canadian *Elise*-case [3] is a similar one.

The same conclusion may be drawn from a Belgian decision [4] and from a Swedish one (*Russian Trade Delegation and others* v. *Carlbom* (I)) concerning an Esthonian nationalization measure involving the ship Toomas [5]. *The Rigmor* [6] and *The Solgry* [7] produced the same results as regards the *situs*.

Somewhat different views appear in American cases.

The Navemar was in Buenos Aires when requisitioned by the Spanish government. The Spanish consul made a note on the ships papers, but gave permission to sail to New York with private cargo. In New York the consul again boarded the ship and this time ordered the master to hold himself at the disposal of the Spanish government. A committee set up by the crew sent the master ashore and pretended to take over in the name of the Spanish government. In the lawsuit that ensued state immunity was not granted, since the court took the view that at that very moment the ship was not in the actul possession of the Spanish government. The Navemar was not in Spain's possession when she arrived in New York, but was seized by a committee from the crew. Well then, immunity "cannot be set up as a bar to jurisdiction where an attempt has been made to seize property within the territorial limits of the U.S. in violation of the orderly

---

[1] (1951) 84 Ll.L.L.R. 513, *I.L.Q.* 1951, 379, *Brit. Yearb.* 1951, 395.

[2] (1939) 63 Ll.L.L.R. 83 and (1939) 63 Ll.L.L.R. 331; cf. also (1937) 59 Ll.L.L.R. 119; from the first two decisions it is clear that no distinction was made between ships and other tangibles.

[3] *Estonian State Cargo and Passenger Steamship Line* v. *Proceeds of the Steamship Elise and Messrs Laane and Baltser*, *A.J.I.L.* 1950, 201, reversing the decision discussed in *A.J.I.L.* 1949, 816 and *Brit. Yearb.* 1949, 427.

[4] *Urrutia & Amollobieta* c. *Martiarena*, *Trib. civil* of Antwerp 18-2-1937, *Revue de dr.i. et de lég. comp.* 1938, 331 and *Bulletin* vol. 39, 338.

[5] *Ann. Dig.* 1943–1945, 61.

[6] *Ann. Dig.* 1941–1942, 240.

[7] *Ann. Dig. Suppl. Vol.*, 153.

process of the local law". This was a judgment on the main point of the dispute and in the first instance it was decided that the requisition could not have binding force extra-territorially and consequently could not affect the Navemar. On appeal a quasi-territoriality was assumed, although the same views prevailed as regards immunity. The reasoning was that the requisition decree became effective while the ship, en route from Buenos Aires to New York, was on the high seas. Quasi-territoriality is therefore assumed on the high sea, but not in foreign ports. In other words, it could not be said that foreign legislative measures of a *penal character* applied *within American jurisdiction*, so that the rights of the Spanish government were maintained [1], [2].

It is clear from this case that the American judiciary interprets the territorial notion of confiscation in a less restricted sense than appeared from the preceding cases.

Some French decisions went still further, although expressly indicating that no confiscation was involved but only requisition without a confiscatory character. Here a Spanish measure was held binding even with regard to ships moored in French ports [3].

A Dutch decision did not touch the *situs* question. The Sendeja [4] was about to sail from IJmuiden as the Spanish (Republican) government requested her arrest. The Spanish government therefore had no actual possession of the ship and could not invoke immunity, the more so since it submitted voluntarily to Dutch jurisdiction. The ship in question was registered at Bilbao and according to a decree of June 28th, 1937 (Spanish Official Gazette of June 29th, 1937) all ships registered at the port of Bilbao were to be requisitioned by the Spanish (Republican) government. Of course that was what the Spanish government referred to. The President of the Haarlem District Court, however, considered that when the decree was enacted Bilbao was already under

---

[1] *Ann. Dig.* 1938–1940, 176; ditto *The Motomar, Bulletin* vol. 41, 270.

[2] The further developments of this case were rather interesting. The Franco-regime afterwards requested the return of the ship, which was still under U.S. jurisdiction, to the original owners, since it did not want to appear as if effectuating confiscatory measures of its predecessors.

[3] *Société Cementos Resola* c. *Larrasquita et Etat Espagnol, Cour d'Appel* of Poitiers 20-12-1937, *Clunet* 1938, 287, *Ann. Dig.* 1935–1937, 196; *Agusquiza* c. *Société Sota y Aznar, Cour d'Appel* of Bordeaux 28-3-1938, *Nouvelle Revue de dr.i.pr.* 1938, 332, *Ann. Dig.* 1935–1937, 195.

[4] President Haarlem District Court 24–7–1937, *N.J.* 1937, No. 863, *Ann. Dig.* 1935–1937, 203.

control of the Franco regime for a week. The republican government now demanded the assistance of the Bilboans in fighting the enemy at considerable risk, but it was evident, that it could not meet its obligations as regards protection of life, liberty and property belonging to its subjects living at Bilbao. Under these circumstances the requisition was held to be contrary to the "rules of public policy, governing this country", which opened the port of IJmuiden. It is not altogether clear whether it follows *a contrario* from this decision that judgment would have been given for the plaintiff, if only the Spanish government had been in actual control of Bilbao. Neither was it clear whether the distinction confiscatory as opposed to non-confiscatory requisition played any part.

For the rest it is doubtful whether the French decisions started from a supposed quasi-territoriality. Indeed they went far in recognizing the measure in issue, but this need not be founded on quasi-territoriality. This is clearly shown by the decision of the People's Court at Batum [1]. Here an extra-territorial claim was upheld without any fiction of quasi-territoriality.

3. The Problem

Studying the relationship between confiscation and *situs* one gets the impression that the problem is essentially simpler than often presented. If we are not mistaken, a criterion may be used which goes for both tangibles and intangibles, with the understanding that any artificial idea should be avoided. Apart from solving the *situs* problem with regard to other legal relations, it is advantageous to avoid the artificial *situs* notion especially where intangibles are concerned. Avoiding the artificial notion is feasible, if closer consideration is given to the root of the distinction made by the courts between territorial and extra-territorial confiscation.

In essence the difference between territorial and extra-territorial confiscation coincides both with confiscations which may be executed by the state through its own organs without any external assistance and with those which are effective only when

---

[1] Concerning the ships Georges and Edwich, *Clunet* 1923, 663.

a foreign state co-operates either actively, or passively by tolerating the measure on its territory. For tangibles this means that the *situs* is clearly decisive though with respect to tangibles the underlying question is also whether the object can be seized without foreign assistance. This criterion coincides with the (physical) *situs* of tangibles, but in the case of intangibles there is no reason whatever to operate with a perfectly artificial *situs* notion, the only question being: can the property at issue be seized? This is the only standard to be applied. Here the borrowing of a *situs* notion from other situations undoubtedly gives rise to strange constructions. This is avoided in the way suggested above.

Our view is in full harmony with legal reality. In most cases the courts use motivations which time and again are open to argument. In formulating this point it would be desirable to pay more attention to the following words of Lord Loughborough in *Folliot* v. *Ogden* [1]: "The penal laws of foreign countries are strictly local and effect nothing more than they can reach and can be seized by virtue of their authority..." [2].

Our conception naturally does not eliminate all difficulties and does not pretend to do so. It only presents a solution for the artificial *situs* notion and is not a method for judging the desirability of the recognition or the enforcing of a confiscatory measure itself. This becomes apparent from the following illustration: B (debtor) owes A (creditor) a debt arising from a contract that has been completely performed within the territory of state X. B goes abroad where he has the disposal of part of his fortune, leaving other property in X. State X confiscates the fortune of A and collects the debt. Now one might ask: Has A, if he goes abroad, the right to claim the debt from B by virtue of the principle, that any part of a debtor's property may be seized and sold for payment, or has the claim become null and void as a result of the confiscation? There is a risk of double payment here. If B has to pay both inside state X (on account of his property there) and abroad, then in fact confiscation takes place with repect to B. If the claim of A is dismsised abroad, then there is confiscation as regards A.

It goes without saying that a court dealing with such a case is

[1] (1789) 1 H.Bl. 123, (1790) 3 T.R. 726, cit. Re, 129.

[2] Niboyet, IV, 675, too, makes a suggestion in this sense.

placed in an awkward position, but the question whether a territorial or an extra-territorial confiscation is involved, is simple: since state X is able to execute its confiscatory measure without outside assistance by collecting the debt, the confiscation is a territorial one.

Comparison of our view and the various cases already discussed shows that above all our criterion excludes doubts and is simple to apply.

E.g. in the case of the Carthusian liqueur any discussion about the *situs* question (i.e. has the trade-mark one *situs* or more?) had been avoided if the question had been examined whether the French state apparatus could have confiscated without external assistance [1]. Certainly this was not the case: active outside assistance was indispensable for the liquidator's case and consequently his claims could be safely denoted as extra-territorial. This is perfectly realistic in view of the divergent economic values that the trade-mark could have in various countries.

This example further shows that the practical outcome was not different from what our criterion would have produced. This appears also from other cases. Our view, then, only claims to put the problem more clearly, to approach it rather on its own merits, by which in any case a definite policy can be followed.

For tangibles this becomes clear; in our opinion it leads to the same consequences with regard to ships as other tangibles. The confiscation has to be held extra-territorial, if in executing the measure the states own organs are insufficient.

Finally our test is still more enlightening with respect to intangibles: here the *situs* notion can be radically thrown overboard, so that one is rid of at least one artificial construction.

---

[1] This would have considerably clarified the discussion of Lyon-Caen and Millerand, pleading for the liquidator, on the one side and Weisz and Köhler, opposing the liquidator's case on the other; cf. *Revue Darras* 1907, 415.

CHAPTER III

TERRITORIAL CONFISCATIONS

I. INTRODUCTION

Views diverge regarding the validity of territorial confiscations. This is apparent from the case law which in this respect has come into existence. The question of validity may appear in different ways. Most frequent is the following case. The confiscating state, or its assignee, exports the confiscated goods and an action for recovery is brought before a foreign court either against the confiscating state, where the latter still claims a title to property, or against its assignee, where the goods have already been alienated [1]. It is evident that in such cases the courts are asked to give different decisions from those in matters of extra-territorial confiscation. In adjudging a territorial confiscation to be valid, the courts will play a more passive part, than in a case where they validate an extra-territorial confiscation. In the latter case their part would be an active one since they would aid in the execution of a foreign confiscatory measure. On the one hand the question is whether "the validity or legality of what that foreign government *has done* may be examined and possibly invalidated and set aside. This situation, as may be noticed, deals with what is a *fait accompli*. The question is one of undoing what a foreign government has already done within its own territorial jurisdiction" [2]. Therefore, effectuating the validity of the confiscation has to be regarded as a matter of recognition, while on the other hand effectuating the validity of an

---

[1] Classic example: *Luther* v. *Sagor* [1921] 1 K.B. 456 and [1921] 3 K.B. 532; instead of an action for recovery an action for damages may be brought (*Hertzfeld* v. *U.S.S.R. Trib. civil de la Seine* 18-10-1933, *Clunet* 1934, 636) or the confiscating state, that has lost possession of the good, goes to law in order to recover it (*Saez Murua* v. *Pinillos and Garcia*, Belgian Court of Cassation 23-11-1939, *Ann. Dig.* 1938–1940, 289).

[2] Re, 49.

extra-territorial confiscation really is an enforcement. In this case "the courts of the *forum* should have aided in the execution of the foreign legislation" [1].

First of all we shall consider the denial of all validity to territorial confiscation.

II. NON-RECOGNITION OF TERRITORIAL CONFISCATIONS

1. *Non-recognition of the Confiscating State or Government*

In a first category of decisions the non-recognition of territorial confiscations is based on grounds which as a matter of fact have nothing to do with the idea of confiscation. A French court, in refusing an appeal as to the validity of the confiscation, in the case *Héritiers A. Bouniatian* c. *Société Optorg* [2], did so on the ground that the non-recognition of Soviet-Russia involved the ignoring of Soviet Russian law. As regards the confiscation itself this judgment was irrelevant; here the Soviet law was outlawed *in toto*.

The same ground for the decision is to be found in England. The *Luther* v. *Sagor* case [3] clearly states: "If a foreign government or its sovereignty is not recognized by the government of this country, a judicial court of this country either cannot, or at least need not, or ought not to, take notice of, or recognize such a foreign government or its sovereignty" [4]. In the case law of several countries the same view is taken [5].

2. *Public Policy: Conflict with the Law of Nations*

Meanwhile validity has been denied to territorial confiscation on other grounds as well. Here the principle of public policy or a comparable principle enters. In France this principle was employed after the Soviet Union had been recognized and subsequently non-recognition of confiscatory measures could no longer

---

[1] Re, 49.
[2] *Trib. civil de la Seine* 12-12-1923, *Clunet* 1924, 133.
[3] [1921] 1 K.B. 456.
[4] To the same effect: *The Annette, The Dora* [1919] P. 105.
[5] *Supra*, 27 ff.

be based on non-recognition of the Soviet government [1]. It may be considered important that here we are confronted with a decision on the subject itself.

Operating with the principle of public policy as a last resort will logically arise only when initially concluding that without invoking public policy the law of the confiscating state would be applicable. In this case the law of the confiscating state has to be regarded as applicable under the *lex rei sitae* principle; if its application is not desired, public policy is the only alternative.

Perhaps an example in this respect may be found in the French *Ropit*-case. This suit however had a special aspect, since it did not refer to territorial confiscation in so many words, such reference being denied in the English counterpart [2] of this action. The case concerned ships which had been confiscated at Odessa by the local Soviet. After Odessa had been occupied by French troups the ships fell again into the hands of their former owners. Consequently the granting of validity to the confiscation for all purposes would have amounted to enforcement rather than to recognition [3]. This case in the first instance came before the District Court of Marseilles [4]. A short time after the recognition of the Soviet Russian government this court had to decide a claim of the Soviet Russian state against the Ropit. Under the decree nationalizing the merchant fleet [5] Soviet Russia claimed possession of the ships which had taken refuge in France and contested the appointment of an *administrateur provisoire*, since the corporation was extinct as a legal entity. This claim was rejected. The court held that, since Soviet law could no longer be ignored *in toto* in view of the recognition of Soviet Russia, the principle of *ordre public* continued to be applicable. "*Attendu ... que reconnaître le gouvernement d'un pays ... n'est en aucune*

[1] H. Henrich (*Die russischen Enteignungsdekrete und ihre Rechtswirkung im Ausland*, Hamburg, 1933, 79) prophesied that after the recognition an appeal to the principle of public policy would prove unacceptable, since before that the rejection of the confiscation had been based solely on the non-recognition. This prophesy however did not come true. Cf. also Bartin, I, 62. For the rest the forecast was unfounded and illogical.

[2] *The Jupiter* (*No. 3*) [1927] P. 122.

[3] Cf. Seidl-Hohenveldern 25, 26.

[4] *Etat russe* c. *Cie Russe de Navigation à Vapeur et de Commerce* (*Ropit*), *Trib. comm.* of Marseilles 23-4-1925, *Clunet* 1925, 391.

[5] Labry, 371; Bunyan & Fisher, 611; Hahn und von Lilienfeld-Toal, 106; decree of January 26/February 8, 1918.

façon convenir de faire siennes, pour en assurer l'exécution, les moeurs et les lois de la Nation dirigée par le gouvernment reconnu". The decree in question was considered to be repugnant to the public policy, *"que ce décret ... n'est en réalité qu'un fait de spoliation"*, and therefore it cannot be enforced in France. The court even went further in remarking that *"les dispositions ... du droit ... des pays russes présentent au premier chef un caractère politique et social en opposition formelle avec notre législation qui repose sur le respect de la propriété individuelle"*. This called in question the applicability of a great part of Russian law on the ground of its political character [1]. The court further observed that Russia herself was defending the purely domestic operation of her own decrees. This view had been laid down in two circulars, the first one dated the 12th of April, 1922, from the People's Commissariat of Foreign Affairs [2] and addressed to the Soviet representatives abroad; the second one dated 26th September, 1923, from the People's Commissariat of Justice [3] and addressed to the notaries public. This *territoriality* was interpreted by the court as a restriction of operation relating to the Soviet territory only, without any further consequences. On appeal the *Cour d' Appel* at Aix [4] upheld the court's decision. Again the consideration was that there always had to be decided whether a measure might be involved *"portant atteinte aux principes essentiels de l'organisation politique et sociale de la France"*; in the present case the matter was a *"confiscation pure et simple, un coup de force de l'Etat contre l'individu"*, aiming at the abolition of private property and the establishment of the dictatorship of the proletariat; so *"il heurte les bases mêmes de droit français"*. The argument of the purely domestic operation of the decree was also adopted [5].

---

[1] It is considered to be a *privilegium odiosum*: cf. J. Delehelle in *Revue Darras*, 1927, 216; P. Arminjon: *Les lois politiques et le droit international privé*, Revue Darras, 1930, 385; *Les lois politiques, fiscales, monétaires en droit international privé*, Annuaire, 1950 II, 1.

[2] Circular 12-4-1922, No. 42, *Clunet* 1925, 568.

[3] Circular 26-9-1923, No. 194, *Clunet* 1925, 569.

[4] *Cour d'Appel* of Aix 23-12-1925, *Clunet* 1926, 667.

[5] As to the observation that Soviet Russia herself was advocating the purely domestic validity, it may be remarked that the circulars in question did not have force of law and consequently a decision could hardly be based upon them. Moreover the People's Commissariat of Foreign Affairs in a subsequent circular (No. 329 dated October 23, 1925, *Clunet* 1927, 531) issued an explicit statement, calling the interpretation given to the circular of 12–4–1922 quite wrong. Its only purpose was to

In the cassation-suit the principle of public policy also settled the matter [1].

We meet with the same principle in a decision of the President of the District Court of le Havre [2], sustaining an attachment against a French corporation laid by the Mexican Eagle (an oil-company operating and afterwards expropriated in Mexico). The validity of the obviously territorial measure of the Mexican government was rejected with an appeal to the *ordre public*, referring to section 545 *Code Civil*. On appeal things took a different course. In trying the principles of the claim [3], as a sequal to the sentence of its President, the District Court ruled that in this case there was no conflict with public policy. The Court of Appeal of Rouen [4] completely upheld this decision. Attention may be drawn however to the fact that the possibility of applying public policy was not involved. Its application remained the leading principle [5].

This also appears from decisions connected with the Spanish civil war. The *Potasas Ibericas* factory was being run chiefly with French capital and mostly under French direction. When the din of war drew near, the management fled to France. This caused the Spanish government to enact some decrees, which under penalty of expropriation of the factory, required the immediate return of the refugees. The request was not surprisingly left unheeded and the corporation was expropriated. Thereafter a parcel of potash from *Potasas Ibericas* came to

---

provide foreign representatives with an instruction how to act. For the rest it is to be noted that the argument that the Soviets themselves wished their legislation to be taken in a purely domestic sense was of secondary importance only.

[1] 5-3-1928, *Clunet* 1928, 674.

[2] *Banque et Société de pétrole* c. *Cie mexicaine de pétroles El Aguila* 18-10-1938, *Bulletin* vol. 41, 65.

[3] *Trib. civil* of Le Havre, 22-7-1939; particulars regarding the decisions, mentioned in this note and the next one were found in a decision *Trib. civil* of le Havre 17-11-1948, dealing with a claim of compensation against the Mexican Eagle (El Aguila). Through the kind intermediary of N.V. De Bataafsche Petroleum Maatschappij the text of this decision was put at our disposal.

[4] *Cour d'Appel* of Rouen 2-12-1942.

[5] In this connection the decision *Re Comp. Mexican Eagle, Cour d'Appel* of Rouen 27-7-1943 (cf. Niboyet, *Traité*, IV, 437) S. (*Table Quinq.* 1941–45) 214, seems rather strange. On the one hand it stated that this was not a case of outright confiscation since compensation had been promised. On the other hand it remarked that "*dans ces conditions les tribunaux français ne peuvent censurer un acte d'un gouvernement étranger*," since the public policy principle could only be applied if a question on French territory was at issue and here only a question between foreigners and a foreign state was at stake.

France and the board of directors immediately claimed ownership. This matter was raised for the first time in an action before the Commercial Court at Marseilles [1]. There the validity of the expropriation was rejected on the ground of inconsistency with French public policy. The *Cour d'Appel* of Aix [2] upheld this judgment. Although the *Cour d'Appel* of Montpellier in *Potasas Ibericas* c. *Bloch* dissented from the above-mentioned ideas and wished to consider the confiscation as a *fait accompli*, the *Cour de Cassation* ruled that the validity of the confiscation had to be refused on account of inconsistency with public policy [3]. A particular feature of this case was the promise of compensation after the expropriation had taken place and after the potash had been transported to France. The *Cour de Cassation* however argued as follows: The potash has been expropriated without compensation, and therefore confiscated; after that it has been conveyed to France and there claimed by the original owner. Because the application in France of such confiscation is inconsistent with French public policy, the original owner succeeds. After the confiscation however a compensation had been promised. At that time the potash was already in France and since the initial expropriation had the character of a confiscation and consequently could not be recognized in France, the original owner had a *droit acquis*, not liable to be affected even by a *post factum* grant of compensation. Moreover a decree granting such a compensation cannot take effect in relation to goods in French territory. The *Cour d'Appel* at Nîmes, to which the matter was referred, took a similar view [4].

The Italian judgment of the 26th of October 1923 (Rome) [5] considered public policy to be an impediment to recognizing the act of confiscation in Soviet Russia. Before the Court of Cassation however [6], the validity of the confiscation was upheld on the

[1] 25-5-37, *Clunet* 1937, 535, S. 1938.2.105, *Ann. Dig.* 1935–1937, 191, *re Moulin* c. *Volatron*.

[2] 25-3-1939, *Ann. Dig.* 1938–1940, 24, *re Volatron* c. *Moulin*.

[3] *Cour de Cassation* 14-3-1939, *Clunet* 1939, 615, *Ann. Dig.* 1938–1940, 150, S. 1939. 1.182.

[4] *Bloch* c. *Potassas Ibericas*, *Cour d'Appel* of Nîmes, 19-5-1941, *Gaz. du Palais* 1941 II 105.

[5] *Consorzi agrari di Piacenza* c. *Commissariat pour le commerce étranger de l'R.S.S.R.*, *Clunet* 1924, 257.

[6] *Ostrecht* 1925, 178; decision of 25-4-1925.

ground that a preliminary commercial agreement with Soviet Russia in which claims of former owners had been forgone had been concluded. Already before the latter decision the preliminary Italo-Russian agreement was referred to in *Italian Black Sea Comp.* v. *Russian Soviet Government* [1]; section 10 of this agreement provided that merchandise and goods of every kind, imported and acquired in both countries, should not be subject to sequestration or judicial action.

In Germany recent times have produced a number of decisions in which the principle of public policy likewise prevails [2]. Conflict with the law of nations is also involved as a *ratio decidendi*.

Though in England the courts are of a different opinion, the applicability of the principle of public policy by English courts is maintained by some authoritative jurists [3]. Maybe this conception has influenced the decision in the case of the *Anglo Iranian Oil Co* v. *Jaffrate et al.* (the Rose-Mary). In this case the Supreme Court of Aden [4] held that the validity ot the territorial confiscation could not be accepted on the ground of inconsistency with both public policy and the law of nations. In the Anglo-American sphere this decision forms an exeption. The Italian case *Anglo-Iranian Oil Co* v. *Societá Unione Petrolifera Orientale* (the Miriella) [5], connected with the same subject, showed a contrary result. Here public policy was invoked as well, but the court refused this appeal with reference to the promised compensation.

---

[1] Court of Appeal of Milan, 26-7-1922, *Ann. Dig.* 1919–1922, 26.

[2] *L. G.* Kassel, 20-7-1948, *Z.A.I.P.* 1949, 138; *A. G.* Waiblingen, 26-6-1948, *Z.A.I.P.* 1949, 139; *A.G. Dingolfing*, 7-12-1948, *Z.A.I.P.* 1949, 141; *O.L.G.* Nürnberg 1-6-1949, *Bruns Z.* 1951–52, 265; *L.G.* Berlin-West 13-10-1950, *N.J.W.* 1951, 238. A different view was held by *L.G.* Hildesheim 18-11-1947, *Z.A.I.P.* 1949, 137; *L.G.* Cottbus, 5-4-1950, *Bruns Z.* 1951–52, 264.

[3] E. g. Wortley, *Rec. des Cours* 1939, I, 424 and 1947, II, 82; Fachiri, *Brit. Yearb.* 1931, 95; Schmitthof, 59.

[4] *A.J.I.L.* 1953, 325; cf. H. W. Baade: *Die Anerkennung im Ausland vollzogener Enteigungen*, in Jahrbuch für Internationales Recht III, 132 and M. Philonenko: *Une des affaires de l' Anglo-Iranian*, Clunet 1954, 380. The Tokyo District Court and the Tokyo Higher Court held that public policy might be invoked in cases of territorial confiscatory measures, though they recognized the Iranian measure in a similar case, *Anglo-Iranian Co., Ltd.* v. *Idemitsu Kosan Co* (the tanker Nissho Maru), 1953, D. P. O'Connell, *I.C.L.Q.* 1955, 267 ff.

[5] Venice 11-3-1953, *A.J.I.L.* 1953, 509.

III. RECOGNITION OF TERRITORIAL CONFISCATIONS

In comparison with this denial of the validity of territorial confiscation one finds the more current view that a confiscation which is entirely confined to the territory of the confiscating state must be universally accepted as a *fait accompli.*

In this respect the case law of the U.S.A. shows a rather firmly established rule, which is supported by a long line of precedents. Proceeding from the principle of jurisdictional immunity [1] a rule has been developed in relation to our subject that may be called the act of state doctrine [2]. It asserts that acts of governments which bear the character of *ius imperii* may be tested in this respect only; further details, like possible constitutionality etc. and the result attained, are not open to discussion.

This conception is clearly indicated in *Underhill* v. *Hernandez* [3]. Underhill, a citizen of the United States, brought an action against Hernandez, a Venezuelan general, whose faction by means of a revolution had succeeded in assuming power and was recognized by the United States as the legitimate government. As commander in chief Hernandez was responsible for some acts directed against Underhill, including confiscatory measures. Here Chief Justice Fuller delivering the United States Supreme Court's judgment coined the famous phrase: "Every sovereign state is bound to respect the independency of every other sovereign state, and the courts of one country will not sit in judgment on the acts of the government of another done within its own territory". Although a recognized government was involved, the judgment made it clear that the "act of government" was not of necessity to emanate from a recognized government. In this matter the effectiveness is of great importance [4].

Based on this decision, and even going slightly further was the

---

[1] *The Schooner Exchange* v. *M'Faddon,* 7 Cranch 116, U.S. 1812, Hudson, 306.

[2] Cf. e.g. Fedozzi, *Rec. des Cours* 1929, II, 145; Holdsworth, *Col. L.R.* 1941, 1313; King, *A.J.I.L.* 1948, 811; Mann, *L.Q.R.* 1943, 42 and 155; Van Panhuys, *R. M. Themis,* 1953, 217; Van Praag, *Revue de dr.i. et de lég. comp.,* 1923, 436; Re, 19.

[3] 168 U.S. 250 (1897); earlier decisions: as to England: *Duke of Brunswick* v. *King of Hannover,* 2 H.L. Cas. 1 (1848) cf. Re 29; as to the U.S.A.: *Hatch* v. *Baez,* 7 Hun 596 (N.Y. 1876), cit. Re, 35; *Waters* v. *Collot,* 2 Dall. 247 (U.S. 1796) cit. Re, 23.

[4] "The immunity of individuals from suits brought in foreign tribunals for actt done within their own states, in the exercise of governmental authorities ... musr necessarily extend to the agents of governments ruling by paramount force as a mattes of fact."

finding in the case *American Banana Co.* v. *United Fruit Co* [1]. Here the action was not directed against a government or a governmental official, but the conflict in which these two United States companies were involved, was linked up with a governmental act. Though not the only ground for the refusal, the same principle was clearly evident again: "a seizure by a state is not a thing that can be complained of elsewhere in the courts".

The rule attained its clearest formulation in *Oetjen* v. *Central Leather Co.* [2] and *Ricaud* v. *American Metal Company* [3].

In the *Oetjen*-case the plaintiff, as an assignee of the original owner, claimed a parcel of hides. The defendant had bought them from an enterprise, which in turn had obtained them from General Villa, the Mexican general, who had come to power after a revolt. General Villa had seized the hides by way of military contribution. When the case was brought up for trial, his faction in the mean time had been recognized *de iure* by the U.S.A. as the Mexican government. Now the U.S. Supreme Court considered, that "when a government which originates in revolution or revolt is recognized by the political department of our government as the *de iure* government of the country in which it is established, such recognition is retroactive in effect and validates all the actions and conduct of the government so recognized from the commencement of its existence". The passage from the *Underhill*-case was quoted: "... every sovereign state is bound to respect the independence of every other sovereign state, and the courts of one country will not sit in judgment on the acts of the government of another, done within its own territory". Having regard to this the outcome was clear. The action of General Villa "is not subject to re-examination and modification by the courts of this country". It is true that according to the text one of the considerations in this case was that the seizure had taken place at the expense of a Mexican citizen, but this consideration is not essential to the rule [4].

The case *Ricaud* v. *American Metal Company* dealt with a confiscatory measure, taken by the Carranza regime before having

[1] 213 U.S. 347 (1909).
[2] 246 U.S. 297 (1918).
[3] 246 U.S. 304 (1918).
[4] This is apparent from the cases *Underhill* and *Ricaud* and results from the nature of the rule.

been recognized by the U.S.A. as the legitimate government of Mexico. Meanwhile recognition *de iure* had taken place. It stands to reason that the retroactivity of the recognition, which had also played a part in the *Oetjen*-case, was immediately stressed. Referring to the *Oetjen*-case the retroactivity was accepted. The court then stated that "the courts of one country will not sit in judgment on the validity of the acts of another done within its own jurisdiction", but qualified this by remarking that this principle does not deprive the court of jurisdiction in the case but "requires only that when it is made to appear that the foreign government has acted in a given way on the subject-matter of the litigation, the details of such action or the merit of the result cannot be questioned, but must be accepted by our courts as a rule for their decision". As regards the applicability of the rule it made no difference that the action was directed against an American citizen, the principle being equally applicable to citizens of the confiscating state as well as to citizens of another country, including citizens of the state of the *forum*.

The case *Shapleigh* v. *Mier* [1] does not contradict this position. It is true that in this case the constitutionality of the confiscation was reviewed, which seems to point in a different direction; however the court considered itself to be a court of a country, having succeeded the confiscating state in its sovereignty and not a court of a foreign government [2].

The rule developed in these decisions equally finds expression in several state decisions and decisions of lower federal courts, though here the unanimity which marks the decisions of the U.S. Supreme Court does not prevail.

Reference may be made for instance to the case *O'Neill* v. *Central Leather Co.* [3], which being founded on the *Underhill*-case exceeded the latter. Here it was assumed that the Carranza-regime had to be put on a level with a government, notwith-

---

[1] 299 U.S. 468 (1937); this was an action for the title to land. The land in question was part of Mexico and was in 1926 cut by avulsion from the southern (Mexican) bank of the Rio Grande to the northern (U.S.) bank and so became part of the U.S. In the first instance (*Ann. Dig.* 1935–1937, 31) however, it was stated that the act of state doctrine was applicable: according to the court this was a "fait accompli, whose validity of justice may not be inquired into by a court of this country ..." Reference was made to the cases *Oetjen* and *Ricaud*.

[2] Cf. Re 115, 116.

[3] 37 A.L.R. 748 (1925).

standing a pronouncement of the State Department, stating that the United States had never recognized any government in Mexico headed by Carranza or Villa or forces operating under their command as belligerents. Since the right to confiscate property was considered also to be "one of the rights of the military occupant of a territory", the title of property of an assignee was not "open to inquiry in our courts".

Molina v. *Comision Reguladora Del Mercado de Henequen* [1] was rather similar; here the rule was applied with reference to the retro-activity of the recognition.

In *Monte Blanco Real Estate Corporation* v. *Wolvin Line et al.* [2] the decision was very much in the sense of the *Ricaud*-case. It was the same in *Terrazas* v. *Holmes* and *Terrazas* v. *Donahue* [3]. Again an interesting case was *Cia Minera Ygnacio Rodriguez Rames S. A.* v. *Bartlesville Zinc Co et al.* [4]; unlike in *O'Neill* v. *Central Leather Co.* a thorough investigation was made whether a governmental act was involved. It was found that this was not the case here with an appeal to *Williams* v. *Bruffy* ("The validity of its acts ... depends entirely upon its ultimate success. If it fail to establish itself permanently, all such acts perish with it").

In *Wulfsohn* v. *Russian Socialist Federated Soviet Republic* [5], though the principle of jurisdictional immunity played an important part, the same conception was apparent as the court said: "It may be conceded that its (i.e. the R.S.F.S.R.'s) actions should accord with natural justice and equity. If they do not however, our courts are not competent to review them".

The case *Salimoff and Co* v. *Standard Oil Co.* and the same v. *Vacuum Oil Co.* [6] was in line with the pattern set by the U.S. Supreme Court, in ruling that, though the U.S.S.R. had not been recognized by the U.S.A. still it was the *de facto* government of Russia, and "the existing government cannot be ignored by the courts of this state, so far as the validity of its acts in Russia is concerned".

In the same way *Starke* v. *Howe Sound Co. et al.* [7] was in entire

[1] 92 N.J.L. 38, 104 Atl. 450 (1918), cit. Re, 167.
[2] *Ann. Dig.* 1919–1922, 53.
[3] *Ann. Dig.* 1925–1926, 59.
[4] *Ann. Dig.* 1925–1926, 67; reference to *Williams* v. *Bruffy*, 96 U.S. 176 (1877).
[5] *Ann. Dig.* 1923–1924, 39.
[6] *Ann. Dig.* 1933–1934, 22.
[7] *Ann. Dig.* 1933–1934, 27.

accordance with the rule here developed and *Banque de France* v. *Equitable Trust Co of New York* and *Banque de France* v. *Chase National Bank* [1] were equally in accordance with it. The French bank had a goldstock on deposit with the Russian National Bank; this deposit dated from before the revolution. The gold was confiscated. Now a German firm sent the defendant, for account of the Russian National Bank, a certain amount of this gold of which the French bank proved to be the original owner. However, the French claim was rejected. In the court's opinion the Soviet Russian government, though unrecognized, had to be considered an existing and factual government and therefore competent as regards measures on Russian territory. Hence this confiscation was judged to be valid.

In the matter of the Mexican measures relating to oil, an interesting action was fought in the case *Eastern States Petroleum Co.* v. *Asiatic Petroleum Corp.* [2]. Here again the finding was completely based on the leading cases of the Supreme Court (*Underhill* v. *Hernandez*, etc.) and it was stated that "the acts of a foreign sovereign in expropriating property within its own territory are not reviewable in our courts". The court held that it did not have "jurisdiction ... to adjudge as to the validity of the title acquired ... through the expropriation by the Mexican Government".

The case *Banco de España* v. *Federal Reserve Bank* [3] was entirely in the same sense: "The governmental acts of a foreign country done within its own border are not subject to examination in our courts" [4].

Equally consistent was the decision *Bernstein* v. *Van Heyghen Frères S.A.* [5]. Mr. Bernstein, a German Jew and owner of a shipping business was confined to a concentration-camp; in 1939 he emigrated on the condition that all his interests in the shipping-concern should fall to the German government, of course without compensation. The enterprise was sold to a Belgian firm and in 1942, when one of the ships was lost, Bernstein put in a claim for

---

[1] *Ann. Dig.* 1929–1930, 43. The risk of double payment was also mentioned here.

[2] *Ann. Dig.* 1938–1940, 90; 139 A.L.R. 1211.

[3] *Ann. Dig.* 1938–1940, 12.

[4] Not even when, as in this case, an examination *expressis verbis* was asked for by the Franco-government, which meanwhile had been recognized; cf. Re, 114-171.

[5] *Ann. Dig.* 1947, 11, *Clunet* 1950, 228, *A.J.I.L.* 1948, 217, *Col. L.R.* 1947, 106.

damages. This claim was rejected because the confiscation had taken place entirely on German territory. A similar conclusion was arrived at in *Bernstein* v. *Ned. Amerik. Stoomvaart Mij* [1]. The decision notably in the light of recent events has called forth quite a lot of fervent criticism [2].

The English conception emanates from the same principle, though definitely on the condition that the confiscation be executed by a recognized government. The essential importance of recognition is evident from the case *Luther* v. *Sagor* [3]; in the first instance the confiscation was considered invalid, since the Soviet Union had not yet been recognized diplomatically. The case on appeal was heard after recognition had taken place. Considering the conclusive importance attributed by the lower court to the fact of non-recognition, it is easily understood that the appellant now laid full stress on the recognition, which had occurred in the meantime. Again some letters of the Foreign Office (under date April 20 and 22, 1921) were produced, the first stating clearly: "I am to inform you that His Majesty's Government recognize the Soviet Government as the *de facto* Government of Russia". This statement was a very important one; from now on the final decision depended on whether the recognition possessed retroactivity, the conflict having arisen at an earlier date. Since the English case law offered no authority on this point [4], the American case law was consulted, and four decisions [5] adhering to the principle of retroactivity were found and referred to. "It is also the result of the interpretation by this court of the principles of international law, that when a government ... is recognized ... as the *de iure* government of the country in which it is established, such recognition is retroactive in effect and validates all the actions and conduct of the government so recognized from the commencement of its existence". Since no essential difference was made between recognition *de facto* and *de iure* and since the

---

[1] *Ann. Dig.* 1948, 20, *A.J.I.L.* 1948, 726 and *A.J.I.L.* 1949, 180, *A.J.I.L.* 1950, 182.
[2] E.g. *Yale L.J.* 1947, 108; *Col. L.R.* 1947, 1061, cf. Re 150, 169, 170.
[3] [1921] 3 K.B. 532.
[4] Cf. on this *supra*, 35 ff.
[5] *Williams* v. *Bruffy* 96 U.S. 176 (1877); *Underhill* v. *Hernandez* 168 U.S. 250 (1897); *Oetjen* v. *Central Leather Co.* 246 U.S. 297 (1918) and *Ricaud* v. *American Metal Co.* 246 U.S. 304 (1918).

question concerning the commencement of the recognition did not produce any difficulties (the commencement was in any case prior to every date material in this action), Lord Justice Bankes came to the conclusion that the appeal should be allowed. In his opinion no conflict with justice or morality arose. The confiscatory decree underlying the transfer of property to Soviet Russia served the highest interests of that state, though British views are different. "It must be quite immaterial for present purpose that the same views are not entertained by the government of this country, are repudiated by the vast majority of its citizens and are not recognized by our laws". Lord Justice Warrington joined in this decision. Lord Justice Scrutton finally advised great care; one should not be too apt at considering the legislation of a recognized state to be repugnant to justice. In this connection he pointed to the high taxes in England. "But it appears a serious breach of international comity, if a state is recognized as a sovereign independent state, to postulate that its legislation is contrary to essential principles of justice and morality".

A second sensational case was *Princess Paley Olga* v. *Weisz* [1]. Claimant, the wife of Grand Duke Paul of Russia, in 1928 recognized in England several objects of art she had formerly owned [2]. She claimed them as her property alleging that she had been deprived of her proprietary rights unlawfully. The judgment in the first instance (not reported) rejected the claim for three reasons. The goods involved had been in a museum in Russia since 1918 and all the contents of the musea had been declared state-property by a decree of 18-3-1923; secondly the decree of 19–11–1920 declared that all movables of emigrants and refugees (to which category of citizens the princess of course belonged) were state-property. In the third place the court held that, even though things had been spoliated by the Soviet government, this had been validated afterwards; now that the Soviet Union

---

[1] [1929] 1 K.B. 718; this Russian princess is the authoress of a booklet containing a striking description of her last years in Russia, entitled: *Souvenirs de Russie, 1916–1919* (Paris, 1923).

[2] Under similar circumstances further actions may perhaps be expected. According to the New York Times (International Air Edition) of 12-6-1950 Russia offered for sale in Belgium large quantities of diamond, viz. diamonds cut before the revolution and taken from the owners by way of confiscation.

had been recognized (*de iure* as well) British courts were bound to respect the acts and decrees pertaining to goods within the jurisdiction of the Soviets. On appeal this judgment was upheld. Lord Justice Scrutton among other things remarked: "Our government has recognized the present Russian Government ... and our Courts are bound to give effect to the laws and acts of the Government so far as they relate to property within that jurisdiction when it was affected by those laws and acts." Lord Justice Sankey quoted with approval the well-known words from the case *Oetjen* v. *Central Leather Co.* [1]: "... the Courts of one country will not sit in judgment on the acts of the Government of another done within its own territory". To this Lord Justice Russell added: "This court will not inquire into the legality of acts done by a foreign government against its own subjects in respect of property situate in its own territory".

So both in this case as in the case *Luther* v. *Sagor* it was clearly stated that whenever confiscations of property situated in Russian territory were concerned, non-application of confiscatory regulations was out of the question. With regard to goods like these Soviet Russian law is conclusive, leaving no room for the principle of public policy.

Previously in *Carr* v. *Fracis Times & Co.* [2] a similar decision following the act of state doctrine had already been arrived at.

Several Dutch decisions in this matter are also known, but a definite practice cannot yet be extracted since the Supreme Court only once has been confronted with a case of this kind. That single decision was in line with the Anglo-Saxon conception.

The series of Dutch judgments start with a decision by the President of the District Court at Middelburg of August 2, 1938 [3]. In this case the N.V. de Bataafsche Petroleum Maatschappij had attached a considerable quantity of oil, in its opinion the property of the Mexican Eagle (also called El Aguila), one of its daughter-companies, which was in her debt. In reply the Mexican government asked for annulment of the attachment, claiming

---

[1] 246 U.S. 297 (1918).

[2] [1902] A.C. 176; cf. Mann, *L.Q.R.* 1943, 164; here a seizure of arms was at issue within the territorial waters of Muscat under the authority of the Sultan of Muscat.

[3] *Mexico* v. *B.P.M.*, *N.J.* 1938, No. 790, *Ann. Dig. Suppl. Vol.*, 16.

the oil in question to have become state property by expropriation; to this the B.P.M. replied that the expropriation was a pseudo-one and in point of fact a confiscation, and so contrary to the Mexican constitution. Now the decision of the President was remarkable in two respects. First, Dutch courts were denied the right to test the expropriation measures for their constitutionality, obviously in connection with section 13a of the General Principles of Legislation Act (stating that jurisdiction of the Dutch courts is limited by the exceptions recognized in public international law). In the second place the decision also ruled out the existence of a conflict with public policy since compensation had been promised. In Dutch law, it is true, a prompt compensation (and not a promise only) is required, but this element was not deemed essential to the principle of public policy, although the existence of compensation was.

A similar decision was rendered by the District Court at Dordrecht on August 23, 1938 [1].

The President of the District Court of Rotterdam was also more than once confronted with this question. The judgment of September 1, 1938 [2] once more dealt with an attachment. The Mexican Eagle had attached a lot of petrol at the expense of a French corporation, which claimed to be the owner. In this case things took a different course because the Mexican Eagle proved that the petrol had been won before the expropriation. Indeed it had been in Mexico at the time of the expropriation but the applicability of the expropriation-decree was disputed. In his decision the President first stated that the ownership had to be decided according to French law, since the French corporation had bought the petrol in France from a third party, which in turn had obtained it through others from the Mexican government. The first question to be examined was whether the French corporation had been acting in good faith. Now this, in the opinion of the President, was doubtful, since at the time of the transaction it was common knowledge that there was a flutter in the dove-cote. But even if *bona fides* was taken for granted the ownership could not be decided in favour of the French corporation, since an examination of the expropriation-decree proved

[1] *Annuaire Grotius*, 1939, 121.
[2] *Petroservice* v. *El Aguila*, *N.J.* 1939, No. 115, *Ann. Dig. Suppl. Vol.*, 16.

that petrol which was already won before the enactment of the decree, was exempt from expropriation. Therefore the expropriation as actually executed by lower Mexican officials had been illegal. To the remaining question whether acts of a sovereign government may be reviewed the answer of the President was in the affirmative, because the government in question was not a party in this suit. Consequently the attachment in favour of the Mexican Eagle was upheld. This judgment was appealed from and eventually taken to the Supreme Court. Before dealing with these further decisions we would first like to cite some other cases.

The Pakhuismeesteren, into whose warehouses a lot of oil from Mexico had been stored, asked the President of the Rotterdam District Court to annul the attachment of the oil by the Mexican Eagle. Now, in the opinion of the President, the Mexican Eagle for the present succeeded in making out a *prima facie* case as to its title to property, whereas the Pakhuismeesteren confined themselves to a mere denial of this title, without further proof. Therefore the attachment was upheld [1].

At Arnhem too a case was brought before the President of the District Court [2] and this case also dealt with the annulment of an attachment effectuated by the Mexican Eagle against a French corporation. The President declared the legality of the confiscation to be rather doubtful and considered a compensation due only after ten years not sufficiently complete, so that a confiscation rather than an expropriation should be spoken of. Consequently the matter was a difficult one. Obviously the President hesitated to introduce the principle of public policy in so many words. At length, by weighing up the interests, the case went in favour of the Mexican Eagle. What weighed heaviest was the consideration that, as a result of lifting the attachment, the oil would disappear from the Netherlands, leaving the Mexican Eagle deprived of the means of legal remedy. Hence the attachment was upheld. On appeal, shortly after, this judgment was upheld though on different grounds [3]. Whether it was a matter of confiscation was considered immaterial, since in the opinion

---

[1] *Fa Pakhuismeesteren* v. *El Aguila* 6-4-1939, *N.J.* 1939, No. 782.
[2] *Petroservice* v. *El Aguila* 13-6-1939, *N.J.* 1940, No. 19.
[3] *Petroservice* v. *Mexican Eagle* 19-9-1939, *N.J.* 1940, No. 20.

of the Court a *prima facie* case was made out that the oil in question had been won before the expropriation-decree was enacted, and so under the provisions of that decree had not been expropriated. Therefore inconsistency with public policy, which the Mexican Eagle had advanced as an alternative, did not come under discussion.

A little different was the next action, again instituted at Rotterdam [1]. Once more it aimed at the annulment of an attachment by the Mexican Eagle against an American corporation. This time it could be proved that the oil was won after the expropriation had taken place. The President found that since compensation had been promised, confiscation could not be spoken of. Consequently the Mexican Eagle's title to the property had not been made out and the attachment was smashed. This meant that in the present case, according to the President, there was no room for the application of the principle of public policy. What the decision had been if the case were to be considered a case of confiscation is unknown since this point did not come up for discussion.

We now will deal with the action succeeding the decision of the Rotterdam President under date September 1, 1938. On the 4th of December 1939 the Court of Appeal at the Hague [2] decided not to uphold the decision of the Rotterdam President. The court deleted an inquiry into the question of the ownership of the petrol, by ruling that Dutch courts may not sit in judgment on the legality of the acts of the Mexican government. The Supreme Court [3] upheld this decision. The Supreme Court presumed that the Court of Appeal, in accepting the view of the Mexican government without an inquiry into its legality had evidently done so in virtue of section 13a of the General Principles of Legislation Act. If not, the Court had been erring with regard to the application of the law of nations, which according to Dutch views cannot lead to cassation. So the primary thesis that the petrol was not subject to expropriation could not result in cassation. As an alternative it was urged that, legal as the expropriation under Mexican law might be, Dutch public policy was involved since

[1] *Davis & Cy v. El Aguila* 31-7-1939, *N.J.* 1939, No. 747, *Ann. Dig.* 1938–1940, 25.
[2] *Petroservice* v. *El Aguila, N.J.* 1940, No. 27, *Ann. Dig. Suppl. Vol.*, 16.
[3] *El Aguila* v. *Petroservice* 7-12-1941, *N. J.* 1941, No. 923, *Ann. Dig. Suppl. Vol.*,16.

the compensation could not be considered real. To this the Supreme Court replied that, although payment was not secured — because compensation had only been promised and not paid immediately — still the safe-guarding of Dutch public policy under the circumstances offered no objection to the view that the Mexican government was the owner.

The judgment of the District Court of Antwerp 21-2-1939 in the case of *Propetrol, Petroservice and Petrolest* c. *Compania Mexicano de Petroleo and Tankage and Transport* [1] was quite in line with the Anglo-American decisions.

The Swiss case *Pettai* v. *Schinz* [2] arrived at a similar conclusion.

In German case law the conclusions of the courts were in the beginning identical with those of the Anglo-American courts, although not based on quite the same *ratio decidendi*.

Thus a couple of decisions of the *Landesgericht* at Hamburg may be pointed to re the Russian confiscations. The case *Caucasian Licirice Company Ltd.* g. *Katz* [3] dealt with the following. A parcel of liquorice, at the time owned by claimant and confiscated by the Soviet Russian government was sold by this government to defendant. The claim for recovery by the original owner could not succeed, according to the court, because under the *lex rei sitae* principle Russian law was relevant. The presumed inconsistency with section 30 of the *Einführungsgesetz* (stating non-application of foreign law if such application would be inconsistent with the *gute Sitten*-morality — or in conflict with the *Zweck eines deutschen Gesetzes* — purpose of a German statute —) could not be argued. Section 30 *E.G.* could not be introduced because this would run counter to Section 2 of the Treaty of Rapallo [4]. This treaty, it is true, mentions *deutsche Reichsangehörige*, but a foreign corporation was not held to be entitled to

[1] *Ann. Dig.* 1938–1940, 25.
[2] Zürich 19-12-1928, *Z.f.O.* 1929, 1403.
[3] Decision 13-6-1924, *Ostrecht* 1925, 165.
[4] "*Deutschland verzichtet auf die Ansprüche, die sich aus der bisherigen Anwendung der Gesetze und Masznahmen der RSFSR auf deutsche Reichsangehörige oder ihre Privatrechte ... gegen Reichsangehörige oder ihre Privatrechte ergeben, vorausgesetzt, dasz die Regierung der RSFSR auch ähnliche Ansprüche dritter Staaten nicht befriedigt.*" Text Martens, *Nouveau Rec.*, *3e Serie*, XII, 70.

a more favourable treatment than a German one. Quite in the same sense was the decision in the case *Keil* g. *Nathan, Philipp & Co* [1].

In the cases concerning *Kunsthaus Lepke* [2] the result was identical. They dealt with objects of art confiscated by the Russian government and now put up for auction by the Lepke-concern. The original owners commenced an action for recovery, involving Section 30 *E.G.*. In deciding the matter, the court first of all, under the rules of German private international law, considered Russian law to be applicable according to the *lex rei sitae* principle, to which it added, that its validity would only fail if running counter to section 30 *E.G.*. However section 30 *E.G.* was held to be inapplicable, because the matter in question was a *Hoheitsakt* (and so pertaining to public and not to private law), whereas section 30 *E.G.* only had a bearing on matters of private law; moreover, also because a *fait accompli* was at issue here. Apart from this an expropriation without compensation in times of war or in case of urgency could not be considered contrary to morality or any German law, and therefore section 30 *E.G.* could not be applied. Consequently the suit of the former owners had to be rejected.

The foregoing decisions are marked by two main features: The Treaty of Rapallo dominates though the act of state doctrine is perceptible as well. Nonetheless the rule is not so clearly developed as in Anglo-American case law. This also appears from more recent decisions, though these were taken by lower courts [3].

Some Swedish decisions [4] likewise were based on the act of state

---

[1] *L.G.* Hamburg 26-12-1924, ***Ostrecht*** 1925, 170.

[2] E.g. ***Scherbatow*** g. ***Lepkes Kunstauktionshaus*** *L.G.* Berlin 1-11-1928, ***Clunet*** 1929, 184; *L.G.* Berlin 11-12-1928, *Z.f.O.* 1929, 1366.

[3] Rejection of validity in *L.G.* Kassel 20-7-1948, ***Z.A.I.P.*** 1949, 138 (public policy, violation of the principles of public international law); *A.G.* Waiblingen 26-6-1948, *Z.A.I.P.* 1949, 139 (public policy); *A.G.* Dingolfing 7-12-1948, *Z.A.I.P.* 1949, 141 (public policy, violation of the principles of the law of nature and public international law); *O.L.G.* Nürnberg 1-6-1949, ***Bruns Z.*** 1951/52, 265 (violation of public international law); *L.G.* Berlin-West 13-10-1950, *N.J.W.* 1951, 238. Recognition of the validity however in *L.G.* Hildesheim 18-11-1947, *Z.A.I.P.* 1949, 137 and *L.G.* Cottbus 5-4-1950, ***Bruns Z.*** 1951/52, 264.

[4] Supreme Court 11-6-1941, ***Weiss*** v. ***Simon***, ***Ann. Dig. Suppl. Vol.***, 108, ***Z.A.I.P.*** 1940/41, 833; Supreme Court 10-6-1942, ***Z.A.I.P.*** 1949/50, 497.

doctrine. In an Austrian decision concerning restitution of Jewish property a similar conception is encountered: a seizure in Czechoslovakia by the German occupant is not reviewable by an Austrian court [1].

From our survey it is apparent that in most countries the act of state doctrine is dominant. How far this is right will be more closely examined.

---

[1] *Oberste Rückstellingskommission* (*O.R.K.*) 30-10-1948, *J.Bl.* 1949, 18, overruling *Rückstellungsoberkommission* Vienna 10-9-1948, *J.Bl.* 1949, 18, 231. To the same effect *O.L.G.* München 10-2-1950, *Clunet* 1951, 1226: seizure by occupant in the Netherlands.

CHAPTER IV

EXTRA-TERRITORIAL CONFISCATIONS

I. INTRODUCTION

In contrast to the conceptions of the validity of territorial confiscations those concerning the validity of extra-territorial confiscations show a greater unanimity. Thus the validity of extra-territorial confiscations is with few exceptions [1] rejected by the case law. This is not to be wondered at. When a government aims at extending such a drastic violation of the principle of protection of private property beyond its frontiers, the foreign *forum* will, by nature as it were, oppose it. For, since it is not in the power of the confiscating government actually to execute a confiscatory measure also outside its frontiers, it is up to the foreign court to decide whether or not it will concur in the confiscatory measure. It is obvious that such concurrence is more than a mere recognition. What is claimed here, is very often called enforcement [2]. This is evident from the various ways in which

---

[1] Lithuania: decision of December 7,/21, 1931, *Z.f.O.* 1933, 818, based on interpretation of peace treaty, cf. *infra*, 90; Georgia: the decision of the People's Court of Batoum October 1922, *Clunet* 1923, 663, concerning the ships Georges and Edwich is explained by the political relation between Soviet Russia and Georgia; it is not, as Ripert supposes in his note, solely based on the recognition of Soviet Russia by Georgia; Tunis: *Rey* c. *Lecouturier*, *Trib. civil* of Tunis 11-5-1907, S. 1908.2.115; explicable by the special constitutional relation to France; U.S.A.: the case law based on the Litvinov Assignment, cf. *infra*, 91 ff. In all cases excepting the Tunesian one (Carthusian liqueur) the validity of Soviet Russian measures was involved. Moreover some Dutch decisions pertaining to *Kommissarische Verwaltung* are to be mentioned: In *Manes* v. *Kommissarische Verwalter*, Cantonal Court of Hilversum 13-12-1938, *N.J.* 1939 No. 51, *Ann. Dig. Suppl. Vol.*, 20 and *Firm of Komotau* v. *Kommissarische Verwalter*, Cantonal Court of The Hague 14-6-1939, *N.J.* 1939 No. 764, *Ann. Dig. Suppl. Vol.*, 21, the real nature of this *Verwaltung* was not recognized, the competence of the *Verwalter* in the Netherlands being taken for granted. The Italian decision *re Eulenberg*, District Court Milan 4-6-1940, *Modern L.R.* 1942/1943, 167 is accounted for by the political relations. Cf. also the cases in which a decision was founded on jurisdictional immunity, *supra*, 36 ff.

[2] E.g. Re, 49.

extra-territorial validity is put in issue [1]. Thus it may happen that the confiscating government puts in a claim for certain goods which in its opinion are covered by the confiscation. To do this, however, the government requires the active co-operation of the court of the *forum* where such property is situated. Not infrequently concurrence in a different form is required: the recognition of the powers of a trustee who really acts as the representative of the confiscating government; the claims of any assignee of the confiscating government; the opinion that debts have been cancelled.

Although the views on extra-territorial validity lead to an almost unanimous result, viz. its rejection, some variety in the arguments may be noted. On the one side the principle of public policy [2] is encountered; in this case the stress is laid on the principles of law of the *forum*. On the other hand the point is taken that confiscatory measures by nature have no extra-territorial effect or do not intend to have, because they are to be considered *lois de police et de sûreté* [3], penal in nature [4] or *odiosa* [5] and, accordingly, may find only strictly territorial application. Very often several of such arguments are used simultaneously, while strictly territorial validity is sometimes attained without comment, whether [6] or not [7] by interpretation of the intention of the confiscating government. Finally, non-recognition of the confiscating state or government sometimes also plays a part [8].

II. NON-ENFORCEMENT OF EXTRA-TERRITORIAL CONFISCATIONS

1. *Non-recognition of the Confiscating State or Government*

Just as in confiscation executed entirely within the territory of the confiscating state, recognition has also played a part in confiscation intending to have extra-territorial effect. In the

[1] A very detailed survey is given by Seidl-Hohenveldern, 55.
[2] *Infra*, 81 ff.
[3] *Infra*, 84.
[4] *Infra*, 85 ff.
[5] *Infra*, 87.
[6] *Infra*, 87, 88.
[7] *Infra*, 88.
[8] *Infra*, 89 ff.

U.S.A. it was clearly stated several times that in principle the rule to regard legislation and other acts of an unrecognized state or government as a nullity was to be adhered to and that the toning down of this rule was to be considered an exception. Judge Cardozo formulated this limitation in *Boris N. Sokoloff* v. *National City Bank of New York* [1] by stating that an unrecognized state or government "may gain for its acts and decrees a validity quasi governmental, if violation to fundamental principles of justice or to our own public policy might otherwise be done". After the claim of Boris N. Sokoloff, who had a deposit with the Russian branch of the National City Bank of New York, had been dismissed in the first instance, because the nationalization of this branch had caused frustration of contract, the decision was reversed by the Appelate Division. The highest New York Court, the Court of Appeals, affirmed the decision of the Appelate Division, though on other grounds. It is true, it was decided *in casu*, that the exception to the dogmatic rule of non-application of the decrees of an unrecognized government was not at issue, but the fundamental possibility of such an exception was put forward. This decision proved to be the guiding principle for several of those which followed. In *Fred. S. James* v. *Second Russian Insurance Cy* [2] the exception was not deemed applicable either: the "principles of justice" or the "public policy" did not demand such in *casu*. The same reflected in the decision in the first instance re *Russian Reinsurance Co and Paul Rasor* v. *Francis R. Stoddard and the Bankers Trust Cy* [3] as well as in *Fred. S. James & Co* v. *Rossia Insurance Cy of America* [4] and *Petrogradsky Bank* v. *National City Bank* [5].

Also in more recent case law [6] the U.S.A. continued to apply the general rule as amended by the *Sokoloff*-case, although the rule was also used without mention of the Cardozo-amendment.

---

[1] *Ann. Dig.* 1923–1924, 44, 37 A.L.R. 712, *Clunet* 1925, 446.

[2] *Ann. Dig.* 1925–1926, 57.

[3] *Clunet* 1925, 451.

[4] *Clunet* 1928, 789.

[5] *Ann. Dig.* 1929–1930, 38.

[6] *Johnson* v. *Briggs* (anti-Jewish measure, non-recognition of the annexation of Austria), *Ann. Dig.* 1938–1940, 87; *Amstelbank N.V.* v. *Guaranty Trust Cy of New York*, *Ann. Dig.* 1941–1942, 584 (anti-Jewish measure, non-recognition of the occupation of the Netherlands); *Kon. Lederfabriek "Oisterwijk" N.V.* v. *Chase National Bank of City of New York*, *Ann. Dig.* 1941–1942, 588 (the same).

The latter proved from *The Kotkas* [1], *The Regent* [2], *The Signe* [3], *Latvian State Cargo and Passenger Line* v. *Clark* [4], *The Maret* [5] *A/S Merilaid & Co* v. *Chase National Bank* [6], in which decisions measures of the Baltic Soviet republics were in dispute.

The Irish decision *The Ramava* follows the same lines [7].

2. *Public Policy*

The principle of public policy is frequently employed. In France the principle was set forth so explicitly in the well-known *Ropit*-case [8], that it was also adopted as a yard-stick by later case law. It is true that in this case it was a difficult question of fact whether a territorial or an extra-territorial confiscation was at issue — the court avoided the answer to this question — but the application of the principle appeared also in cases, where this point was evident indeed. Thus public policy appeared to present the *ratio decidendi* in the struggle which the original owner of the copyrights of the works by Rimsky-Korsakoff and Moussorgski fought successfully [9]. These copyrights had been confiscated in Soviet Russia by decree of November 26, 1918. It may further be assumed that in the various cases concerning the liquidation of corporations affected by Soviet Russian nationalization measures, inconsistency with public policy was always implicitly the ground for the rejection of extra-territoriality of the confiscatory element included in nationalization [10]; in some decisions this is expressly stated [11]. Also later French case law continued to use the principle of public policy; the German anti-Jewish measures,

---

[1] *Ann. Dig.* 1941–1942, 70.

[2] *Ann. Dig.* 1941–1942, 70.

[3] *Ann. Dig.* 1941–1942, 86.

[4] *A.J.I.L.* 1949, 380, *Ann. Dig.* 1948, 45; to the same effect *Latvian State Cargo and Passenger Line* v. *U.S.*, *A.J.I.L.* 1954, 332.

[5] *Ann. Dig.* 1943–1945, 29.

[6] *A.J.I.L.* 1948, 231, *Ann. Dig.* 1947, 6.

[7] *Ann. Dig.* 1941–1942, 91 (Esthonian confiscation).

[8] *Supra*, 59 ff.

[9] *Bessel* c. *Société des auteurs et compositeurs dramatiques*, *Trib. civil de la Seine* 14-2-1931, *Clunet* 1932, 114.

[10] *Infra*, 112.

[11] E.g. *Crédit National Industriel* c. *Crédit Lyonnais*, *Cour d'Appel* of Paris 18-2-1926, *Clunet* 1927, 1061, cf. *infra*, 113.

as far as confiscation was concerned, were denied any extra-territorial effect [1].

In Belgium the same concept was found. Thus Belgian courts were confronted with German anti-Jewish measures leading to pure confiscation. Very positively the Brussels Commercial Court defeated the extra-territorial validity by a plea of public policy: "... *en effet, elle autorise une expropriation sans préalable indemnité et heurte, par conséquent, le principe d'ordre international belge*" [2]. In some other Brussels decisions this view was affirmed [3].

As regards the Carthusian liqueur legal proceedings were carried on in Germany and other countries. In Germany the claim of the liquidator of the Congregation of the *Pères Chartreux* to use exclusively the trade-mark of the liqueur was rejected as a confiscatory claim, by a plea of public policy [4].

In the Netherlands public policy was likewise used. In *Helvetia* v. *De Nederlanden van 1845* where the dispute was about the Russian insurance company Moskowskoie, expropriation without compensation was held contrary to public policy [5]. This was also

---

[1] *Aronsfrau* c. *Gimpel*, *Cour d'Appel* of Paris 9-1-1939, *R.C.D.I.P.* 1939, 300; *X.* c. *Lévit et Walter*, *Trib. comm. de la Seine* 23-6-1939, *Ann. Dig. Suppl. Vol.*, 25 and *Jellinek* c. *Levy*, *Trib. comm. de la Seine* 18-1-1940, *Gaz. du Palais* 7-3-1940, *Ann. Dig. Suppl. Vol.*, 24.

[2] Decision of 9-6-1938 *re Eismann* c. *Melzer*, *J. des Trib.* 54, 3558, *Belg. Jud.* 1938, 563.

[3] Decision Brussels District Court 17-11-1938, *Bulletin* vol. 41, 262, *re Schönberg* c. *Sarna* and decision of 26-10-1939, *Bulletin* vol. 42, 57, *J. des Trib.* 54, 3589 (anti-Jewish measures); *re Compagnie Belgo-Lithuanienne d'Electricité*, Brussels Court of Appeal 25-6-1947, *Clunet* 1950, 864 (Lithuanian nationalization). In the same way the Antwerp District Court applied the principle of public policy in *Urrutia & Amollobieta* c. *Martiarena*, decision of 18-2-1937, *Revue de dr.i.et de lég. comp.* 1938, 331; in the appeal case, however, this judgment was reversed, cf. *supra*, 42.

[4] *Rey et Dr Levy* c. *Lecouturier*, Court of Appeal of Hamburg 5-11-1907, *Revue Darras* 1907, 949; Supreme Court of Leipzig 29-5-1908, *Entsch. Rg.* 69, 1, *Revue Darras* 1908, 815; this result was preceded by the decision of the Hamburg District Court of 4-5-1905, *re Rey et Dr Levy* c. *Lecouturier*, *Revue Darras* 1907, 950, which preliminarily prohibited Abbé Rey (the priest under whose name the trade-mark was registered) to use the trade-mark; and by *Rey et Dr Levy* c. *Lecouturier*, Hamburg District Court 23-2-1906, *Revue Darras* 1907, 415, from which a kind of truce emerged. Rey was not allowed to use the trade-mark, nor was the liquidator. In *Rey et Dr Levy* c. *Lecouturier*, Hamburg District Court 11-12-1908, *Revue Darras* 1909, 314, extra-territorial effect was rejected since the present legislation was held a *loi de police et d'exception*.

[5] The Hague District Court 9-3-1933, *N.J.* 1933, 1662, *Ann. Dig.* 1933–1934, 80; The Hague Court of Appeal 3-6-1937, *N.J.* 1937, 1675, *Ann. Dig.* 1935–1937, 204.

stated in *Herani* v. *Wladikawkas Railway Co.* [1] and *Banska* v. *Hahn en Sibeha* [2] (Czech nationalization). In *The Sendeja* [3] the President of the Haarlem District Court had to adjudicate upon a requisition by the Spanish government. The President laid down, after considering that the government in question had no *de facto* authority over the port of Bilbao, where the Sendeja had her home port at the time of enactment of the requisition decree, that any collaboration with such requisition would be inconsistent with public policy. In the German measures against the Jews the confiscatory element was diagnosed and their extra-territorial validity rejected; in this respect the Amsterdam District Court pleaded public policy [4].

In Rumania, too, the principle of public policy was put forward, although it did not exclusively support the decision; non-recognition also played a role [5].

In the first instance Danish decision *Banska a Hutni* v. *Hahn* [6] the term public policy was also used. The appeal decision, however, though upholding the decision in the first instance, deemed the *ratio decidendi* public policy a fallacy.

Switzerland already applied the principle in the dispute about the Carthusian liqueur [7] and also adhered to this view regarding Soviet Russian confiscations. In the well-known case *Banque Internationale de Commerce de Pétrograd* c. *Hausner* [8] *"la con-*

---

[1] Amsterdam District Court 11-6-1940, *N.J.* 1940, 1607, *Ann. Dig. Suppl. Vol.*, 21; Amsterdam Court of Appeal 4-11-1942, *N.J.* 1943, 687, *Ann. Dig. Suppl.* Vol., 21.

[2] Arnhem Court of Appeal 11-3-1952, *N.J.* 1952, 554; the decision in the first instance, Arnhem District Court 22-3-1951, *N.J.* 1951, 611, did not engage this argument, but rejected extra-territorial effect because the present debt was beyond the reach of the nationalization.

[3] Haarlem District Court 24-7-1937, *N.J.* 1937, 863, *Ann. Dig.* 1935–1937, 203.

[4] *Hunzedal* v. *Smit*, Amsterdam District Court 3-1-1940, *N.J.* 1940, 1002, *Ann. Dig. Suppl. Vol.*, 33; however cf. *supra*, 78.

[5] Rumanian Supreme Court 13-2-1929, *Z.f.O.* 1930, 673; 5-12-1932, *Clunet* 1935, 718 (Soviet Russian nationalization).

[6] Mentioned in the appeal case Court of Western Denmark 12-5-1952, *Clunet* 1954, 480, cf. *infra*, 153 (Czech nationalization).

[7] *Rey* c. *Jaccard*, Supreme Court 13-2-1906, *R.O.* 32 I 148, *Revue Darras* 1907, 282; in *Compagnie Fermière de la Grande Chartreuse* c. *Rey*, Supreme Court 11-7-1913, *R.O.* 39 III 640, the character of the measure as a *loi de police et d'exception* was also pointed to.

[8] Supreme Court 10-12-1924, *R.O.* 50 II 507, *Clunet* 1925, 488.

fiscation pure et simple du patrimoine des banques" was regarded as contrary to public policy. This also appeared from *Wilbuschewitz* c. *Autorité tutélaire de la Ville de Zürich et Dépt. de justice du Canton de Zürich* [1]. In other Swiss decisions public policy was used as well [2].

While U.S. courts are shy of applying the principle of public policy, though not to such extent as the English courts, it is remarkable that yet this principle is encountered in the U.S.A.. Other *rationes decidendi* were also used and an Anglo-American court would, so to speak, generally prefer to apply any other consideration to public policy. Although the principle was not the main argument of the decision, yet it was explicitly used by the New York Appelate Division in *Russian Reinsurance Co and Paul Rasor* v. *Francis R. Stoddard and the Bankers Trust Cy* [3]. In *Wladikawkazky Railway Co* v. *New York Trust Co* [4] it was stated even more clearly if possible: "It is hardly necessary to state, that ... the confiscation ... is contrary to our public policy and shocking to our sense of justice and equity". Also in *Plesch* v. *Banque Nationale d'Haiti* [5] the argument of public policy was used as well as in *Bollack* v. *Société Générale* [6] and *A/S Merilaid & Co* v. *Chase National Bank* [7].

3. Nature and Intention of Confiscation as a Ground for Non-enforcement

a. Police and Order

Besides public policy also other arguments were used to resist extra-territorial effect. The concept that confiscation by a

[1] Supreme Court 13-7-1925, *R.O.* 51 II 259, *Clunet* 1926, 1110.
[2] Geneva District Court 31-10-1917 (*re Société de Sosnowice*), *Revue Darras* 1918, 190 (German war-measure); *Bankhaus Thorsch* g. *Thorsch*, District Court of Zürich 7-12-1938, *Bulletin* vol. 40, 251, Court of Appeal Zürich 1-3-1939, *Bulletin* vol. 42, 87, *Z.A.I.P.* 1951, 601; *Böhmische Unionbank* g. *Heynau*, Supreme Court 22-12-1942, *R.O.* 68 II 377; Court of Appeal of Bern 7-11-1944, *Z.A.I.P.* 1951, 603 (the last four decisions concern *Kommissarische Verwaltung*).
[3] *Clunet* 1925, 451; final decision *Clunet* 1925, 1070, *Ann. Dig.* 1925–1926, 54.
[4] *Ann. Dig.* 1933–1934, 65; although the decision in *Johnson* v. *Briggs*, *Ann. Dig.* 1938–1940, 87, was chiefly based on the non-recognition of the annexation of Austria by Germany, all the same the principle of public policy was operated with in this case.
[5] *A.J.I.L.* 1948, 739, 1949, 814, *Ann. Dig.* 1948, 13.
[6] *Ann. Dig.* 1941–1942, 147.
[7] *Ann. Dig.* 1947, 15, *A.J.I.L.* 1948, 231.

measure of police and order may only be applied as such strictly territorially, was held in various countries where legal proceedings were carried on about the Carthusian liqueur. In Belgium it was clearly stated that the attack on the trade-mark registered in Belgium could not succeed: here it was a question of a *"loi de police et de sûreté, dont l'application expire aux limites du territoire français"* [1]. Argentine and Brazil, too [2], spoke of a *loi de police* and so did Holland [3]. The measure enacted by the Greek government on March 6, 1935 after the revolt in the 1930's, whereby all the possessions of the rebels and their nearest relatives were seized, were as *loi de police et de sûreté* and having *manifestement un caractère politique* also allowed only strictly territorial operation in the French decision of April 3, 1935 [4].

b. Penal Law

Confiscation with extra-territorial intention is sometimes regarded as penal law and therefore rejected. In England the French Associations Act of 1901 was regarded as penal [5]. Remarkably enough this argument was not used in rejecting the extra-territoriality of the Soviet Russian confiscations. Only in *A/S Tallina Laevauhisus Ltd.* v. *Tallina Shipping Co and Estonian State S.S. Line* [6], where the nationalization of the Esthonian shipping companies, a measure taken after Esthonia's union with Soviet Russia, was in dispute, the penal nature of the measure was used as a ground for non-enforcement of extra-territoriality. This was also the case when an attempt was made also to extend the confiscation

---

1 *Rey c.s.* c. *Fouyer*, Brussels Commercial Court 13-2-1907, *Revue Darras* 1907, 273 and Brussels Court of Appeal 20-5-1910, *Revue Darras* 1911, 732.

2 *Rey* c. *Lecouturier*, Supreme Court 10-5-1907, *Clunet* 1907, 1171 and *Rey* c. *La Junte Commerciale de Rio*, Court of Appeal of Rio de Janeiro 14-5-1907, *Clunet* 1908, 579.

3 *Rey* c. *Lecouturier*, The Hague Court of Appeal 28-10-1907, *W.* 8615, *Revue Darras* 1908, 313; Supreme Court 5-3-1908, *W.* 8691, *Revue Darras* 1908, 843.

4 *British Investors Banking Cy* c. *Gouvernement Grec*, *Trib. civil* of Le Hâvre (*Réf.*), 3-4-1935, *Clunet* 1935, 940, *R.C.D.I.P.* 1935, 408.

5 *Lecouturier* v. *Rey* [1910] A.C. 262, *Revue Darras* 1910, 914; in a lower instance also the argument of unfair competition had been used [1908] 2 Ch. 715, *Revue Darras* 1908, 270; in the first instance the claim of the Carthusian Congregation had been dismissed, *Revue Darras* 1908, 270. Earlier decisions concerning the exclusion of penal law: *Folliott* v. *Ogden* (1789) 3 T.R. 726; *Wolff* v. *Oxholm* (1817) 6 M. & S. 92 (cit. Dicey, 18).

6 (1946) 79 Ll.L.L.R. 245, *Brit. Yearb.* 1946, 384 and *A/S. Tallina Laevauhisus* v. *Estonian State S.S. Line* (1947) 80 Ll.L.L.R. 99, *Brit. Yearb.* 1947, 416.

of King Alfonso's property by the Spanish republic to his possessions in England[1]. In *Frankfurther* v. *Exner*[2] finally, where the extraterritorial authority of a *Verwalter*, appointed under the Austrian legislation of April 13, 1938 came at issue, any such authority was rejected, since confiscatory laws were involved, which "though not strictly penal ... are regarded here in the same light as penal laws ..."

Canada used the expression in the well-known *Elise*-case referring to the *Tallina*-case [3]; the trial in the first instance of the *Elise*-case is interesting in that the court did not raise objections to extra-territorial operation: "I have grave doubts that I would consider nationalization with 25% compensation as being regarded in Canadian law as contrary to the essential principles of justice and morality". [4]

Legal proceedings regarding the property of King Alfonso of Spain were, besides in England, also taken in Italy; here, too, extra-territorial effect was rejected on the ground of the penal nature of the measure [5].

Non-enforcement of extra-territorial operation on the ground of the penal character of the measure was encountered in the suit about the trade-mark of the Carthusian liqueur [6] in the U.S.A.

c. Odiosa

The thought of *odiosa restringenda* was encountered in the Argentine decision regarding the same measure [7]. On the other

---

[1] *Banco de Vizcaya* v. *Don Alfonso de Borbon y Austria* [1935] 1 K.B. 140.

[2] [1947] 1 Ch. 629; to the same effect *Novello & Co* v. *Hinrichsen Edition Ltd.* [1951] Ch. 595, [1951] Ch. 1026, cf. J. G. Fleming in *I.L.Q.* 1951, 377 and M. Saporta in *Clunet* 1951, 1120.

[3] (1946) 79 Ll.L.L.R. 245, (1947) 80 Ll.L.L.R. 99.

[4] *Estonian State Cargo and Passenger S.S. Line* v. *Proceeds of the Steamship Elise and Messrs Laane and Baltser*, *Brit. Yearb.* 1949, 427, *A.J.I.L.* 1949, 816 and *Messrs Laane and Baltser* v. *Estonian State Cargo and Passenger S.S. Line*, *Brit. Yearb.* 1953, 512, *A.J.I.L.* 1950, 201.

[5] *Alfonso di Borbone* v. *Credito Italiano and Banco de Vizcaya*, District Court of Rome 30-8-1933, Court of Appeal of Rome 5-6-1934, *Ann. Dig.* 1935–1937, 198; *Alphonso XIII* v. *Banco commerciale italiana et Banco Urquijo*, District Court of Milan 17-1-1935, *Clunet* 1935, 1056.

[6] *Baglin* v. *Cusenier*, *Revue Darras* 1907, 972 (decision of Circuit Court of New York); 221 U.S. 580 (1911); the English and the American decisions have influenced each other: in *Lecouturier* v. *Rey* [1908] 2 Ch. 715, the American decision *Revue Darras* 1907, 972 was cited with approval; so was done in *Baglin* v. *Cusenier*, 221 U.S. 580 (1911) with the English decision *Lecouturier* v. *Rey* [1910] A.C. 262.

[7] *Lecouturier* v. *Rey*, Court of Buenos Ayres 23-12-1905, *Revue Darras* 1907, 612; mention was made of a *loi politico-sociale*.

hand this thought was also perceptible in other decisions such as the French *Venizelos*-case [1].

d. Public Law

The nature of a confiscatory measure as a measure of public law caused more than once strictly territorial application [2].

e. Intention of the Measures

Besides these reasons for strictly territorial application lying in the nature of the confiscatory measures, a ground for the rejection of extra-territorial validity is sometimes the intention of the measure concerned. The act or decree in question is then interpreted and its intention, it is believed, may be deduced from it.

This view is expressed in the French *Arno-Mendi*-case [3]; moreover this feeling had already been expressed elaborately before in the *Ropit*-case [4]. In the latter case the Court observed, and this was upheld on appeal, that in Russia herself the Soviet Russian acts were considered to have strictly territorial application. This had been laid down in a circular of April 12, 1922 from the People's Commissariat of Foreign Affairs, addressed to the representatives of Soviet Russia abroad, and also in a circular of September 26, 1923 from the People's Commissariat of Justice, adressed to the notaries [5].

In English case law, too, the argument of extra-territoriality not being intended by the measure itself was used a few times. It is to be found in *The Jupiter (No 3)* [6], *Russian Commercial and Industrial Bank* v. *Comptoir d'Escompte de Mulhouse and others* [7], *Banque Internationale de Commerce de Pétrograd* v. *Goukassow* [8] and in several other decisions on Soviet Russian nation-

---

[1] *Supra*, 85.

[2] The Netherlands: *Scheepvaart en Steenkolen Mij* v. *Schneider*, Court of Appeal of The Hague 8-11-1946, *N.J.* 1947, No. 31, *Ann. Dig.* 1946, 17; in this case the decision of the Rotterdam District Court of 22-12-1943, which accepted the competence of the *Verwalter* on the ground of *Reichskommissar* Seyss Inquardt's decree nr 179 dated 17-10-1940, was reversed. Switzerland: Court of Appeal of Zürich 11-11-1942, *Z.A.I.P.* 1951, 602, *Schweiz. Jahrb. für intern. R.* 1944, 210, 234 (*Kommissarische Verwaltung*).

[3] *Ann. Dig.* 1935–1937, 195 (Spanish requisition).

[4] *Supra* 59 ff.

[5] *Supra* 60; cf. also *U.S.* v. *Pink*, 315 U.S. 203 (1942).

[6] [1927] P. 122, [1927] P. 250.

[7] [1923] 2 K.B. 630, [1925] A.C. 112.

[8] [1923] 2 K.B. 682, [1925] A.C. 150.

alizations. In *Frankfurther* v. *Exner* [1] the intention was also investigated and it was concluded that extra-territoriality was the object.

The Dutch decision [2] where the powers of an Austrian *Verwalter* were at issue, was also founded on the interpretation of the measure, which was not intended to have extra-territorial effect.

In the U.S.A. the intention of mere territorial operation was advanced in the *Moscow*-case [3]; here the *Jupiter* (*No 3*)-case [4] was also cited.

On the other hand strictly territorial effect was insisted on several times without much further explanation. Thus decisions are to be found in Austria [5], Denmark [6], England [7], the Netherlands [8], France [9], Sweden [10] and the U.S.A. [11].

---

[1] [1947] 1 Ch. 629.

[2] *Manes* v. *Van Duren*, Arnhem Cantonal Court 19-12-1938, *N.J.* 1939, Nr 16, *Ann. Dig. Suppl. Vol.*, 20.

[3] *Moscow Fire Insurance Co* v. *The Bank of New York*, *Ann. Dig.* 1938–1940, 141.

[4] [1927] P. 122, [1927] P. 250.

[5] *O.G.H.* 10-3-1948, *Z.A.I.P.* 1949, 479, *J.Bl.* 1949, 70, *re National Soz. Lehrerbund* (German measures); *Verwaltungsgerichtshof* 25-1-1950, *Clunet* 1951, 624; *Verwaltungsgerichtshof* 2-2-1950, *Clunet* 1950, 732, *J.Bl.* 1950, 192, *re* Law No. 5 of the Allied Control Council.

[6] Anti-Jewish measures: *Eisner* v. *Nilwa*, Commercial and Admiralty Court 17-2-1939, *Clunet* 1954, 492, *Z.A.I.P.* 1941–42, 822, *Bulletin* vol. 41, 263; *Östl. Landgericht* 11-5-1939, *Z.A.I.P.* 1941–42, 823, *Bulletin* vol. 41, 263.

[7] *First Russian Insurance Cy* v. *London & Lancashire Ins. Cy.* [1928] 1 Ch. 922; *The El Condado* (1939) 63 Ll.L.L.R. 83, (1939) 63 Ll.L.L.R. 331.

[8] *Germany* v. *Van der Hoeven*, Utrecht District Court 31-5-1922, *W.* 10935, *N.J.* 1922, 1110; Amsterdam Court of Appeal 3-11-1925, *W.* 11440, *Ann. Dig.* 1925–1926, 145: no German seizure of goods within Dutch territory; to the same effect Amsterdan Court of Appeal 7-10-1921, *N.J.* 1922, 1268; *Bohm* v. *Hozemann*, Rotterdam District Court 13-1-1939, *Bulletin* vol. 41, 263 (*Kommissarische Verwaltung*); *Anninger* v. *De Monchy*, Rotterdam District Court 11-10-1939, *N.J.* 1940, No. 168, *Ann. Dig. Suppl. Vol.*, 21 (*Kommissarische Verwaltung*).

[9] *Rosa Catana* c. *Potocki*, *Trib. civil de la Seine* 7-5-1873, *Clunet* 1875, 20: the ukase from the Czar ordering guardianship over Count Potocki was not recognized in France.

[10] Soviet Russian nationalization: *Stockholms Enskilda Bank* v. *Amilakvari*, Supreme Court 12-11-1938, *Ann. Dig. Suppl. Vol.*, 107; *Azov-Don-Bank*, Supreme Court 19-10-1945, *Z.A.I.P.* 1949–50, 499.

Anti-Jewish measures: District Court of Borås 2-2-1939, *Bulletin* vol. 41, 263; District Court of Göteborg 7-2-1939, Court of Appeal of Jönköping 30-6-1939, *Bulletin* vol. 41, 264; *Weisz* v. *Simon*, Supreme Court 11-6-1941, *Ann. Dig. Suppl. Vol.*, 108, *Z.A.I.P.* 1941–42, 833 and Supreme Court 10-6-1942, *Z.A.I.P.* 1949–50, 497.

Claim of British Enemy Property Custodian rejected: *Hopf Products Ltd.* v. *Paul Hopf and Skandinaviska Banken Aktiebolag*, Supreme Court 25-9-1944, *Ann. Dig.* 1943–1945, 63, Supreme Court 16-10-1944, *Z.A.I.P.* 1949–50, 497.

[11] *Stern* v. *Steiner*, *Bulletin* vol. 41, 263; *Anninger* v. *Hohenberg*, *Ann. Dig.* 1938–1940, 19; *Loeb* v. *Manhattan Co*, *Ann. Dig.* 1938–1940, 20; *Zwack* v. *Kraus Bros & Co*, *A.J.I.L.* 1951, 377; *Augstein* v. *Banska a Hutni Akciova Spolecnost*, *A.J.I.L.* 1954, 513.

f. Legislation of the Forum

Occasionally rejection of extra-territoriality appeared to be founded on legislation of the *forum* [1].

III. ENFORCEMENT OF EXTRA-TERRITORIAL CONFISCATIONS

Nearly all exceptional cases in which extra-territorial effect of confiscations was upheld prove on further consideration to be based upon special reasons. The most sensational have been the American decisions on Soviet Russian nationalizations where extra-territoriality was accepted with reference to the Litvinov Assignment.

Only a few isolated cases are further known, where extra-territorial effect was upheld. Thus this was decided in Georgia, when she did not yet form part of Soviet Russia [2]; in Tunis, too, a similar decision was rendered in respect of the Carthusian liqueur [3]. Unfortunately, some Dutch decisions on *Kommissarische Verwaltung*, naive to say, did not recognize the true nature of the measure [4], whilst also an Italian decision granted a *Verwalter* extra-territorial power [5].

In most cases the reason for enforcement was found in a treaty. But it is remarkable that even in treaties expressly concluded in respect of confiscatory measures the point of extra-territorial operation was defined rather vaguely. Thus it is the question whether the treaties concluded between Soviet Russia and the Eastern European states and that concluded between Soviet Russia and the U.S.A., known as the Litvinov Assignment even mentioned extra-territoriality itself.

---

[1] *Bollack* v. *Société Générale* ..., *Ann. Dig.* 1941–1942, 147; reference was made to the New York Civil Practice Act.

[2] People's Court of Batoum October 1922, *Clunet* 1923, 663, re the ships Georges and Edwich; cf. *supra*, 78.

[3] Tunis District Court 11-5-1907, S. 1908.2.115; cf. *supra*, 78.

[4] *Manes* v. *Kommissarische Verwalter*, Cantonal Court of Hilversum 13-12-1938, *N.J.* 1939, Nr 51, *Ann. Dig. Suppl. Vol.*, 20; *Firm of Komotau* v. *Kommissarische Verwalter*, Cantonal Court of The Hague 14-6-1939, *N.J.* 1939, Nr 764, *Ann. Dig. Suppl. Vol.*, 21; cf. *supra*, 78. Several other Dutch decisions, however, rejected the claims of *Verwalter*; cf. *supra*, 87, 88.

[5] *Re Eulenberg*, Milan District Court 4-6-1940, *Modern L.R.* 1942–43, 167; cf. *supra*, 78.

1. *Eastern European Countries*

Under the Riga Peace Treaty of March 18, 1921 [1] Poland and Soviet Russia entered into diplomatic relations. Section 12 of this treaty provided that the property in Poland of the Russian state should pass to the Polish state. On the face of it this might lead to the conclusion that the assets of the branches of the nationalized Russian corporations passed to the Polish state. Reasoning in this way, however, a *petitio principii* is made, as Rundstein [2] rightly observes, for it should be decided first whether such assets were in fact to be regarded as Soviet property. The Treaty did not make any pronouncement on it and such extra-territoriality has never been recognized in Poland [3].

The Peace Treaty between Latvia and Soviet Russia (the Riga-Treaty, August 11, 1920 [4]) contained a similar provision. Here, too, assignment of property was made from the Russian to the Latvian state, but it was expressly stipulated that the claims of the former banks on the peasants were cancelled. It might be concluded from this *a contrario* that in respect of other assets extra-territoriality was accepted. This did not appear, however, from the Latvian regulation following the treaty [5].

The Dorpat Peace Treaty of February 2, 1920, concluded between Esthonia and Soviet Russia [6] contained in section 12 the stipulation that the property in Esthonia of the nationalized Russian banks was expressly allocated to the Esthonian creditors.

Also the Moscow Treaty of July 12, 1920, concluded between Lithuania and Soviet Russia [7] contained a provision by which the assets in Lithuania of Soviet Russia passed to the Lithuanian state. With regard to the claims of the nationalized banks on peasants a provision similar to that in the treaty with Latvia was also to be found. Poland, Latvia and Esthonia rejected extra-territoriality [8], as is apparent from the regulations follow-

[1] Martens, *Nouveau Rec. 3e série*, XIII, 141.
[2] S. Rundstein, *Zweigniederlassungen russischer Aktiengesellschaften in Polen*, Ostrecht 1925, 330.
[3] *Infra*, 115 ff., 124.
[4] Martens, *Nouveau Rec. 3° série*, XI, 888.
[5] *Infra*, 116, 124.
[6] Martens, *Nouveau Rec. 3° série*, XI, 864.
[7] Martens, *Nouveau Rec. 3° série*, XI, 877.
[8] *Infra*, 124.

ing the treaties, but in contrast the Lithuanian Supreme Court [1] recognized extra-territoriality under the Moscow Treaty.

2. *The U.S.A.; the Litvinov Assignment*

In the U.S.A. the extra-territoriality of Soviet Russian confiscatory measures was always rejected; Soviet legislation, as legislation of an unrecognized government, was rejected and the Cardozo-amendment, at least in respect of extra-territoriality, was deemed not to be applicable [2]. This situation lasted till 1933.

At that time the U.S.A. was the only big Western power not to have recognized Soviet Russia. Germany had led the way early [3], Great Britain had followed in 1921 [4] and France granted recognition in 1924 [5]. The U.S.A., however, continued to oppose recognition [6]. This changed under Roosevelt's presidency. Of course there had always been a tendency urging recognition and a desire to dissociate recognition from approval of the regime. The latter tendency eventually gained the upper hand and after several preliminary discussions recognition was accorded in 1933, on which occasion various diplomatic notes were exchanged [7]. What was particularly of importance was the so-called Litvinov Assignment, consisting of a letter from Litvinov to Roosevelt, dated November 16, 1933 and Roosevelt's reply of the same date. The case law after the recognition mainly relates to this assignment. It stated among other things that "... preparatory to a final settlement of the claims and counter-claims between the government of the U.S.S.R. and the U.S.A. and the claims of their nationals, the government of the U.S.S.R. will not take any steps to enforce any decisions of courts or initiate any new litigations for the amounts admitted to be due or that may be

---

[1] *Ministry of Home Affairs* v. *Helperin & Ewald*, decision of Kaunas 7/21-12-1931, *Z.f.O.* 1933, 818, severely criticized by J. Robinson and G. Chklaver.

[2] *Supra*, 30 ff.

[3] Treaty of Brest-Litovsk 3-3-1918, Martens, *Nouveau Rec. 3° série*, X, 773; after the rupture of this treaty soon the Rapallo-Treaty was made, Martens, *Nouveau Rec. 3° série*, XII, 70.

[4] See *Luther* v. *Sagor* [1921] 3 K.B. 532.

[5] Recognition was granted through a telegram under date October 28, 1924, J. Delehelle, *La situation juridique des Russes en France* (Lille, 1926),124, 125.

[6] For a concise survey of the period 1917–1933 see Ch. P. Anderson, *Recognition of Russia*, A.J.I.L. 1934, 90.

[7] *A.J.I.L.* 1934, Suppl., 1.

found to be due it, as the successor of prior governments of Russia or otherwise, from American nationals, including corporations ... and will not object to such amounts being assigned and does hereby release and assign all such amounts to the government of the U.S.A., the government of the U.S.S.R. to be duly notified in each case of any amount realized by the government of the U.S.A. from such release and assignment". The Federal government soon maintained that it had therefore obtained from the Soviet Russian government the right to the assets of the nationalized corporations, arguing as follows: the assets have passed to Soviet Russia by nationalization and the Federal Government now acts as the successor to Soviet Russia. Criticism was made that by doing so the confiscation was granted extra-territorial effect. The Federal Government eventually got the better of the argument. The *Pink*-case [1] has definitely decided the fate of the assets in the U.S.A. of some Russian corporations, chiefly insurance companies. A strenuous battle, however, preceded the *Pink*-case.

In *U.S.* v. *Belmont* [2] we see the first skirmish. A Russian corporation from Petrograd had deposited a sum of money with the banker Belmont before 1917. The business was nationalized; nobody was making any claim on the sum; so it was dormant and bore interest. After the Litvinov Assignment, however, the Federal Government of the U.S.A. as the successor to the Soviet Government claimed the amount. The Supreme Court allowed the claim on various grounds. In the first place reference was made to several precedents and the well-known passage was quoted: "Every sovereign state is bound to respect the independence of every other sovereign state and the courts of one country will not sit in judgment on the acts of the government of another done within its own territory" [3]. Further the Supreme Court emphasized that the Litvinov Assignment and recognition were to be regarded as one and the same transaction: "The effect ... was to validate ... all acts of the Soviet government here involved from the commencement of its existence". The transaction was to be considered a treaty between the U.S.A.

---

[1] *U.S.* v. *Pink*, 315 U.S. 203 (1942).
[2] 301 U.S. 324 (1937).
[3] *Underhill* v. *Hernandez*, 168 U.S. 250 (1897).

and Russia, which had validity beyond law and "policy" of an American state (the state of New York). Finally the very important question arose whether the decision was in conflict with the Fifth Amendment to the American constitution. The Supreme Court answered: No; the constitution had no extra-territorial operation (except with regard to Americans) and therefore did not protect any Russian business. It is important to remember that the Federal Government was the sole claimant. Therefore the question of creditors and the like did not arise. Belmont resisted the claim solely as he wanted to make sure that he had discharged his debt.

The Federal Government did not give up. Its object were some Russian insurance companies in liquidation, viz. the Northern Insurance Company of Moscow, the Moscow Fire Insurance Company and the First Russian Insurance Company. These companies, nationalized in Russia, had branches in New York which had continued their operations. In the long run, however, this was no longer possible under the state insurance law of New York, so that liquidation was directed under the supervision of the Superintendent of Insurance. At the time of the Litvinov Assignment these companies were being wound up. The situation regarding foreign insurance companies was such that they were allowed to operate by means of a branch in New York, provided they deposited a fixed portion of the premium-reserve in New York as security for the contracts concluded there. After the settlement of the business of the three companies mentioned, a considerable balance appeared to be left. This sum, it was assumed, was to be allotted to creditors and shareholders. The Superintendent of Insurance had already given instructions to that effect. But then the Federal Government interfered. In the first instance a decision had already been handed down before the *Belmont*-case. In *U.S.* v. *Bank of New York and Trust Co* and *U.S.* v. *Manhattan Co* [1] the claims of the U.S.A. on the balances of the Moscow Co and the Northern Co were at stake, or at least the suspension of its distribution. This claim lodged with the federal courts was dismissed on appeal: the District Court mentioned inconsistency with public policy: "the subsequent

[1] *Ann. Dig.* 1933–1934, 70.

recognition ... in no way changed the confiscatory nature of the decree in as far as these particular funds were concerned." The Circuit Court and the Supreme Court left this undecided and dismissed the claim on procedural grounds. The Federal Government then once more instituted proceedings in the state courts. It succeeded with regard to the Northern Co [1] and became entitled to the balance left after satisfaction of creditors. The decision was founded on the *Belmont*-case and did not go any further. In this development the *Moscow*-case (*Moscow Fire Insurance Co* v. *Bank of New York* [2]) was a retrograde step. It is true that the case cannot be regarded as a binding precedent, since the final decision was given by an equally divided court (3-3) [3], but it is obvious that the final decision reached in the *Pink*-case, was not arrived at overnight. In the *Moscow*-case it was considered that the rights to the property of the Moscow Co did not become vested in Soviet Russia, nor in the U.S.A. "its assignee"; in the first place the Soviet decrees were not intended to have extra-territorial effect (this was supported with reference to several English cases and by interpretation of the context) and moreover "confiscatory decrees do not affect the property claimed here". At last the final decision came: the Supreme Court clearly expressed and went even further than in the *Belmont*- and *Manhattan*-cases that the claim of the Federal Government came before the claims of foreign creditors and shareholders [4]. This *Pink*-case [5] diminished the struggle. The point at issue was the liquidation of the First Russian Insurance Cy., where the Federal Government lodged a claim on the assets. The Supreme Court considered several points in this case. In the first place it argued that the case in question was not be to compared with the *Moscow*-case. Further it was noted that the fact whether the nationalization decrees had any extra-territorial effect would indeed be decisive, because "the United States acquired, under the Litvinov Assignment, only such rights as Russia had." It appeared, however, that extra-territorial operation was intended and this was shown by means of an official statement dated

[1] *U.S.* v. *Manhattan Co*, A.L.R. 1942, 1220, cit. Herzfeld, 4.
[2] *Ann. Dig.* 1938–1940, 141.
[3] Cf. on this Hollander, 56, 66.
[4] The domestic creditors had already been paid.
[5] *U.S.* v. *Pink*, 315 U.S. 203 (1942).

November 28, 1937 by the Russian People's Commissar of Justice from which it appeared that "... the funds and property of former insurance companies constitute the property of the State, irrespective of the nature of the property and irrespective of whether it was situated within the territorial limits of the R.S.F. S.R. or abroad". This statement was accepted as binding. The *Belmont*-case was also referred to, when at the same time the Litvinov Assignment was mentioned. The recognition of Soviet Russia, the entering into diplomatic relations and the Litvinov Assignment, the Court argued, were representing "all parts of one transaction, resulting in an international compact between the two governments". And "this treaty has supremacy" over "state law and policies". In this respect the *Moscow*-case should not be followed, "for the *Moscow*-case refuses to give effect or recognition in New York to acts of the Soviet Government which the United States by its policy of recognition agreed no longer to question". Should, indeed, the prevalence of the public policy of the State of New York (where legal proceedings had been carried on) be pursued in accordance with the *Moscow*-case, this would "tend to restore some of the precise impediments to friendly relations which the President intended to remove on inauguration of the policy of recognition of the Soviet Government". Strictly speaking the decision in the *Moscow*-case would amount to "a rejection of a part of the policy underlying recognition by this nation of Soviet Russia." Such a power should not be granted to a State (as distinct from the Federal Government): "To permit it would be to sanction a dangerous invasion of Federal authority. For it would imperil the amicable relations between governments and vex the peace of nations". "Power over external affairs is not shared by the states; it is vested in the national government exclusively". "And the policies of the states become wholly irrelevant to judicial inquiry when the United States, acting within its constitutional sphere, seeks enforcement of its foreign policy in the courts". Full stress was laid on the international aspect and Herzfeld [1] is, indeed, right, when he thinks that the Court's opinion was mainly determined by two considerations: the fear of making a bad impression on

[1] Herzfeld, 24.

Soviet Russia by interfering in foreign policy, and the fear of provoking the displeasure of the American creditors of Czarist Russia. Creditors and shareholders of the companies would be satisfied with a rejection of the claim of the Federal Government but allowing the claim would approach the rights of creditors of Czarist Russia; indeed, in view of this the Litvinov Assignment had been made. The Court, therefore, decided: "We hold that the right to the funds of property in question became vested in the Soviet Government as the successor to the First Russian Insurance Cy.; that this right has passed to the United States under the Litvinov Assignment; and that the United States is entitled to the property as against the corporation and the foreign creditors". The *Pink*-case exclusively concerned foreign creditors, who were rejected in favour of the Federal Government; in *U.S.* v. *New York Trust Cy.* [1] American creditors were also turned away. A final decision was reached [2]. The whole affair aroused severe comment [3]; at any rate it was apparent that here it was not a question of a fundamental change of conduct of the American Courts in respect to the extra-territorial operation of confiscatory measures in general, but that the point of view of the Supreme Court was restricted to such cases as were covered by the Litvinov Assignment [4].

IV. NATIONALIZATION OF CORPORATIONS

1. *Legal Personality*

The nationalization of a corporation contains, as we already noted, several phases [5]. The element of extinction may be

[1] *Ann. Dig.* 1946, 29.

[2] The same point of view can be concluded *a contrario* from some decisions only refusing extra-territorial effect on account of limitation of the claim: *Guaranty Trust Comp.* v. *U.S.*, 304 U.S. 126 (1938), *Ann. Dig.* 1938–1940, 184; *U.S.S.R.* v. *National City Bank*, *Ann. Dig.* 1941–1942, 68; *U.S.* v. *Curtiss Aeroplane Co*, *Ann. Dig.* 1943–1945, 17; cf. Hollander, 52, 53 and Seidl-Hohenveldern, 144, 145.

[3] Borchard, *A.J.I.L.* 1937, 675, *A.J.I.L.* 1942, 275; Jessup, *A.J.I.L.* 1937, 481, *A.J.I.L.* 1942, 282; notes in *Harvard L. J.* 1937, 162, 1942, 865; *Yale L. J.* 1937, 292, 1940, 324, 1942, 848.

[4] More recent cases show this clearly: *Plesch* v. *Banque Nationale d'Haiti*, *Ann. Dig.* 1948, 13, *A.J.I.L.* 1948, 739, *A.J.I.L.* 1949, 814; *Bollack* v. *Société Générale* ..., *Ann. Dig.* 1941–1942, 147; *A/S Merilaid & Co* v. *Chase National Bank*, *Ann. Dig.* 1947, 15, *A.J.I.L.* 1948, 231; cf. Seidl-Hohenveldern, 145.

[5] *Supra*, 7, 8.

distinguished from the confiscatory element [1]. The private corporation as such disappears. Now the question arises to what extent this disappearance is recognized elsewhere and what consequences may follow.

It is generally agreed that the personal law of a corporation is applicable to questions of formation and dissolution [2]. This would mean in principle that a corporation, to which Russian law is applicable as personal law, has ceased to exist after nationalization by Russian law. Almost everywhere this conclusion was arrived at. Nevertheless the harshness of the dissolution and its effects were mitigated considerably in several countries.

If the conclusion had been drawn that such an abrupt end of the corporations as took place particularly in Soviet Russia, immediately produced equally abrupt effects elsewhere, this would have caused too unsatisfactory a situation [3]. Then the inference should have been drawn that the — no longer existing — corporation could no longer enforce any rights, while, on the other hand, no rights could be enforced any more against itself. Enrichment either at the cost of the corporation or at the cost of the creditors and other claimants would unavoidably take place. In order to meet this unsatisfactory situation case law and also legislation have shown various solutions. With a few exceptions both case law and legislation proceeded from the actual extinction of the corporation. It is obvious that there was no alternative. When a corporation with headquarters in Russia governed by Russian law as its personal law, was dissolved by Russian law, the fact that this was not taken into account would become entirely unreal. The articles of association could no longer be applied consistently and there would be all kinds of questions as to what was to be regarded as the old corporation. How was it to operate; who would have power to act in its behalf etc. In fact, it could only be admitted: "*Qu'on assassine des gens à Moscou*

---

1 Sometimes it will occur that the confiscating state does not formally extinguish the corporation, but only seizes the shares; cf. Seidl-Hohenveldern, 130.

2 Cheshire, 193, 478; Dicey, 476; Wolff, 305; Wolff, *Das I.P.R. Deutschlands*, 117; Schnitzer, I, 303; Rabel, II, 85. On the question of this personal law, see e.g. Wolff, 297.

3 This is apparent from the German decision *Reichsgericht* 20-5-1930, *Clunet* 1934, 147, *J.W.* 1931, 141, not granting the nationalized corporation access to the court, so that the claim at issue remained outstanding.

ou qu'on assassine des sociétés, l'homme assassiné est mort" [1]. Even the mitigation of the effects presented serious difficulties. The courts were confronted with altogether new problems. Situations had to be solved, which only too often amounted to a state characterized by Lord Justice Maughan as "... a submerged wreck floating on the ocean of commerce. It has had for the past fifteen years neither compass nor officers nor crew" [2].

The effects were mitigated in various ways. Almost everywhere this amounted to liquidation in a certain form. Only in view of such winding-up were the fragments of the nationalized corporations assumed to have a limited legal personality. When regarding the views in various countries, it is evident that legal existence in general is considered to be extinct when not confined particularly to liquidation. Otherwise such a concept was not at once common property of the case law. France at first operated with the idea *société de fait*; English and American case law also experienced a particular evolution.

a. Belgium

From the Belgian decision *Benoist et Levieux* c. *National City Bank of New York* [3] it is apparent that the Belgian court regarded the existence of the Banque Russo-Asiatique nationalized by Soviet Russia extinguished.

b. France

In French case law a rather extensive evolution is to be observed, which had its main origin in the cases regarding Soviet Russian nationalizations. Non-recognition of Soviet Russia initially played an important part. In the decisions *re Banque Russe pour le Commerce Etranger* [4] and *Vlasto* c. *Banque Russo-Asia-*

---

[1] Niboyet, *Travaux* 1935, 31; cf. also Lerebours-Pigeonnaire, *Travaux* 1934, 157, who compares the *succursales* with " ... *des rameaux poussés sur un tronc. Le tronc étant mort, les rameaux le sont aussi* ..."

[2] Re *Russian Bank for Foreign Trade* [1933] 1 Ch. 745 at p. 764.

[3] Brussels District Court 20-12-1934, *Clunet* 1935, 671; Brussels Court of Appeal 11-7-1936, *R.C.D.I.P.* 1937, 121 and Brussels Court of Appeal 11-7-1938, *Bulletin* vol. 41, 273; in *Deckers en Van der Heyden* c. *Soc. Tannerie de l'Azoff*, Liège District Court 25-3-1938, *Bulletin* vol. 41, 273, it was even stated that a corporation after confiscation in Soviet Russia is to be held as still existing until liquidation is demanded elsewhere.

[4] *Trib. comm. de la Seine* 16-1-1922, *Clunet* 1923, 539.

tique [1] there was no doubt of the continuance of the corporations, since non-recogniton of Soviet Russia involved ignoring of nationalization measures. Otherwise the fact could not be blinked at that there had been a revolution in Russia. Application of the old Russian law was therefore often amended by using the term *force majeure* [2], the result being that, on the whole, French case law met the amputated Russian corporations as much as possible during this period. The question of the cognizance of French courts was always answered in the affirmative. Where this was denied with reference to section 420 of the *Code de procédure civile* (*"Le demandeur pourra assigner, à son choix, devant le tribunal du domicile du défendeur* etc.) the courts regarded a *domicile de fait* also as a domicile within the meaning of law [3]. So the actual transfer of the management of a corporation to France gave sufficient grounds [4].

Naturally, in this initial period the situation was rather confused. People had fled out of Russia hurriedly and had gone to France. In some cases there was a *succursale* in the latter country where the management of the *maison mère* attempted to continue the business. In other cases business had sometimes been done in France without a branch being there; at most a representation was used. The interested parties (shareholders, creditors) requested French courts to appoint an *administrateur provisoire*, especially in the case of a representation, though also in the case of a branch, whose management was disorganized.

---

[1] *Trib. comm. de la Seine* 26-4-1922, *Clunet* 1923, 933; to the same effect *Affaire Kharon, Trib. civil de la Seine* 20-5-1921, *Clunet* 1923, 533.

[2] This is evident e.g. in *Vlasto* c. *Banque Russo-Asiatique, Trib. comm. de la Seine* 26-4-1922, *Clunet* 1923, 933: a valid departure of the articles of association – held a part of Russian law – in view of the *évènements de force majeure dont la Russie est le théatre*. Cf. Grouber et Tager, *Clunet* 1924, 8. However, the principle of *force majeure* was not consistently carried through: *Banque Industrielle de Moscou* c. *Banque du Pays du Nord, Trib. comm. de la Seine* 21-5-1924, *Clunet* 1927, 350 (powers of the management,appointed in1916 for the course of 5 years were to be considered finished); *Mkeidze* c. *Banque Russo-Asiatique, Trib. comm. de la Seine* 20-8-1924, *Clunet* 1925, 385 (*"la nationalisation des banques russes ayant rompu tous liens et toute solidarité avec les succursales ..."*); cf. Picard et Tager, criticizing these cases:" ... *on risquerait d'aboutir le plus souvent a une dénie de justice*", *Clunet* 1927, 368.

[3] *Banque russe pour le commerce étranger, Trib. comm. de la Seine* 16-1-1922, *Clunet* 1923, 539.

[4] *Bronstein* c. *Banque Russo-Asiatique, Trib. comm. de la Seine* 3-6-1921, *Clunet* 1927, 349; *Société Sago* c. *Société Russe de Transport et d'Assurances, Trib. comm. de la Seine* 2-11-1923, *Clunet* 1927, 349; *Société X* c. *Société Y., Trib. comm. de la Seine* 29-11-1923, *Clunet* 1927, 350.

That the courts declared their willingness appeared for instance from the decision relating to the *Ropit*-case [1]; in the case concerning *Société Peroune* [2], where a corporation was under consideration whose *siège social* was established in Petrograd, but which had *bureaux commerciaux* in Paris, the court considered itself competent to appoint an *administrateur provisoire*. It stated that such appointment was made in the interests of the corporation and the creditors, since the *siège social* could not be consulted, no normal meeting of shareholders could be held and a conflict among the members of the management had arisen.

After the recognition of Soviet Russia by France the situation changed. Rejection of the Soviet legislation *en bloc* by reason of the non-recognition was no longer possible and the dissolution of the corporation had to be judged on its own merits. Here some measures taken in France after the Soviet revolution should also be referred to. The necessity was then felt to take conservatory measures with regard to property belonging to the Russian state. For there was no doubt that the Russian state as such continued to exist; the difficulty, however, was in ascertaining who exercised the state authority. In this connection a committee was set up on June 29, 1920, which was called *Commission de liquidation russe* (a *commission interministrielle*, as the official decision ran), which had the task *"d'établir l'arrêté général des sommes dont l'ancien Etat russe est débiteur envers l'Etat français"*. It also received a few other instructions [3]. On the eve of the recognition of the Soviet Russian government it appeared to have ceased to exist. The vacancy had to be filled, particularly now that Soviet Russia was to be given diplomatic recognition. This could involve the possibility that Soviet Russia would set up claims to property of Russian origin. To prevent this (on October 22, 1924, six days before the recognition!) an *administrateur-séquestre* was appointed by the President of the *Tribunal civil de la Seine* at the request of the *Procureur de la République*. The *administrateur* was to take care of all property administered by the former committee, and of all other matters *"qui seraient*

---

[1] *Shramchenko* c. *Tcheloff e.a.*, *Trib. comm.* of Marseilles 3-12-1920, *Clunet* 1924, 141.
[2] *Société Péroune*, *Trib. comm. de la Seine* 5-1-1921, *Clunet* 1924, 139.
[3] *Journal officiel de la République française* 1-7-1920, 9266 and *Clunet* 1920, 838.

également à l'abandon par suite des mêmes circonstances" [1]. The instruction was extended a month later (November 29, 1924); now the sequestrator was, in addition, given the task of conducting the provisional administration of the branches (*succursales*) of the Russian corporations. Mr. Jaudon whose name appeared later in various cases was appointed as a sequestrator. Besides the freezing of a possible recovery by Russia there was also the thought that by doing so the claims of the French government were secured, and that this security could be seized for the benefit of the French creditors [2]. According to Henrich [3] the sequestrator was also appointed for the very reason that it was realized that after the recognition the principle of public policy could no longer be pleaded. In the first place this would harm good relations — the Russian commercial representative Krassin had left the country in a rage at the decision *in re Bouniatian* [4]. In the second place this would be illogical because prior to the recognition the courts did not apply any Soviet law on the very ground of the non-recognition, from which it could be inferred *a contrario* that Russian law could be applied integrally after the recognition took place. Bartin [5], too, considered the view of the courts before the recognition dangerous. Otherwise, the courts have not gone the way foreseen by Henrich.

In France various large Russian firms had branches, independent establishments; of other enterprises, on the other hand, only a few managing directors who had fled out of Russia with assets, were present. It is understandable that many legal proceedings were instituted. The passing away of the legal existence of the corporations could be a stroke of luck for the debtors, but not for the creditors. Hence a debtor sometimes chanced an action. Naturally, whether the corporation preferred to regard itself as existing depended on the financial status of the nationalized corporation in France. Now, the case law has given various solutions for the often extremely thorny problems which were submitted to the courts.

---

[1] *Clunet* 1925, 530.
[2] See Goeldlin de Tiefenau, 27, 28.
[3] Henrich, 79.
[4] *Héritiers A. Bouniatian* c. *Société Optorg, Trib. civil de la Seine* 12-12-1923, *Clunet* 1924, 113.
[5] Bartin, I, 62.

We can divide the case law into different groups, according to the corporations concerned.

In the first place it appears that several Russian corporations tried to transform themselves into French corporations. This was done before the recognition of the Soviet government; it is difficult to trace exactly how such transformation was made [1]. An instance of this is presented by the Banque Russe pour le Commerce Etranger, transformed into Banque générale pour le commerce étranger [2].

More extensive was the case law in respect of those corporations, which as Perret [3] describes, had a certain organization in France.

Finally there were nationalized corporations, which, without having an existing organization in the form of a branch, tried to continue doing business as best they could after a precipitate flight out of Russia taking records and assets with them.

The firms which had a form of organization at their disposal in France, notably banks, at first continued operations energetically and transferred "*au siège de cette succursale le centre de leurs opérations*" [4]. In the beginning there was a tendency to proceed to liquidation with the least possible delay and thereby to admit that life had been extinguished. This tendency was manifest especially in the instruction, extended on November 29, 1924, [5] of the *administrateur-séquestre* appointed on October 22, 1924. This certainly did not hold for such corporations as could successfully pretend transformation into French corporations. In these cases the sequestration was withdrawn. But also where the pretension to have become a French corporation was not

---

[1] Sollogoub, 98; Perret, 4, 36; Loussouarn, 144, 460.

[2] Cf. *Ordonnance* of the President of the *Tribunal de la Seine* 23-12-1924, *Clunet* 1925, 419 (cf. *Clunet* 1927, 358); *Veuve Lalande* c. *Banque russe pour le commerce étranger, Trib. comm. de la Seine* 29-6-1932, *Clunet* 1934, 663; however, from *Rabinovitch* c. *Banque russe pour le commerce étranger, Trib. comm. de la Seine* 15-5-1925, *Clunet* 1927, 354 and *Société pour l'Approvisionnement et l'Industrie des cuirs et peaux* c. *Banque russe pour le commerce étranger, Trib. comm. de la Seine* 26-11-1925, *Clunet* 1927, 354, it was apparent that this matter was judged differently as well: in these cases a factual transfer of the seat to France was not held sufficient by the court: it had to be proved that the transfer took place in a regular way. Picard and Tager vehemently protested, *Clunet* 1927, 366. To the same effect *Dame Krivitsky* c. *Banque russe pour le commerce étranger, Trib. comm. de la Seine* 19-11-1927, *Clunet* 1928, 132.

[3] Perret, 35.

[4] Picard et Tager, *Clunet* 1927, 364.

[5] *Clunet* 1925, 530.

successful, the sequestration was waived: in *Banque Russo-Asiatique* [1], for instance, it was decided that the *succursale* in Paris "*a perdu ce caractère et apparaît comme devenue le siège même de la société*".

The tendency to regard the legal existence of the corporations as unimpaired in France, has manifested itself particularly in the inclination of case law and literature to give form to the *société de fait* idea. The corporations liquidated in Russia and at least very drastically amputated in France were granted the status of *société de fait*. Thus it was made possible for them to continue for the time being. It was not always clear whether the courts granted the status of *société de fait*, or assumed that there was a question of a transformation into a French corporation. As regards the Banque Russe pour le Commerce Etranger a contrast can be found between the *Ordonnance* of 23-12-1924 [2] and the decision *Nahoum* c. *Banque Russe pour le Commerce Etranger* [3]. The former directed the withdrawal of the sequestration, because here a French bank should be involved. The latter spoke of *société de fait*.

By a *société de fait* [4] either of two things can be understood. As a rule a *société* which has defects of birth is concerned; it can also concern a corporation which is unable to continue its otherwise quite normal existence owing to special circumstances and is forced to seek abnormal courses. The corporations nationalized in Russia exemplify the latter. The *société de fait* idea is entirely formed by the case law and is a typical example of judge-made-law in a legal system which is otherwise as a rule wholly based on the system of codification. The case law has decided that the articles of association may be applied as far as possible, as also appears from the case law with regard to our subject matter. It further assumes a certain legal personality, a certain legal existence; the latter, however, is much restricted, because the existence is assumed for the benefit of third parties only; finally, a *société de*

---

[1] *Trib. de la Seine* 23-3-1925, *Clunet* 1927, 352; the instruction to the sequestrator exclusively mentioned competence as to branches; cf. *Banque Russo-Asiatique*, *Trib. comm. de la Seine* 1-10-1926, *Clunet* 1927, 359.

[2] *Clunet* 1925, 419.

[3] *Trib. comm. de la Seine* 3-12-1934, *Clunet* 1935, 125.

[4] See on this Hémard's standard work; for a short survey Perret, 40.

fait cannot bring actions [1]; it can be sued, however, and then it is regarded as a continuance of the old corporation and therefore liable for debts [2].

Of course it had to be proved that the part of the Russian corporation, established in France, was *société de fait,* but it was sufficient if the centre of activities had been transferred to France (*transfert de fait*) and that there were goods belonging to the corporation in France. The end of the corporation established in Russia would also cause the ending of the branch. The courts did not wish this result, particularly in the light of the practical result (the branches in France were sometimes very active and were still doing a substantial business). Hence the term *société de fait* was used. This was the argument of the case law. The inclination to assume *sociétés de fait* was apparent in some decisions [3] and unexpressed in others [4], but the tendency was always paramount. Several decisions somewhat indicated the conception of *société de fait* [5]. The courts assuming a *domicile de fait,* considered this fact sufficient to declare themselves competent and in this way, by accepting the nationalized corporation as party in the action, already implicitly made a certain decision. This was sometimes done explicitly by saying that the branch in question had an existence of its own. The *Cour d'Appel* of Paris made an exception to the case law when it applied much more stringent standards to the existence of a *société de fait.* The court considered

---

[1] Perret (44) properly observes: "*Cette difficulté aurait depuis longtemps amené les sociétés russes à la liquidation si la jurisprudence n'avait autorisé des palliatifs sous forme d'administrateurs provisoires etc. ... ou si au moins au début les débiteurs n'avaient exécuté des paiements volontaires.*"

[2] E.g. *Deutsche Bank und Diskonto Gesellschaft* c. *Banque internationale de Pétrograd, Cour d'Appel* of Paris 29-3-1938, *Clunet* 1938, 749, 1017.

[3] E.g. in *National City Bank of New York* c. *Société Renault Russe e.a., Trib. comm. de la Seine* 12-7-1929, *Clunet* 1929, 1122.

[4] E.g. *Khorosch* c. *Société Rossia, Kamenka e.a., Cour d'Appel* of Paris 7-1-1928, *Clunet* 1928, 687.

[5] *C.* c. *la Société d'Assurance Y., Trib. comm. de la Seine* 1-5-1925, *Clunet* 1927, 353; *Selikman* c. *Société de Naphte de Bakou, Trib. comm. de la Seine* 12-4-1926, *Clunet* 1927, 357; *Kamenka et Epstein* c. *H. et J. Cahn, Trib. comm. de la Seine* 11-1-1927, *Clunet* 1927, 362; *Darlay et Cie* c. *la Succursale de la Banque du Commerce et de l'Industrie, Trib. civil de la Seine* (*Réf.*) 28-2-1927, *Clunet* 1928, 686; *Zelenoff* c. *Banque de Commerce de Sibérie, Cour d'Appel* of Paris 31-1-1928, *Clunet* 1928, 679; in this case a *domicile de fait* was assumed in France, though no business was carried on there; the place where the archives were kept was taken for domicile. In the decision *Banque de Sibérie* c. *Vairon et Cie, Cour d'Appel* of Bordeaux 2-1-1928, *Clunet* 1929, 115, au *existence de fait* was demanded as a condition for the existence of a *société de fait*; in this case an *existence de fait* was not assumed.

it impossible[1] to sue a Russian corporation in France, though it had a branch there, unless it was proved that the branch led an entirely independent existence and the *siège social* was no longer situated in Russia. However, the Parisian *Cour d'Appel* determinedly followed the old course in the decision *Kahn* c. *Société d'assurances Rossia*[2]; there competence was already assumed now that there was a question of a *siège provisoire.* This also remained the predominant tendency of the case law[3] after 1928.

Besides the corporations which were granted the status of *société de fait* by the court, we mention finally such firms which in flight from Russia took their assets with them in whole or in part, but yet remained unorganized; they were rather unstable and tried to save themselves as far as possible. It stands to reason that the legal position of such "corporations" was very precarious. The French case law, therefore, concluded that such corporations must be regarded as dissolved and only continued to exist as long and in so far as this was required for the purpose of winding up[4]. Practice showed that this might take several years.

The case law therefore presumed that either the legal existence

---

[1] *Karagoulian* c. *Banque russe pour le commerce et l'industrie, Cour d'Appel* of Paris 17-5-1927, *Clunet* 1928, 131.

[2] *Cour d'Appel* of Paris 8-3-1928, *Clunet* 1928, 682.

[3] *National City Bank of New York* c. *Société Renault Russe e.a., Trib. comm. de la Seine* 12-7-1929, *Clunet* 1929, 1122; *Deutsche Bank & Diskonto Gesellschaft* c. *Banque Internationale de Pétrograd e.a., Trib. comm. de la Seine* 27-6-1934, *Clunet* 1935, 117, stating "*elle a survécu à sa propre disparition comme société de fait*"; *Ancelle* c. *Société du Naphte Russe, Trib. comm. de la Seine* 22-1-1934, *Clunet* 1935, 125; *Maximoff* c. *Société de Banque Volga-Kama, Trib. comm. de la Seine* 22-1-1934, *Clunet* 1935, 125; *L'association des porteurs de parts de la Banque Internationale de Commerce de Pétrograd et Hennéants* c. *Banque Internationale de Commerce de Pétrograd e.a., Trib. comm. de la Seine* 17-8-1934, *Clunet* 1935, 125; *Nahoum* c. *Banque russe pour le commerce étranger, Trib. comm. de la Seine* 3-12-1934, *Clunet* 1935, 125; *Deutsche Bank* c. *Nobel, Trib. comm. de la Seine* 20-1-1936, *Ann. Dig.* 1935–1937, 193; *Deutsche Bank & Diskonto Gesellschaft* c. *Banque Internationale de Pétrograd, Cour d'Appel* of Paris 29-3-1938, *Clunet* 1938, 749, 1017; *Banque Russe* c. *Technogor, Cour d'Appel* of Paris 3-1-1944, *R.C.D.I.P.* 1948, 81 .

[4] *Cie Nord de Moscou* c. *La Union et Phénix Espagnol, Trib. civil de la Seine* 9-5-1925, *Clunet* 1926, 126 and *Cour d'Appel* of Paris 13-6-1928, *Clunet* 1929, 119; *Banque de Sibérie* c. *Vairon et Cie, Cour d'Appel* of Bordeaux 2-1-1928, *Clunet* 1929, 115; *Cockerill* c. *La Union et Phénix Espagnol, Cour d'Appel* of Paris 23-12-1930, *Clunet* 1931, 400, *Cass.* 4-7-1933, *Clunet* 1934, 662; *Société Wildenberg* c. *Comptoir National d'Escompte, Trib. comm. de la Seine* 15-1-1934, *Clunet* 1934, 653; *Crédit Français* c. *Koulmann, Trib. comm. de la Seine* 23-1-1934, *Clunet* 1934, 653; *Banque Scandinave et Vve Rosenthal* c. *Kamenka e.a.* (*Banque Azof-Don*), *Trib. comm. de la Seine* 21-1-1935, *Clunet* 1935, 134.

of the Russian corporations had been destroyed and led a shady and temporary existence exclusively for winding up or had been reduced to a degenerate form of life — *société de fait* — destined to end in liquidation. "*Le maintien de ces sociétés*", Perret [1] observed, "*même sous forme de sociétés de fait, n'est pas souhaitable, puisque toute vie normale leur est interdite*".

c. Germany

German case law also recognized the dissolution of the nationalized corporations. It is true, the *Kammergericht* of *Berlin* decided in *Ginsberg* g. *Deutsche Bank* [2] on March 3, 1925, that the Soviet Russian nationalization decrees were to be regarded as a political program rather than a concrete nationalization, so that it had to be assumed that the Russian bank concerned had to be held still existing, but this decision based mainly on material supplied in a *Gutachten* by Zaitzeff on the analogy of the English *Mulhouse*-case [3] was soon abandoned. A later decision of the *Kammergericht* differed [4]; it was assumed that the legal personality had disappeared. The *Reichsgericht* decided similarly [5].

d. England

The English case law has undergone a remarkable development. The legal personality of the nationalized Russian corporations was at first considered entirely extinct; this was decided in some early cases. However, the House of Lords held that the existence of the corporations was to be assumed. The issue in *Russian Commercial and Industrial Bank* v. *Comptoir d'Escompte de Mulhouse and others* [6] (the case *Banque International de Commerce de Petrograd* v. *Goukassow* [7] was decided similarly), was as follows: The plaintiff, a Russian bank with branches in London, had concluded an agreement with the defendant to make a

---

[1] Perret, 77.

[2] *J.W.* 1925, 1300, *Ostrecht* 1925, 163, *Clunet* 1925, 1057.

[3] *Russian Commercial and Industrial Bank* v. *Comptoir d'Escompte de Mulhouse and others* [1923] 2 K.B. 630, [1925] A.C. 112.

[4] Dated 25-10-1927, *J.W.* 1928, 1232, *Z.f.O.* 1928, 1583.

[5] *Re Spahn & Sohn A.G.*, *Reichsgericht* 20-5-1930, *J.W.* 1931, 141, *Z.f.O.* 1930, 646, *Clunet* 1934, 147; *Reichsgericht* 11-7-1934, *J.W.* 1934, 2845, *Clunet* 1935, 164.

[6] *Russian Commercial and Industrial Bank* v. *Comptoir d'Escompte de Mulhouse and others* [1923] 2 K.B. 630, [1925] A.C. 112.

[7] *Banque Internationale de Commerce de Pétrograd* v. *Goukassow* [1923] 2 K.B. 682, [1925] A.C. 150.

deposit with a London bank as security for a loan. After the Soviet measures they agreed to liquidate the loan. The plaintiff paid, but the defendant did not return the deposit, alleging that the plaintiff had become extinct by nationalization and that payment to the plaintiff would involve a risk to the defendant of having to pay twice. In the first instance the plaintiff failed. The data to be discussed by us are extracted from the appeal and before the House of Lords. On appeal Lord Justice Bankes examined whether the legal personality of the Russian bank had become extinct by nationalization in the light of the various decrees [1]. He carefully discussed the decree of December 14, 1917, regarding the nationalization of the banks and the decree of January 26, 1918, regarding the confiscation of the stock of the banks. He also pointed to the instruction of the People's Commissar of Finance dated December 10, 1918, which gave technical details of the amalgamation of the banks with the People's Bank. Then he concluded: "The more I study the documents ... the more I become with the conviction that the policy underlying them ... is the policy of destruction, and the absorption is the absorption of extinction" [2]. English courts, as is known, hold the view that foreign law is treated as fact and must be proved accordingly [3]. In such cases experts on Russian law are always seen to act as witnesses. They often contradicted each other, as they did in this case. It was maintained that the legal personality had disappeared but one expert Idelson observed: "... the Russian bank being a joint stock company in order to die must do so in the prescribed way". Idelson argued therefore that the legal personality still existed. Lord Justice Scrutton concurred with Lord Justice Bankes' remarks. Lord Justice Atkin, however, held a different view. He felt that under the decrees in question loss of legal personality need not be presumed, but he also attached great importance to the fact that after the date of the nationalization decree the London branch had still carried on correspondence with Petrograd. In his opinion this was against liquidation by law. So the case by a two to one decision again decided in favour of the defendant, since

[1] An English translation of the decrees formed an appendix to the judgment.
[2] [1923] 2 K.B. 643.
[3] Dicey, 866; Wolff, 218; Cheshire, 127.

the legal existence of the plaintiff was presumed to have disappeared. This also meant that the plaintiff was not condemned in costs, for the court argued, if a non-existent person is unable to receive, he is also unable to pay. The Lords, however, did not concur. They unanimously upheld Lord Justice Atkin's view. Lord Cave, the principal spokesman, also inquired into the decrees at length and referred to Russian Constitutional law. By means of a thorough investigation of the context he concluded that the nationalization decree of December 14, 1917 (particularly having regard to section 4 which referred to a further elaboration which was never published as such in the form of a decree) was to be regarded as a political statement rather than an actual nationalization. Moreover, he deemed the confiscation of the shares (decree of January 26, 1918) inconsistent with the fact that the banks should have been nationalized already on December 14, 1917; for then there could be no question of the title of the shares being transferred. He considered that the nationalization decree spoke of a future nationalization and concluded that the bank still existed. Judgment was given for the bank.

Quite parallel to the *Mulhouse*-case was *Sea Insurance Cy* v. *Rossia Insurance Cy and Employers Liability Assurance Corporation Ltd* [1]. In the first instance legal existence was regarded as having disappeared, but was held unimpaired before the House of Lords, after the final decision in the *Mulhouse*-case had been given. The tendency of the decision in the *Mulhouse*-case manifested itself in various subsequent actions. It was assumed in *Sedgwick, Collins and Cy Ltd.* v. *Rossia Insurance Cy of Petrograd* (*Employers Liability Assurance Corporation Ltd, Garnishees*) [2] that the legal existence of the Russian corporation had not disappeared and the property of the corporation in England was not affected by the Soviet measures. This was likewise decided, with reference to the last-mentioned case, in *Sabatier* v. *The Trading Cy* [3]. In the *First Russian Insurance Cy* case [4] legal existence was also assumed. It was the same in the *Jupiter*-cases,

[1] 17 Ll.L.L.R. 316, 20 Ll.L.L.R. 308.
[2] [1926] 1 K.B. 1, [1927] A.C. 95.
[3] [1927] 1 Ch. 495.
[4] [1928] 1 Ch. 922.

where the Ropit acted[1]. The decision *Woronin, Lütschg and Cheshire* v. *Messrs. Frederick Huth & Co*[2], relying on the *Mulhouse*-case[3], the decision *Sedgwick, Collins and Cy*[4] and *The Jupiter* (*No 3*)[5] also held that the legal personality had not disappeared. There was no question of extra-territorial effect (i.e. the passing of the property of goods in England to Soviet Russia). Otherwise the resemblance to the French conception of *société de fait* was remarkable; here a Russian corporation was concerned without branches abroad, but possessing a very large portion of the assets, with the majority of the shareholders and managing directors in England. This was the ground for assuming residence in England. Further, the articles of association were still considered in force, in so far as they had the force of contract. Neither did the court regard the rights of the shareholders as affected, since the stock as a chose in action, not tied to the seat of the company but to the shareholder's domicile, fell entirely outside Russian jurisdiction.

If the attitude of English courts in the period up to about 1929 could be characterized as conservative, a new interpretation of Russian law changed this in the 1930's, though the Companies Act 1929 rendered it still possible to come to a solution. In 1932 the winding-up period opened with the decision *Lazard Bros & Co* v. *Banque Industrielle de Moscou* and *Lazard Bros & Co* v. *Midland Bank Ltd*[6]. Wortley says[7] that "a bold move was made" by leaving the path of the established case law and deciding that the Russian bank in question had disappeared. This was done on the ground of fresh evidence; once again all the relative Russian documents were examined, including material not discussed in previous cases. A difficult point was the exact date on which the legal existence had disappeared; this was not clearly decided, but it was held by Lord Wright speaking for the Lords that "long before 1930 (the date material in this action) all traces of Czarist banks had vanished".

---

[1] *The Jupiter* (*No. 1*) [1924] P. 236; *The Jupiter* (*No. 2*) [1925] P. 69; *The Jupiter* (*No. 3*) [1927] P. 122, P. 250.

[2] [1925] A.C. 112.

[3] [1927] A.C. 95.

[4] [1927] P. 122, P. 250.

[5] 79 Ll.L.L.R. 262, *Brit. Yearb.* 1930, 235, *Clunet* 1928, 756, *Z.f.O.* 1929, 303.

[6] [1932] 1 K.B. 617, [1935] A.C. 289 and 49 T.L.R. 94.

[7] Wortley, *Brit. Yearb.* 1933, 6.

This decision underlay further case law; for the future similar judgments with regard to the evidence of the foreign law were given. We mention *Russian and English Bank* v. *Baring Bros & Co* [1], which also decided that the legal existence of the bank had vanished, so that the bank could not sue. The court advised winding-up in accordance with section 338 (2) of the Companies Act 1929. Winding-up resulted [2]; after a liquidator had been appointed it was first decided that this did not mean a revival of legal personality [3]. But the liquidator in his capacity could act as a plaintiff [4]. Also in *Re Russian Bank for Foreign Trade* [5] it was held that the legal personality had disappeared. For the first time in *Re Russo-Asiatic Bank* [6] a date was fixed on which the bank had ceased to exist. The date specified by the court was not later than January 1918, at the time of the second decree respecting the nationalization of the banks [7]. From *Deutsche Bank und Diskonto Gesellschaft* v. *Banque des Marchands de Moscou* [8] it likewise appeared that the legal existence of the bank was to be regarded as disappeared.

In this development the *Tallina*-case [9] was remarkable, since here the line indicated by the *Mulhouse*-case [10], but abandoned in 1932 by the decision *Lazard Bros & Co* [11], was again taken. In the *Tallina*-case it was again held that the disputed Esthonian nationalization decree had not *ipso facto* deprived the corporation in question of its existence, but had rather ordered it to be wound up.

e. The Netherlands

Dutch case law on the existence of corporations is not entirely

[1] [1932] 1 Ch. 435.

[2] *Re Russian and English Bank* [1932] 1 Ch. 663.

[3] *Re Russian and English Bank* [1934] 1 Ch. 276.

[4] *Russian and English Bank* v. *Baring Bros & Co* [1935] 1 Ch. 120, [1936] A.C. 405; cf. *infra*, 121.

[5] [1933] 1 Ch. 745.

[6] [1934] Ch. 720.

[7] Cf. Wohl, *Ostrecht* 1925, 113.

[8] (1938) 158 L.T.R. 364.

[9] *A/S Tallina Laevauhisus Ltd* v. *Tallina Shipping Co and Estonian State S.S. Line* (1946) 79 Ll.L.L.R. 245, *Brit. Yearb.* 1946, 384, *A/S Tallina Laevauhisus* v. *Estonian State S.S. Line* (1947) 80 Ll.L.L.R. 99, *Brit. Yearb.* 1947, 416.

[10] *Russian Commercial and Industrial Bank* v. *Comptoir d'Escompte de Mulhouse and others* [1923] 2 K.B. 630, [1925] A.C. 112.

[11] *Lazard Bros & Co* v. *Banque Industrielle de Moscou, Lazard Bros & Co* v. *Midland Bank Ltd* [1932] 1 K.B. 617, [1933] A.C. 289 and 49 T.L.R. 94.

unanimous. Several decisions considered the existence unimpaired, others considered the existence vanished. Thus it was held in *Vseobtchaia Stroitelnaia Kompania* v. *Smit*[1] that the existence had remained unimpaired, though the operation of the corporation in Russia was paralyzed. This was also the case in *Helvetia* v. *De Nederlanden van 1845*, when the existence of the Russian insurance company Moskowskoie was at stake; the Hague District Court[2] considered public policy a bar; the Court of Appeal[3] arrived at continuance on account of the interpretation of the nationalization decree and the circumstances. Also in *Latvian Shipping Co* v. *Montan Export*[4], with no evidence to the contrary furnished, it was held that a nationalized Latvian corporation had not lost its existence.

In *Herani* v. *Wladikawkaz Railway Co*[5], however, it was found that a corporation nationalized by Soviet Russia had ceased to exist.

f. Sweden, Switzerland

Both in Sweden[6] and Switzerland[7] it was found that the existence of the corporations had disappeared by nationalization.

g. Rumania

In Rumania the contrary is the case; otherwise decisions were made here on the ground of the non-recognition of the nationalizing government[8].

[1] Dordrecht District Court 12-1-1927, *N.J.* 1927, 447, *Ann. Dig.* 1927–1928, 71.

[2] The Hague District Court 9-3-1933, *N.J.* 1933, 1662, *Ann. Dig.* 1933–1934, 80.

[3] The Hague Court of Appeal 3-6-1937, *N.J.* 1937, 1675, *Ann. Dig.* 1935–1937, 204.

[4] The Hague Court of Appeal 20-1-1950, *N.J.* 1950, No. 752.

[5] Amsterdam District Court 11-6-1940, *N.J.* 1940, No. 1095, Amsterdam Court of Appeal 4-11-1942, *N.J.* 1943, No. 496, *Ann. Dig. Suppl. Vol.*, 21.

[6] *Forsikringsaktieselskapet Norske Atlas* v. *Sundén-Cullberg*, Supreme Court 18-10-1929, *Ann. Dig.* 1929–1930, 97; *Commercial and Industrial Bank of Russia* v. *Aktiebolaget Göteborgs Bank*, Supreme Court 26-6-1931, *Ann. Dig.* 1931–1932, 142; *Ruditzky* v. *Aktiebolaget Svenska Handelsbanken*, Supreme Court 26-3-1932, *Ann. Dig.* 1931–1932, 143; *Stockholms Enskilda Bank* v. *Amilakvari*, Supreme Court 12-11-1938, *Ann. Dig. Suppl. Vol.*, 107; *Azov-Don Bank*, Supreme Court 19-10-1945, *Z.A.I.P.* 1949–50,499; Supreme Court 30-12-1947, *Z.A.I.P.* 1949–50,501; in the last mentioned case an Esthonian nationalization was at issue, the other cases dealt with Russian nationalizations.

[7] *Banque internationale de Commerce de Pétrograd* c. *Hausner*, Swiss Supreme Court 10-12-1924, *R.O.* 50 II 507, *Clunet* 1925, 488; *Wilbuschewitz* c. *Autorité tutélaire de la Ville de Zürich et Dép.t. de justice du Canton de Zürich*, Swiss Supreme Court 13-7-1925, *R.O.* 51 II 259, *Clunet* 1926, 1110.

[8] *Banque russe pour le commerce étranger* c. *Association d'emprunt et de dépot de Cetatea-Alba*, Court of Cassation 4-11-1921, *Clunet* 1925, 1125; Court of Cassation 5-12-1932, *Clunet* 1935, 718.

h. U.S.A.

In the U.S.A. the same stand was taken as long as the nationalizing government in question was not recognized; the rule to ignore the measures taken by an unrecognized state or government was consistently applied and the amendment given by Cardozo in the *Sokoloff*-case [1] was mentioned on this account, but not used. *Fred. S. James & Co* v. *Second Russian Insurance Cy* [2] was a clear example of it. This conception was also apparent from *Russian Reinsurance Co and Paul Rasor* v. *Francis R. Stoddard and the Bankers Trust Cy* [3]. *Petrogradsky Bank* v. *National City Bank* [4] again accurately formulated the conceptions, stated in the *Sokoloff*-case and likewise arrived at the continuance of the nationalized corporation, as did *Fred. S. James & Co* v. *Rossia Insurance Cy of America* [5]. The last-mentioned decision stated that the conception of the nationalized corporations which retained their existence would have to be reconsidered after a possible recognition of Soviet Russia by the U.S.A.. In this connection the case *Vladikavkazsky Railway Co* v. *New York Trust Co* [6] of 1934, and therefore after the recognition, is remarkable. Here it was indicated that the dissolution of the corporation could not be recognized, since it was contrary to public policy. It was even said that the non-recognition of Soviet Russia was not the real reason why her decrees were denied any effect: "The fact that the present Russian government was not recognized was not the basis of our refusal to give effect to its decrees nationalizing corporations and confiscating their property". On the contrary: "it is hardly necessary to state, that the ... dissolution ... [and] ... the confiscation ... is contrary to our public policy and shocking to our sense of justice and equity". Apart from the fact that no extra-territorial validity was granted to the confiscatory element in the dissolution, dissolution itself was to be regarded as contrary to public policy. This conception is seldom found. From the case law mentioned before, where dissolution was regarded as valid, it follows implicitly that the principle of

---

[1] *Ann. Dig.* 1923–1924, 44, 37 A.L.R. 712, *Clunet* 1925, 446.
[2] *Ann. Dig.* 1925–1926, 57; cf. Goeldlin de Tiefenau, 122.
[3] *Ann. Dig.* 1925–1926, 54, *Clunet* 1925, 451, *Clunet* 1925, 1070.
[4] *Ann. Dig.* 1929–1930, 38, *Clunet* 1930, 782.
[5] 37 A.L.R. 720, *Clunet* 1928, 789.
[6] *Ann. Dig.* 1933–1934, 65.

public policy was not applied. Several decisions even said so expressly. In France it was clearly expressed for the first time in *Banque de Sibérie* c. *Vairon et Cie* [1]. Application of public policy was rejected in *Cie Nord de Moscou* c. *La Union et Phénix Espagnol* [2] as well as in *Cockerill* c. *La Union et Phénix Espagnol* [3]. Here explicit distinction was made between the confiscatory element and the extinction; and then the two aspects were confronted with public policy: "*Sans doute la loi russe ne s'impose pas quand elle est incompatible avec l'ordre public français et la nationalisation sans indemnité est directement contraire aux principes français; mais il n'en reste pas moins que les banques russes ont cessé d'exister et cette suppression en soi, indépendamment de la confiscation qui en a été la suite, n'est pas en contradiction avec le droit français*".

Extra-territorial effect of the confiscatory element was, indeed, universally rejected [4]; conceptions about isolated confiscations did not distinguish themselves from conceptions of confiscations connected with the nationalization of a corporation. We already discussed the few exceptions [5].

2. *Winding up of Nationalized Corporations*

Now that the necessity of liquidation has been established, the practical question arises how to effect such liquidation. This is not so simple. The Soviet Russian confiscations and nationalizations, the first on a large scale in modern history, caught legal public opinion more or less unawares. There was neither liqui-

---

[1] *Cour d'Appel* of Bordeaux 2-1-1928, *Clunet* 1929, 115; *Cass.* 29-7-1929, *Clunet* 1930, 680.

[2] *Trib. Civil de la Seine* 9-5-1925, *Clunet* 1926, 126; *Cour d'Appel* of Paris 13-6-1928, *Clunet* 1929, 119.

[3] *Cour d'Appel* of Paris 23-12-1930, *Clunet* 1931, 400; *Cass.*4-7-1933, *Clunet* 1934, 662. This view is tacitly assumed in several decisions, e.g. *Crédit Français* c. *Koulmann*, *Trib. comm. de la Seine* 23-1-1934, *Clunet* 1934, 653; *Société Wildenberg* c. *Comptoir National d'Escompte*, *Trib. comm. de la Seine* 15-1-1934, *Clunet* 1934, 653; *Comptoir d'Escompte* c. *Rosenfeld et Brzezinski*, *Cour d'Appel* of Paris 6-7-1935, *Clunet* 1936, 916; cf. Bartin, I, 67 and Picard et Tager, *Clunet* 1929, 131.

[4] Cf. *supra* note 3; this is also evident from e.g. *Banque Internationale de Commerce de Pétrograd* c. *Hausner*, Swiss Supreme Court 10-12-1924, *R.O.* 50 II 507, *Clunet* 1925, 488; *Herani* v. *Wladikawkaz Raylway Co*, Amsterdam District Court 11-6-1940, *N.J.* 1940, 1607, *Ann. Dig. Suppl. Vol.*, 21 and many other decisions.

[5] *Supra*, 78, 91 ff.

dation suited to this situation, nor leading cases upon which to rely. It may be said, though, that the very events in Soviet Russia were the occasion of the introduction of a few statutory measures. Such regulations, notably made in the countries of judge-made-law gave at least positive rules, though not made until a considerable time after the Soviet measures. In other countries, where there were no statutory regulations, considerable confusion prevailed and courts had to manage with analogous application of law or had to be guided by what was deemed fair in the given case.

a. Statute Law

As regards statute law we may point to the English Companies Act 1929, of which sections 338 ff. in Part X are devoted to Winding up of Unregistered Companies [1]; to section 977-b of the New York Civil Practice Act [2] added in 1936 and to the legislation which has come into existence in some Eastern European countries in view of the peace treaties with Soviet Russia after World War I [3].

England

The provisions of the Companies Act 1929 in sections 338 ff. obviously referred to the Russian corporations. It may be assumed, therefore, that the Russian nationalizations were the occasion for this legislation. Section 338 (1) (d) provides: "The circumstances in which an unregistered company may be wound up are as follows:

(1) If the company is dissolved, or has ceased to carry on business, or is carrying on business only for the purpose of winding up its affairs;

(2) If the company is unable to pay its debts;

(3) If the court is of opinion that it is just and equitable that the company should be wound up".

From the second subsection of section 338 it follows that the Russian corporations, as unregistered companies might also be wound up: "Where a company incorporated outside Great

[1] The Companies Act 1948 has similar regulations in sections 398 ff.
[2] Section 977-b see Hollander, 171.
[3] Cf. *supra*, 90.

Britain which has been carrying on business in Great Britain ceases to carry on business in Great Britain, it may be wound up as an unregistered company under this Part of this Act, notwithstanding that it has been dissolved or otherwise ceased to exist as a company under or by virtue of the laws of the country under which it was incorporated".

Naturally the subsection had been framed in general terms. So application was not only confined to Russian companies.

New York

This is also the case with the provisions of section 977-b included in the New York Civil Practice Act in 1936. Under these regulations: "an action may be instituted in the supreme court for the appointment of a receiver of the assets in this state of a foreign corporation, whenever such foreign corporation has assets or property of any kind whatsoever, tangible or intangible within the state of New York, and (a) it has heretofore been or is hereafter dissolved, liquidated or nationalized or (b) its charter or organic law had heretofore been or hereafter is suspended, repealed, revoked or annulled, or (c) it has heretofore ceased or hereafter ceases to do business, whether voluntarily or otherwise or by reason of the expiration of the term of its existence or by revocation or annulment of its organic law or by dissolution or otherwise". It is observed expressly ***sub*** 19 that "such liquidation, dissolution, nationalization etc. ... shall not be deemed to have any extra-territorial effect ..."

Poland

In Poland [1] only conservatory measures were taken at first. By the decrees of November 23, 1918, and December 10, 1918, it was provided that the compulsory administration imposed by the occupant was to be taken over by governmental officials. Such administration was mainly applicable to cases in which there was no owner of the corporation. Now these measures were also used in respect of the branches of nationalized Russian corporations (e.g. the Volga-Kama- and Azof-Don-Bank). No decision had as yet been taken about the title of property; even less on the legal

[1] See S. Rundstein, *Ostrecht* 1925, 330; S. Wierzbowski, *Z.f.O.* 1928, 1097; Perret, 96, 120, 163, 191; Rabinowitsch, *Z.f.O.* 1929, 1109.

continuance of the corporations. As regards the latter the decree of June 13, 1922, did not bring anything new either. This decree provided that the branch offices of corporations which had their seats outside Poland before November 1, 1918, could continue work only with special permission. If such permission was not granted within 6 months, they were to cease operations. No decision had yet been taken as regards their legal status. Neither did the mixed settlement committee created by the Riga treaty bring the matter nearer to its solution. Further conservatory measures came in the form of circulars from the Minister of Justice, dated May 14, 1925 [1], addressed to the courts and the notaries public. The decree of May 25, 1927, stated amongst other things that foreign corporations, no longer existing in their home countries or having no possibilities to continue operations in accordance with their articles of association, fell under the above compulsory management. Thus the decree also remained purely conservatory in nature. From the decision of January 26, 1927 [2], however, it might be inferred that the court regarded the legal personality of the Russian corporation as extinguished. A definite regulation [3] was finally made in 1928. By the decree in question winding up of the property of the nationalized Russian corporations situated within the territorial limits of Poland was ordered.

Latvia

The tendency to regulate the position in Latvia already appeared from the Riga peace treaty [4]. For this purpose some special provisions were added to the Companies Act [5], regarding the branch offices of nationalized Russian corporations: such branch offices were to go into liquidation according to their articles of association, unless within 6 months they resumed their operations with the consent of the Minister of Finance. If they had neither wound up, nor resumed operations, compulsory liquidation by the government was to follow. On April 17, 1925, this was

[1] *Z.f.O.* 1928, 1087.
[2] *Z.f.O.* 1928, 1237.
[3] Decree of March 22, 1928, *Z.f.O.* 1928, 1164.
[4] Martens, *Nouveau Rec. 3° serie*, XI, 888.
[5] Act of July 31, 1924, *Z. f. Osteur. Recht* I (1925), 93.

changed [1]: if the reorganization and the re-starting of operations had not yet begun by that time, winding up was only possible. So the option had gone. A special decree was enacted [2] for two insurance companies, the Rossia and the Zizu, to which winding up was applicable. A particular feature of this decree was that compensation was made on a gold basis. On September 16, 1927, there came, at last, the further regulation of the winding up of the banks [3].

Esthonia

On the occasion of the Dorpat peace treaty [4] a legal decree was also made in Esthonia, which was very soon promulgated [5]. It provided for the possibility of the reconstruction of the branch offices of Russian corporations established in Esthonia. If this did not take place, the property was placed under legal control as *bona vacantia*. In 1921 it was still provided [6] that the corporations did not exist any longer and were to be placed under management by the government. Further details about the liquidation are lacking.

China

In China a special regulation was made with regard to the nationalized Banque Russo-Asiatique, which had several branch offices in China [7].

b. Initiative

One encounters various questions in winding up a corporation nationalized elsewhere. Assuming that the remains of the corporation are doomed to disappear the first question arising will be who may take the initiative for winding up.

That shareholders ought to be able to do so is apparent. They are the main interested parties; consequently statutory regulations regarding winding up of corporations in general (apart

---

[1] *Z. f. Osteur. Recht* I (1925), 275.
[2] Decree of September 17, 1926, *Z.f.O.* 1927, 56, 82.
[3] *Z.f.O.* 1927, 1359.
[4] Martens, *Nouveau Rec. 3° série*, XI, 864.
[5] Decree of October 27, 1920, according to Rabinowitsch, *Z.f.O.* 1929, 1113.
[6] According to Wohl, *Ostrecht* 1925, 67, 68.
[7] On this Perret, 96, 120, 163 and *Annexes*.

from nationalization) always empower them to demand dissolution. As regards the present winding up their powers are proved by both statute law [1] and case law [2].

Creditors are also entitled to take the initiative for winding up [3].

Case law has not considered whether both the management of the corporation and a debtor ought to be able to demand winding up. No doubt both are interested and it seems fair that they may also demand winding up [4].

Finally, winding up ordered by the court might be justifiable on the ground of public interest [5].

The question who may take the initiative for winding up gives rise to a second question: when can such initiative be taken? In general this proved possible, if only there was property in the country where the winding up was demanded [6]. English statute law requires that the company "has been carrying on business in Great Britain" [7], to which the case law added that the company was to have or at least to have had a place of business in Great Britain. At first this was strictly applied [8], but afterwards liberally interpreted [9] and finally abandoned completely [10].

[1] New York Civil Practice Act, Section 977-b, sub. 2.

[2] As to England it was stated in *Russian and English Bank* v. *Baring Bros & Co* [1932] 1 Ch. 435, that shareholders had not the right to take this initiative; but in *Dairen Kisen Kabushiki Kaisha* v. *Shiang Kee* [1941] A.C. 373, it was held that they did have the right. The latter point of view was taken in France as well: *L'Association des porteurs de parts de la Banque Internationale de Commerce de Pétrograd et Hennéants* c. *Banque Internationale de commerce de Pétrograd e.a., Trib. comm. de la Seine* 17-8-1934, *Clunet* 1935, 125; *Maximoff* c. *Société de Banque Volga-Kama, Trib. comm. de la Seine* 22-1-1934, *Clunet* 1935, 125. To the same effect the Austrian decision *L.G.* Vienna 3-3-1951, according to Seidl-Hohenveldern, 122 note 31; likewise the Belgian case *Deckers en Van der Heyden* c. *Soc. Tannerie de l'Azoff, Trib. comm.* of Liege 25-3-1938, *Bulletin* vol. 41, 273.

[3] New York Civil Practice Act, Section 977-b, sub 2; *Russian and English Bank* v. *Baring Bros & Co* [1932] 1 Ch. 435; *Re Azoff-Don Commercial Bank* [1954] 1 All E.R. 947; *Banque Scandinave et Vve Rosenthal* c. *Kamenka e.a.* (*Banque Azoff-Don*), *Trib. comm. de la Seine* 21-1-1935, *Clunet* 1935, 134.

[4] Cf. Sollogoub, 150.

[5] Sollogoub, 151.

[6] Cf. e.g. the New York Civil Practice Act, Section 977-b.

[7] Section 338 (2) of the Companies Act 1929; section 400 of the Companies Act 1948.

[8] *Sabatier* v. *The Trading Cy* [1927] 1 Ch. 495; *In re Tea Trading Co and Popoff Brothers* [1933] 1 Ch. 647.

[9] *In re Tovarishestvo Manufactur Liudvig Rabenek* [1944] Ch. 404, a hotel can be considered a place of business.

[10] *Banque des Marchands de Moscou* v. *Kindersley* [1951] 1 Ch. 112, sufficient that there were assets of the bank in this country. To the same effect *Re Azoff-Don Commercial Bank* [1954] 1 All E.R. 947 (cf. *I.C.L.Q.* 1954, 506).

c. What Law is Applicable?

Questions on the taking of the initiative, on winding up in general, will be governed by the law applicable to the winding up. This is, of course, the *lex fori* for those countries where a statutory regulation exists. But this offers also little difficulty for other countries. There, too, the *lex fori* is applied, since the law of the confiscating state is certainly not applicable. Because of the very confiscatory operation it is not applied outside the territorial limits [1]. Moreover, application of the *lex fori* is in accordance with the principle of the *lex rei sitae* [2]. Meanwhile, as far as possible, the corporation's articles of association will be taken as a starting point in which case a wide interpretation may sometimes be required owing to *force majeure* [3].

d. Which Assets?

An important question is what property is wound up and its extent. A corporation is nationalized in a certain country and has certain property, whether or not retained by branch offices in several other countries. In every other country winding up in

---

[1] If nationalization is attended with a total upheaval of the legal system, as for instance was the case in Russia where Czarist law was substituted by Soviet law, it might be possible to consider application of the old law; such application of dead law, however, is to be rejected; cf. *supra*, 30.

[2] Perret, 80; a plain indication of the *lex fori* as governing law is found in *Deckers en Van der Heyden* c. *Soc. Tannerie de l'Azoff, Trib. comm.* of Liege 25-3-1938, *Bulletin* vol. 41, 273.

[3] *Vlasto* c. *Banque Russo-Asiatique, Trib. comm. de la Seine* 26-4-1922, *Clunet* 1923, 933: the "*évènements de force majeure dont la Russie est la théatre*" were to be taken into account; *Banque russe pour le commerce étranger, Trib. civil de la Seine* (*Réf.*) 3-5-1926, *Clunet* 1927, 358; election of the management by co-optation was held valid ("*seul procédé de reconstitution possible en l'absence d'assemblées générales*"); *Fred. S. James & Co* v. *Rossia Insurancy Cy of America, Clunet* 1928, 789: legality of the action of the management was to be tested for fairness and good faith rather than for strictly formal regulations; *Petrogradsky Bank* v. *National City Bank, Ann. Dig.* 1929–1930, 38, *Clunet* 1930, 782: the management was held competent though its powers were expired under the articles of association; *Severnoe Securities Corp.* v. *London & Lancashire Ins. Co* (1931), cit. Hollander, 44: surviving directors, less than a quorum, were held competent to act as conservators of the properties of the company; *Re People by Beha* (*Northern Insurance Co and Moscow Fire Insurance Co*) (1931), cit. Hollander, 44, 45: a sole director of the dismembered company can act as conservator (on condition of surety); *Woronin, Lütschg and Cheshire* v. *Messrs. Frederik Huth & Co* 79 Ll.L.L.R. 262, *Brit. Yearb.* 1930, 235, *Clunet* 1928, 756, *Z.f.O.* 1929, 303: meeting of shareholders not called in line with the articles of association; the same *A/S Tallina Laevauhisus* v. *Tallina Shipping Co and Estonian State S.S. Line* (1946) 79 Ll.L.L.R. 245; *Helvetia* v. *De Nederlanden van 1845*, The Hague District Court 9-3-1933, *N.J.* 1933, 1662, *Ann. Dig.* 1933–1934, 80: liquidator held competent though not appointed by a meeting of shareholders in accordance with the articles of association. Cf. however supra, 99.

accordance with the law of such country, being subject as far as possible to the articles of association materializes sooner or later. It is obvious that such windings up are territorially limited. The winding up in France of a corporation nationalized in Soviet Russia comprises only the property situated in France. Property situated elsewhere cannot be included in such winding up[1]. This rule is apparent [2] from the special legislation on this point. It can hardly be otherwise, as long as international agreements are lacking. The reason for this is that winding up of a branch office in a certain country or of property situated there can never pretend to be full liquidation of the corporation [3]. At any rate it can never include the corporation's property affected by the nationalization. The winding up therefore bears a very peculiar character: no winding up of the entire corporation, but yet winding up of the corporation. No winding up of the entire corporation: the different branch offices are cut off from the centre and are loose fragments. No branch can allege to demand the subordination of any other. They have been degenerated simultaneously and in fact have no connections whatever amongst them, being all fragments of one and the same killed corporation. Hence, there is yet winding up of the corporation. Each fragment is a fragment of the corporation. Hence Perret's *"séparation absolue des patrimoines dans l'espace, unité du patrimoine dans le temps"* [4].

[1] *Benoist et Levieux* c. *National City Bank of New York*, Brussels District Court 20-12-1934, *Clunet* 1935,671; Brussels Court of Appeal 11-7-1936,*R.C.D.I.P.*1937,121 and 11-7-1938, *Bulletin* vol. 41, 273 (*re Banque Russo-Asiatique*); *Nobel* c. *Deutsche Bank e.a.*, *Cour d'Appel* of Paris 15-6-1937, *Clunet* 1937, 812 (appeal case of the decision *Trib. comm. de la Seine* 20-1-1936, *Revue Darras* 1937, 117); *Stockholms Enskilda Bank* v. *Amilakvari*, Swedish Supreme Court 12-11-1938, *Ann. Dig. Suppl. Vol.*, 107; *Re Azov-Don Bank*, Swedish Supreme Court 19-10-1945, *Z.A.I.P.* 1949–50, 499. As to *situs* problems cf. *supra*, 44 ff.

[2] New York Civil Practice Act, section 977-b sub 1: "... the assets in this state ..."; as to Poland, Latvia, Esthonia, China, cf. *supra*, 115 ff.

[3] Meanwhile some decisions supporting this opinion are to be found: *Banque Russe* c. *Technogor*, *Cour d'Appel* of Paris 3-1-1944, *R.C.D.I.P.* 1948, 81; *Helvetia* v. *De Nederlanden van 1845*, The Hague District Court 9-3-1933, *N.J.* 1933, 1662, *Ann. Dig.* 1933–1934, 80, The Hague Court of Appeal 3-6-1937, *N.J.* 1937, 1675, *Ann. Dig.* 1935–1937, 204; *Commercial and Industrial Bank of Russia* v. *Aktiebolaget Göteborgs Bank*, Royal Court of Stockholm 18-3-1930, *Revue Darras* 1930, 695, *Z.f.O.* 1930, 675 and Swedish Supreme Court 26-6-1931, *Ann. Dig.* 1931–1932, 142; German *Reichsgericht* 11-7-1934, *J.W.* 1934, 2845, *Clunet* 1935, 164. As for England it is stated that on the one side exclusively the English assets can be controlled, but on the other hand it is held that it is none the less the corporation which is being wound up and not the English affairs thereof, *Russian and English Bank* v. *Baring Bros & Co* [1936] A.C. 405, at p. 428; cf. M. Mann, *I.C.L.Q.* 1954, 690.

[4] Perret, 143.

e. Powers of the Liquidator

In practice the liquidator possesses all powers which he needs to wind up the business properly. He is allowed to sue and to be sued, and, as regards the *société de fait* sometimes deemed to be present in France, this goes still further than the action of the *société de fait* itself. The rule in France is that the liquidators "*constitueront un conseil de liquidation avec les pouvoirs les plus étendus pour représenter la banque en demande comme en défense, réaliser l'actif en bloc ou en détail, à l'amiable ou autrement, apurer le passif, régler tous les comptes et faire le nécessaire selon les lois et usages du commerce sans aucune exception ni réserve*"[1]. The New York Civil Practice Act also grants extensive powers in section 977-b under (12): "Any receiver ... shall have all the powers and duties in addition to those herein provided for, as are possessed by and conferred upon receivers and trustees by the law of the state of New York". In England the question whether the liquidator should act in his own name or in the name of the corporation has been of importance. As regards the Russian and English Bank, after a liquidator had been appointed, it was first decided that this did not imply a revival of legal personality [2]. Later on the liquidator instituted legal proceedings to recover a certain claim [3], acting on behalf of the Russian bank. The court dismissed the claim because the legal existence of the bank had vanished. There was no alternative for the liquidator but to claim in his own name. The matter at issue was: were the liquidator to collect the amount on behalf of the bank, defendant would run the risk of having to pay again at a later date, because he would have paid to a non-existent person. The House of Lords[4], however, decided otherwise in 1936 (three to two decision!) so that the liquidator was to act on behalf of the bank after all [5].

If possible, the liquidator is appointed in accordance with the

---

[1] *L'Association des porteurs de parts de la Banque Internationale de Commerce de Pétrograd et Hennéants* c. *Banque Internationale de Commerce de Pétrograd e.a., Trib. comm. de la Seine* 17-8-1934, *Clunet* 1935, 125; *Nahoum* c. *Banque russe pour le commerce étranger, Trib. comm. de la Seine* 3-12-1934, *Clunet* 1935, 125; *Ancelle* c. *Soc. de Naphte russe, Trib. comm. de la Seine* 22-1-1934, *Clunet* 1935, 125; *Maximoff* c. *Soc. de Banque Volga-Kama, Trib. comm. de la Seine* 22-1-1934, *Clunet* 1935, 125.

[2] *In re Russian and English Bank* [1934] 1 Ch. 276.

[3] *Russian and English Bank* v. *Baring Bros & Co* [1935] 1 Ch. 120.

[4] *Russian and English Bank* v. *Baring Bros & Co.* [1936] A.C. 405.

[5] *Russian and English Bank* v. *Baring Bros & Co.* 54 T.L.R. 1035.

articles of association, but many situations are conceivable in which another choice is made [1]. The statutory provisions give various positive regulations [2].

It stands to reason that the liquidator must advertise claims. He shall also state a time-limit for the presentation of claims. This is apparent both in the countries where there are statutory enactments [3] as well as from the case law in other countries [4].

f. Distribution

It would not seem to be difficult to indicate in a general formula the order of distribution to be adopted. After settling the claims the creditors should be satisfied, the balance, if any, being applied to satisfy the shareholders. However, this gives rise to many questions.

We have already seen that the assets in question are territorially limited. The liquidator will not be able to sue elsewhere, although there are a few decisions which show exceptions to this [5]. A corporation which is nationalized, has been strangled in principle; foreign branch offices or certain properties deriving their existence or status from their relationship to the corporation are going to be in the air. The connection has vanished and it is difficult to regard such branch offices or loose items other than as fragments which are only good for winding up. In the absence of a world-wide regulation perforce territoriality of the assets is the starting point. The settlement of claims of the branch can therefore only comprise such claims as can be enforced before the *forum* of the branch. Afterwards the creditors come in. Which are they and which debts are concerned? Is there a distinction

---

[1] Cf. the decisions mentioned *supra,* 121, holding that the management, eventually completed, could act as liquidator under the articles of association; differently *Banque Scandinave et Vve Rosenthal* c. *Kamenka e.a.* (*Bank Azoff-Don*), *Trib. comm. de la Seine* 21-1-1935, *Clunet* 1935, 134; here a *mandataire de justice* was appointed in contravention of the articles of association.

[2] New York Civil Practice Act, section 977-b; the English Companies Act; Polish legislation.

[3] E.g. New York Civil Practice Act, section 977-b, sub 11: minimum of 60 days; Polish decree of March 22, 1928, Z.f.O. 1928, 1164, section 9: three months.

[4] *Wilbuschewitz* c. *Autorité tutélaire de la ville de Zürich et Dépt. de justice du canton de Zürich,* Swiss Supreme Court 13-7-1925, *R.O.* 51 II 259, *Clunet* 1926, 1110; *Prochorow's Erben* g. *Obergericht Zürich,* Swiss Supreme Court 26-10-1929, *R.O.* 55 I 289, *Ann. Dig.* 1929–1930, 99; *Deckers en Van der Heyden* c. *Soc. Tannerie de l'Azoff, Trib. comm.* of Liege 25–3–1938, *Bulletin* vol. 41, 273.

[5] *Supra,* 120.

to be made between creditors whose debts have been created prior to the time of the nationalization and those created thereafter? Are the claims of creditors who are to be regarded as local, i.e. whose claims have been created by business done with the branch office to be exclusively admitted? Is there a distinction to be made according to the nationality of the creditors? These are some questions the courts and legislation are confronted with and which have been answered in different ways. If it is assumed, as was done in France, that a corporation nationalized elsewhere with a branch office in France, still had a certain existence as *société de fait* with limited opportunities to continue operations, both creditors before and those after the nationalization must be included in the liquidation. So in this case *unité dans le temps* may be spoken of [1]. This is difficult, if there is no question of *société de fait,* although it will seldom occur that the fragment — entirely dislocated in this instance—was still carrying on business; the fact is that this will often be practically impossible and also be dismissed by the courts. Should it occur, however, that a creditor's claim was created after the nationalization, it is only fair not to exclude him from winding up [2].

How is the category of creditors further determined? There is no uniformity of opinion on this point. A distinct tendency to give priority to creditors possessing the nationality of the country where the winding up takes place, or having claims created in such country, is perceptible, as is a tendency to exclude creditors, whose claims are deemed to be localized in the country where nationalization took place [3]. On the other hand the conception is also found that no distinction should be made and that all creditors have equal rights on the strength of the principle that a debtor is liable for his debts with all his property [4].

In the New York Civil Practice Act Section 977-b, 16, the rule is such that first of all the "creditors with valid attachments ... shall be paid in the order of their priority". After that it is the turn of "persons residing and corporations organized in the

[1] Perret, 143.

[2] This is apparent for example from the New York Civil Practice Act, which also covers a corporation which "has heretofore been ... dissolved, liquidated or nationalized ..."

[3] Cf. Perret, 157.

[4] Cf. Perret, 142.

United States ... and the ... claims based on causes of action which accrued or arose in the State of New York". Finally the "claims of all other creditors" are paid.

In Poland [1] only creditors of Polish nationality were paid and other creditors only in so far as their claims were created on Polish territory (section 14 of the Act of 1928).

A similar provision was made in the regulation enacted in Latvia [2].

The winding up effected in China with regard to the Banque Russo-Asiatique only admitted the claims of such creditors as had carried on business with the Chinese branch offices [3].

In England, according to Perret [4], restriction to local creditors applies; however, in the decision *Russian and English Bank* v. *Baring Bros & Co* this was left open, whereas by *Re Azoff-Don Commercial Bank* and *Re Banque des Marchands de Moscou* the contrary was clearly stated: other than local creditors may also participate [5].

In *Deckers en Van der Heyden* c. *Soc. Tannerie de L'Azoff* [6] Belgium dismissed creditors with the nationality of the confiscating state on the plea that as citizens of such state they benefited indirectly by the confiscation. In another Belgian decision a claim, deemed to be localized in the place where the confiscation was effectuated, was rejected on the ground that the claim became extinguished by confiscation [7]. Otherwise this plea was also used in *Deckers en Van der Heyden* c. *Soc. Tannerie de l'Azoff*.

In Switzerland [8] the decision was to the contrary, just as in France [9]; here claims were admitted of creditors possessing the

---

[1] *Z.f.O.* 1928, 1164.

[2] *Z.f.O.* 1927, 1359.

[3] Perret, 163.

[4] Perret, 147.

[5] *Russian and English Bank* v. *Baring Bros & Co* [1936] A.C. 405; *Re Azoff-Don Commercial Bank* [1954] 1 All E.R. 947; *Re Banque des Marchands de Moscou* (*No. 2*) [1954] 2 All E.R. 746.

[6] *Deckers en Van der Heyden* c. *Soc. Tannerie de l'Azoff*, *Trib. comm.* of Liege 25-3-1938, *Bulletin* vol. 41, 273; cf. Perret, 155, 157; also Niboyet and Travers, *Travaux* 1935, 11.

[7] *Compagnie Belgo-Luthuanienne d'Electricité*, Brussels Court of Appeal 25-6-1947, *Clunet* 1950, 864.

[8] *Wilbuschewitz* c. *Autorité tutélaire de la ville de Zürich et Dép.t. de justice du canton de Zürich*, Swiss Supreme Court 13-7-1925, *R.O.* 51 II 259, *Clunet* 1926, 1110.

[9] *Teslenko* c. *Banque Russo-Asiatique* and *Aratzkoff* c. *Banque Russo-Asiatique*, *Cour d'Appel* of Paris 22-7-1929, *Clunet* 1929, 1095; a different view was held in some

nationality of the confiscating state and of creditors whose claims were deemed to be situated in the confiscating state. It might be conceivable that here there would be reciprocity. From the decisions *Teslenko* c. *Banque Russo-Asiatique* and *Aratzkoff* c. *Banque Russo-Asiatique* [1] it appeared that in France different views were held. Creditors who carried on business with the Chinese branch offices, were allowed to participate in the winding up in France, even though creditors in China, who carried on business with French branch offices were excluded from participation. So the fundamental rule of *égalité des créanciers* was applied. However, proof of the claim and details about the dividends obtained outside France were required, so that settlement might be made.

After the creditors finally the shareholders [2]. What will be their position? Do they have any rights whatever to the balance? The view might be taken that the rights of the shareholder are so closely connected with the country where the headquarters of the corporation are nationalized that such rights have been extinguished with the nationalization. However by doing so the shareholder's rights would be unduly localized and this is contrary to legal reality. Outside the nationalizing country the rights have not vanished, if there are items of property situated abroad. For shareholders [3] as for creditors hardly any other decision can be taken than that of a ratable distribution [4], if no balance is to be left or rights are to be granted to the government. Rights granted to the government is less desirable since the state cannot very well be given the benefit of the confiscation effected

---

decisions of the *Trib. comm. de la Seine*: *Teslenko* c. *Banque Russo-Asiatique* 28-3-1927, *Clunet* 1929, 78; *Rabinovitch* c. *Banque russe pour le commerce étranger* 15-5-1925, *Clunet* 1927, 354; *Société pour l'Approvisionnement et l'Industrie des cuirs et peaux* c. *Banque russe pour le commerce étranger* 26-11-1925, *Clunet* 1927, 354.

[1] *Supra*, 124.

[2] Cf. Seidl-Hohenveldern, 125.

[3] *Dairen Kisen Kabushiki Kaisha* v. *Shiang Kee* [1941] A.C. 373; *Wilbuschewitz* c. *Autorité tutélaire de la ville de Zürich et Dép.t. de justice du canton de Zürich*, Swiss Supreme Court 13-7-1925, *R.O.* 51 II 259, *Clunet* 1926, 1110; *Prochorow's Erben* g. *Obergericht Zürich*, Swiss Supreme Court 26-10-1929, *R.O.* 55 I 289, *Ann. Dig.* 1929–1930, 99; *Deckers en Van der Heyden* c. *Soc. Tannerie de l'Azoff*, *Trib. comm.* of Liege 25-3-1938, *Bulletin* vol. 41, 273; *Compagnie Belgo-Lithuanienne d'Electricité*, *Cour d'Appel* of Brussels 25-6-1947, *Clunet* 1950, 864; *Stockholms Enskilda Bank* v. *Amilakvari*, Swedish Supreme Court 12-11-1938, *Ann. Dig. Suppl. Vol.*, 107.

[4] Ripert, *Travaux* 1935, 29; Perret, 186.

by another state [1]. As in the case of creditors exclusion of shareholders of the nationality of the nationalizing country might also take place here. Several times, however, it was decided otherwise [2].

If not a single shareholder turns up after being duly called upon the problem of disposing of the surplus arises. This is not a problem in England [3] because the Crown asserts its rights; but otherwise a situation arises similar to that in *U.S.* v. *Belmont* [4]. In this case no claimant turned up and the U.S.A. obtained a right to the balance, solely by virtue of the Litvinov Assignment. From this it might be inferred that in other cases the state's rights are by no means certain. Be that as it may, whether or not the state is granted rights, the result in both cases is unsatisfactory. In the former case the state benefits by a confiscation, in the latter the balance is doomed to remain suspended.

---

[1] In England it has been suggested in this connection that the Crown might assert rights on *bona vacantia*: Dicey, 296; M. M. Wolff, *Z.f.O.* 1933, 723; Wortley, *Brit. Yearb.* 1933, 3; cf. Seidl-Hohenveldern 115-116. From the decision *In Re Banque Industrielle de Moscou* [1952] 1 Ch. 919 it is apparent that, not a single shareholder playing a part, only the "surplus and no more than that surplus, was saved to the Crown"; to the same effect *Re Azoff-Don Commercial Bank* [1954] 1 All E.R. 947; cf. Perret, 187. As to France it is argued by Niboyet, *Travaux* 1935, 34, that no proportional distribution should take place but that the State must be entitled to the surplus.

[2] From *Deckers en Van der Heyden* v. *Soc. Tannerie de l'Azoff*, *Trib. comm.* of Liege 25-3-1938, *Bulletin* vol. 41, 273, it is apparent that neither the confiscating state nor citizens of that state may participate; different opinion, however in *Prochorow's Erben* g. *Obergericht Zürich*, Swiss Supreme Court 26-10-1929, *R.O.* 55 I 289, *Ann. Dig.* 1929–1930, 99; *Stockholms Enskilda Bank* v. *Amilakvari*, Swedish Supreme Court 12-11-1938, *Ann. Dig. Suppl. Vol.*, 107; cf. also Seidl-Hohenveldern, 126.

[3] *Supra*, n. 1.

[4] 301 U.S. 324 (1937); cf. *supra*, 92, 93.

CHAPTER V

WEIGHING OF OPINIONS — CONCLUSIONS

I. INTRODUCTION

It is clear from our study that the views on the validity of confiscations are rather unanimous. Yet it can hardly be said that the law of various countries contains concrete rules in this respect. It is even remarkable that in England and the United States where common law plays the major role, part of the questions connected with confiscation are covered by legislation [1], which is not the case in most other countries. Judges therefore have taken a very important part in law making. This can also be seen from the fact that a great number of various arguments are used though most cases came to the same result.

The question we have to consider now is whether, in spite of the variability of the arguments employed, certain principles can be found which produced the *rationes decidendi*.

With respect to this question the arguments used by the courts must be weighed one by one and be tested on their merits. It is obvious, however, that two points are of great importance. First of all, state sovereignty plays a prominent part: this is illustrated in territorial confiscations by the act of state doctrine and in extra-territorial confiscations by the rejection of the operation of foreign state authority on domestic territory. Secondly it must be well borne in mind that a confiscation always leads to harsh results. A decision while refusing the validity of a confiscatory measure in respect of a certain person, will in fact often cause confiscation of the property of an other [2]. This illustrates the great difficulties in which judges are involved. Sovereign state authority on the one side and the interest of the individual on the other are the two poles of the problem.

---

[1] *Supra*, 114 ff.

[2] Cf. *infra*, 142 ff.

II. TERRITORIAL CONFISCATIONS

1. Solutions of the Problem in Various Countries

Mainly two opinions are at issue in the recognition of the validity of territorial confiscations; this is obvious from the cases. On the one side it is stated that a domestic confiscation is to be accepted by foreign courts. As a rule this point of view is based upon the opinion that a confiscation is an act of state and therefore is not reviewable by the courts of a foreign country. On the other hand courts take the standpoint that a territorial confiscation cannot have legal consequences elsewhere; this opinion is mainly based upon the ground that a confiscatory decree or measure cannot have legal consequences since it is repugnant to the public policy of the *forum*.

Recently the argument of conflict with the law of nations is used in some cases which refuse to grant validity to territorial confiscation of the property of aliens.

Non-recognition of the confiscating state or government as a ground for rejection of a confiscatory measure needs no further discussion. This ground is not specially connected with confiscations but is used to reject the legislation of the unrecognized state or government in a very general way; all legislative measures are considered to be a nullity [1].

In considering the *rationes decidendi* we must go back to the heart and the essence of confiscation [2]. Confiscation is undoubtedly a typical conception in the field of public law; it is an act of state which emanates as such from the *ius imperii*. It is the act of a sovereign government knowing no earthly master but only equal partners. Since a government has the factual power to execute its acts within its own territory irrespective of the nationality of the inhabitants, this means an unconditional validity to its acts within the limits of its own territory. These acts, it is true, will be realized as a rule through normal channels, so that redress can be sought in the domestic courts. The very feature of the act of state, however, is its absolute validity and effectiveness

---

[1] Cf. *supra*, 27 ff.

[2] Cf. *supra*, 5 ff.

on domestic territory within the scope given to it by the acting government.

When foreign courts encounter such acts of state they must take a stand: recognition or rejection. The conflict is whether the principle of respect due to the acts of a foreign government, or the principle of the inviolability of private property will prevail. As a rule a difference in evaluating the confiscatory measure is also at issue: in the act of state doctrine the character of sovereignty of the confiscation decides the matter; in the other view the consequences on the law of property are decisive.

2. *Non-reviewability of Territorial Confiscations*

a. The Act of State Doctrine: Secondary Immunity

By the act of state doctrine the sovereignty character of the confiscatory measure is considered of decisive importance: as the sovereign in his immunity shows a certain magic inviolability — which sovereign will sit in judgment upon his equals? — so a certain nimbus enwraps the *act* of the sovereign. And consequently the immunity *ratione personae*, which this immunity *ratione materiae* [1] was evolved from, is very closely connected with the latter. In this respect we can speak of *secondary immunity*. This character is clear from the Anglo-American conceptions: "Every sovereign state is bound to respect the independence of every other sovereign state, and the courts of one country will not sit in judgment on the acts of the government of another done within its own territory" (*Underhill* v. *Hernandez* [2]). "... a seizure by a state is not a thing that can be complained of elsewhere in the courts" (*American Banana Co.* v. *United Fruit Co* [3]). The action ".... is not subject to re-examination and modification by the courts of this country" (*Oetjen* v. *Central Leather Co* [4]). "The courts of one country will not sit in judgment on the validity of the acts of another done within its own jurisdiction"; this principle does not deprive the court of jurisdiction over the case but "requires only that when it is made to appear that the foreign

---

[1] Cf. Mann, *L.Q.R.* 1943, 46 and Re, 27.
[2] 168 U.S. 250 (1897).
[3] 213 U.S. 347 (1909).
[4] 246 U.S. 297 (1918).

government has acted in a given way on the subject-matter of the litigation, the details of such action or the merit of its result cannot be questioned, but must be accepted by our courts as a rule for their decision" (*Ricaud* v. *American Metal Company* [1]). In English decisions the same wordings are used, often even citing the American precedents [2].

It is interesting to trace the nature of this secondary immunity and to seek its limits. The Anglo-American decisions, it is true, state that the principle of secondary immunity prevents a review by the courts. Some formal conditions, however, are made, either expressly or tacitly.

First Requirement: a Purely Domestic Confiscation

First, a purely domestic confiscation must be at stake. This is expressly stated in e.g. *Underhill* v. *Hernandez* [3] (".... acts .... done within its own territory"). Tacitly, this inference can be drawn from its contrast to many decisions which refuse to grant extra-territorial operation to confiscations. The latter view must indeed be taken, though the wordings of some decisions are very general :".... when a government .... is recognized .... such recognition is retroactive in effect and validates *all* the actions and conduct of the government so recognized from the commencement of its existence" (*Oetjen* v. *Central Leather Co* [4]).

Second Requirement: a Governmental Act

Secondly the confiscation must be a *governmental* act (whether the government is recognized is set aside). This is clear from many decisions and is illustrated for instance by *Cia Minera Ygnacio Rodriguez Ramos S.A.* v. *Bartlesville Zinc Co* [5]. In this case the governmental character of the act was thoroughly inquired into. But when it is established that "the foreign government has acted in a given way...." (*Ricaud* v. *American Metal Company* [6]) no further inquiries are allowed to be made, neither investigations

[1] 246 U.S. 304 (1918).
[2] E.g. *Luther* v. *Sagor* [1921] 1 K.B. 456, [1921] 3 K.B. 532.
[3] 168 U.S. 250 (1897).
[4] 246 U.S. 297 (1918); Mann has the view that the act of state doctrine involves recognition even of extraterritorial effect, Mann, *L.Q.R.* 1943, 170.
[5] *Ann. Dig.* 1925–1926, 67; in *O'Neill* v. *Central Leather Co*, 37 A.L.R. 748 (1925) a deviating view is held; cf. *supra*, 66 and Re, 87.
[6] 246 U.S. 304 (1918).

into the formal validity. Consequently Van Panhuys [1] explains the opinion of McNair [2] in this respect by stating that it is only necessary to prove that the act is an act of the government or of a governmental official, who is not in advance unqualified to take measures of a certain kind. It may even be wondered whether this condition may be made. From the cases it appears to be satisfactory when the act has governmental character. In *American Banana Co* v. *United Fruit Company* [3] Mr Justice Holmes stated: "The very meaning of sovereignty is that the decree of the sovereign makes law". Following in the footsteps of this case it was said in *Eastern States Petroleum Co.* v. *Asiatic Petroleum Corp* [4]: "A foreign sovereign power must, in our courts, 'be assumed to be acting lawfully'". To the same effect it was stated in *Banco de España* v. *Federal Reserve Bank* [5] that "the question of the validity under Spanish law of the secret decree, or any other step in the purported acquisition of title to the silver by the Spanish government, is not open to examination by us".

b. Act of State Doctrine Irrespective of Nationality

The Anglo-American view does not go beyond these two conditions, the *domestic* confiscation and the *governmental* character of the act. It does not discriminate as to the nationality of the victims, though this point is not always wholly clear. In *Oetjen* v. *Central Leather Co* [6] it was also considered that the principle of non-reviewability was limited to cases where the property "at the time (of the seizure) was owned and in the possession of a citizen of Mexico". This limitation, however, was soon dropped. It was not applied in *Underhill* v. *Hernandez* [7] and *American Banana Co* v. *United Fruit Co* [8]; in *Ricaud* v. *American Metal Company* [9] it was rejected in so many words: "The fact that the title to the property ... may have been to an American citizen who was not in or a resident of Mexico at the time it was seized ... does not

[1] Van Panhuys, 228.
[2] McNair, *Legal Effects of War*, Cambridge, 1948, 375.
[3] 213 U.S. 347 (1909).
[4] *Ann. Dig.* 1938–1940, 90, 139 A.L.R. 1211 (1942).
[5] *Ann. Dig.* 1938–1940, 12.
[6] 246 U.S. 297 (1918).
[7] 168 U.S. 250 (1897).
[8] 213 U.S. 347 (1909).
[9] 246 U.S. 304 (1918).

affect the rule of law that the act within its own boundaries of one sovereign state cannot become the subject of re-examination and modification in the courts of another".

It is quite obvious that the principle of non-reviewability of the foreign act of state would be partly deprived of its material features if nationality would play a role. The nature of the rule is based on the respect due to the foreign sovereign. This sovereign has executed a certain act and, by "the force of territorialism", was able to do so. To him the nationality of the victims is of no importance: his sovereignty covers his whole territory. Courts while discriminating with regard to nationality, would interfere with the principle of secondary immunity, because they would evaluate the act. The very essence of the rule is that "the merit of its result cannot be questioned" [1].

c. *The Act of State Doctrine is not a Rule Purely of Private International Law*

The real nature of the rule becomes evident: it is not a rule purely of private international law. Re even points out that the rule is to be considered "more than a principle of the conflict of laws" [2]. Apart from the question of "more or less", obviously this rule yet has a character different from the normal rules of private international law. This difference must be well borne in mind. The rule being purely one of private international law, there would be reason for the parties to prove the foreign confiscatory law as matter of fact, as usual in England and the U.S.A. [3]. Inquiry into the legality of the confiscatory measure would be possible, or the constitutionality of the measure could be tested. And the correction of public policy could be applied in the end.

It is clear, however, from all precedents that the rule is not to be considered a rule of private international law, though it is in harmony with the *lex rei sitae* principle. The very essence of the rule is that the merit of the result is not reviewable. Acceptance of the principle means unconditional submission to the act of state and it can therefore be said that the rule is derived

---

[1] *Ricaud* v. *American Metal Company*, 246 U.S. 304 (1908).
[2] Re, 159.
[3] Cf. *supra*48, .

from the law of nations, closely allied with the immunity *ratione personae*. Since in the law of nations questions are settled under the rules of this sphere of law, quite different from the categories of private international law, it is conceivable that the act of state doctrine has been called a rule: "unfortunately in fact amoral"; for whatever conceptions of justice or morality the courts of the *forum* may have they are to accept the result and "there is no question of evaluating the result in the light of the existing public policy" [1]. In the American cases this has been pointed out more clearly than in the English and other precedents. This is illustrated by the sensational case *Bernstein* v. *Van Heyghen Frères S.A.* [2].

d. Case Law is not always Wholly Clear

In English case law the principle is not put with the same vigour. In *Luther* v. *Sagor* [3] it was said indeed referring to American precedents that ".... recognition is retro-active in effect and validates *all* the actions and conduct of the government so recognized from the commencement of its existence"; and it was stated (by Lord Justice Bankes): "It must be quite immaterial for present purpose that the same views are not entertained by the government of this country, are repudiated by the vast majority of its citizens and are not recognized by our laws". On the other hand, however, the eventual conflict with public policy was considered by Lord Justice Scrutton. His Lordship advised great caution in this respect. He referred to the heavy taxes in England and stated: "But it appears a serious breach of international comity, if a state is recognized as a sovereign independent state, to postulate that its legislation is contrary to essential principles of justice and morality". By this consideration the principle of non-reviewability is impaired. As to this rule even the slightest notion of an alternative ought to be out of the question, because the two conceptions do not bear with each other. Once the principle of non-reviewability is accepted, it would be a logical error not to discuss the merit of the result, but to take

---

[1] Re, 161.

[2] *Ann. Dig.* 1947, 11, *Clunet* 1950, 228, *A.J.I.L.* 1948, 217, *Col. L.R.* 1947, 106; cf. Re, 146.

[3] [1921] 1 K.B. 456, [1921] 3 K.B. 532.

this view only in such cases which do not cause too much injustice. It is absolutely illogical first to seek out the result and, if this might have been worse, to take the argument that "the court of one country will not sit in judgment on the validity of the acts of another". Once the suggestion of an alternative is made, the act of state doctrine is in fact thrown overboard, since this rule has an absolute character [1].

In a Dutch case the same view is taken. The Hague Court of Appeal [2] stated that a Dutch court is not allowed to pass upon the validity of the acts of a foreign (*in casu* Mexican) government. This judgment was upheld by the Supreme Court of the Netherlands [3], but the court added that Dutch public policy did not prevent accepting the validity of the title to property as things were. Here an alternative was also suggested.

With even more vagueness the principle was used in German case law. In *Scherbatow* g. *Lepkes Kunstauktionshaus* [4] the plaintiff referred to the conflict with public policy. The plea was rejected on the grounds that a *Hoheitsakt* (governmental act) cannot be excluded by public policy. This argument is reminiscent of the act of state doctrine. On the other hand it was expressly considered that in the given case no inconsistency with public policy was at issue.

The principle as such notably employed in Anglo-American case law, is outlined clearly by now: only the governmental character of the act may be tested and, if it turns out that a governmental act is at stake, the domestic confiscation is to be accepted unconditionally.

---

[1] This point is not put quite clearly by Seidl-Hohenveldern, 48. Though commending the utmost reserve as to the use of public policy, still he does not decline the possibility. However, the principle of respect due to the foreign governmental act is relativized in this way.

[2] *Petroservice* v. *El Aguila*, The Hague Court of Appeal 4-12-1939, *N.J.* 1940, No. 27, *Ann. Dig. Suppl. Vol.*, 16, note.

[3] *El Aguila* v. *Petroservice*, Supreme Court 7-2-1941, *N.J.* 1941, No. 923, *Ann. Dig. Suppl. Vol.*, 16, note. Paul Scholten, in his note to this decision (*N.J.* 1941, No. 923) rightly holds the possibility of an alternative wrong; but he does regret such consequence; cf. also Offerhaus, *Mededelingen Ned. Ver. voor Intern. Recht* (Transactions of the Netherlands Branch of the International Law Association) 1948 (No. 26), 32.

[4] *L.G.* Berlin II, 11-12-1928, *Z.f.O.* 1929, 1366.

3. Refusal of the Consequences of Territorial Confiscations

In France the question is put quite differently. Here the consequences of the confiscation in the field of the law of property are emphasized and the governmental character of the act is relegated to the background. The act may be tested in accordance with this conception; the constitutionality and the intention of the decree may be investigated; and public policy may also be invoked. This was pointed out very clearly in the *Ropit*-case [1]: "*.... reconnaître le gouvernement d'un pays ... n'est en aucune façon convenir de faire siennes, ... les moeurs et les lois de la Nation dirigée par le gouvernement reconnu*". And so public policy does come into play: "*.... que ce décret .... n'est en réalité qu'un fait de spoliation*" and "*il heurte les bases mêmes de droit français*".

4. The View of Seidl – Hohenveldern

Besides the two opinions mentioned above, the view of Seidl-Hohenveldern should also be noted. This takes another line and operates with three maxims, viz. the respect due to the foreign governmental act, the principle of protection of private property and the principle of territoriality [2]. The latter principle, based by Seidl-Hohenveldern on state sovereignty, is to the effect that every state has to decide exclusively upon the title of property situated within its own territory (an "*international anerkannten Rechtsgrundsatz, der seinerseits auf dem Prinzip der Staatensouveränität beruht. Danach besitzt jeder Staat die ausschlieszliche Zuständigkeit, über die Rechtmäszigkeit des Erwerbes von Eigentum zu entscheiden, das innerhalb seines Gebietes gelegen ist*"). In our opinion the view of Seidl-Hohenveldern is not exactly right. First, the maxim of the respect due to the foreign act of government becomes meaningless unless the results are not open to discussion. Seidl-Hohenveldern impairs this point by relativizing the maxim. Besides, the acceptance of a principle of territoriality need not cause the inevitable and unconditional acceptance of all the

---

[1] *Etat russe* c. *Cie Russe de Navigation à Vapeur et de Commerce* (*Ropit*), *Trib. comm.* of Marseilles 23-4-1925, *Clunet* 1925, 391, *Cour d'Appel* of Aix 23-12-1925, *Clunet* 1926, 667, *Cour de Cassation* 5-3-1928, *Clunet* 1928, 674.

[2] Seidl-Hohenveldern, 7, 8.

consequences of this principle by the courts. Taking this line appears to be a *petitio principii*, because public policy consequently would be excluded in every case governed by the *lex rei sitae*. Seidl-Hohenveldern does not go that far. Finally, the main objection to the view of Seidl-Hohenveldern is to be found in his opinion that territorial confiscations are to be considered by preference valid elsewhere mainly on the ground that two out of the three maxims speak in favour of the principle. In this "two to one decision", however, the learned author has relativized the issue in a dangerous way.

5. *Our Own Opinion*

a. The Problem

The conflict between the two conceptions, as we see it, turns on the question whether the respect due to the foreign act of state or the respect for the inviolability of private property as incorporated in the law of the *forum* ought to prevail.

In the first place it can be ascertained that under the act of state doctrine a domestic confiscatory measure is to be held valid elsewhere. But in the French conception such a confiscatory decree is governing law in principle as well. The former view is based on the rule of secondary immunity, derived from public international law; in the latter view the confiscatory decree is applicable by virtue of a rule derived from private international law: the confiscatory law is considered governing law under the *lex rei sitae* principle. So far the same results are achieved. But now the roads begin to part: in the Anglo-American view the result is not open to discussion but French courts do question it. Confronting the two conceptions the first question will be whether the rule applied by Anglo-American courts is really a rule of public international law. Would this be the case then the matter would also be decided as regards countries such as e.g. the Netherlands, whose legislation contains the rule that the jurisdiction of the courts is limited by exceptions recognized in public international law [1].

---

[1] Section 13a of the Act giving General Principles of Legislation of the Kingdom.

b. The Act of State Doctrine is not Unconditionally Applicable

As lawsuits between private persons are concerned with public international law, ascertaining the proper law is always a very difficult question. How frequently does not the law presented as public international law have a national flavour [1]? One thing is quite apparent: the immunity *ratione personae,* as for acts *iure imperii* at least, is considered a rule of public international law throughout the world. But the immunity *ratione materiae,* the secondary immunity, is a controversial subject; opinions about the question whether the secondary immunity is a rule of public international law differ. This rule is in conflict with another rule, viz. the principle of the inviolability of private property. This principle is not only entrenched in the law of the overwhelming majority of countries but has also been developed into a principle of the international sphere (cf. Universal Declaration of Human Rights). Consequently we are faced with a controversy of two international duties. The issue is whether a rule which as a rule of public international law is controversial, or a rule of international character which orders respect for the inviolability of private property, will be applied. In that light we are of the opinion that a court must have full scope to adopt the latter view. This need not by any means lead to the opinion that to do so would cause embarassment to the Executive or would "imperil the amicable relations between governments and vex the peace of nations" [2], or even "become a *casus belli*" [3]. For what in fact is the case if a court applies this view? The court need not go into the question whether a confiscation is valid and has full operation within the boundaries of the confiscating state. This is not unthinkable indeed, but really of no importance. Moreover this could be considered indeed a violation of the foreign sovereignty.

c. Foreign Courts Need Only Sit in Judgment on the Consequences of a Confiscation

The confiscatory measure had better not be impaired so far as

[1] Occasionally this field of law is indicated to be international law as interpreted and applied by our courts; cf. the title of Hyde's *International Law, chiefly as interpreted and applied by the United States.*

[2] *Underhill* v. *Hernandez,* 168 U.S. 250 (1897); *American Banana Co.* v. *United Fruit Co.,* 213 U.S. 347 (1909).

[3] *Luther* v. *Sagor* [1921] 1 K.B. 456, [1921] 3 K.B. 532.

the operation, validity and consequences within the boundaries of the confiscating state are at issue. The foreign judge has nothing to do with such questions. It is only his task to pass upon the consequences claimed as regards his own territory. In that case his own jurisdiction is involved. He need not state that the measure in itself is unconstitutional or is inconsistent with the principles of justice and morality [1]. It is sufficient to point out that the consequences demanded cannot be adopted under the jurisdiction of his country; they are excluded by the principle of public policy. If the court sees no inconsistency with public policy, then the consequences are accepted.

d. Test for Constitutionality or Legality of Confiscatory Decree is undesirable

It is conceivable, we said, that a court will go into the legality or constitutionality of a confiscatory decree. A confiscatory measure has always two kinds of features: the measure in itself belongs to the domain of public law, but its consequences are related to the law of property. If the latter element is put in the forefront the view might be taken that the rule of foreign law is to be applied the same way the foreign judge would do [2]. If the latter has the right to go into the legality or constitutionality of the measure, then the court of the *forum* must also be free to make examinations on this point. It is quite obvious, however, that many reservations are to be made. A confiscatory law has indeed important consequences on the law of property, but undeniably in itself it is an act of the sovereign. It is undesirable that foreign courts pass upon the validity of such act; this is to be left to the courts of the acting state. In our view only the consequences of

[1] Meanwhile this did happen: in *Ver. voor de Effectenhandel* v. *de Bataafsche*, Supreme Court of the Netherlands, 13-3-1936, *N.J.* 1936, No. 281, the Supreme Court held it possible to judge of the question whether according to Dutch opinions a foreign act in itself is contrary to the principles of a due and lawful legislation; to the same effect Jansma, 32. Ditto *Wladikavkazsky Railway Co.* v. *New York Trust Co*, *Ann. Dig.* 1933–1934, 65 (U.S.A.); *Etat russe* c. *Cie Russe de Navigation à Vapeur et de Commerce* (*Ropit*), *Trib. comm.* of Marseilles 23-4-1925, *Clunet* 1925, 391, *Cour d'Appel* of Aix 23-12-1925, *Clunet* 1926, 667, *Cour de Cassation* 5-3-1928, *Clunet* 1928, 674; *Moulin* c. *Volatron*, *Trib. comm.* of Marseilles 25-5-1937, *Clunet* 1937, 535, S. 1938.2.105, *Ann. Dig.* 1935–1937, 191, *Cour d'Appel* of Aix 25-3-1939, *Ann. Dig.* 1938–1940, 24; *Potasas Ibericas* c. *Bloch*, *Cour de Cassation* 14-3-1939, *Clunet* 1939, 615, S. 1939.1.182, *Ann. Dig.* 1938–1940, 150; *Bloch* c. *Potasas Ibericas*, *Cour d'Appel* of Nîmes 19-5-1941, *Gaz. du Palais* 1941.2.105.

[2] Mann, *L.Q.R.* 1943, 157.

confiscation are to be faced; since they play their part in the law of property consequently they may be held to come within the principle of the *rei sitae* rule, unless public policy is invoked. So the governmental character of the act itself calls for restraint as regards the review of such measure, but on the other hand certainly does not prevent an appreciation of the consequences as to the jurisdiction of the *forum*.

e. Opposition to the Act of State Doctrine

Strictly speaking in the act of state doctrine the term *lex rei sitae* had better not be mentioned, since this might be confusing. It is the very essence of the rule, regarded as a rule of public international law, not to examine the consequences. The term *lex rei sitae* is typically one of private international law and is not here to be used. It is true, however, that the act of state doctrine is in harmony with the *rei sitae* rule as regards the fundamental application of a domestic confiscatory measure elsewhere. Hence e.g. Mann [1] is induced thinking that in the act of state doctrine the *rei sitae* principle is in the end decisive. On his standpoint this is conceivable since he considers the consequences of the act of state doctrine, the amoral doctrine, in fact unacceptable consequences. Consequently he supposes that it becomes possible to invoke public policy. However, this would deprive the act of state doctrine of its essence.

Other suggestions to avoid the amoral consequences have also been made. In the U.S.A. the act of state doctrine culminated, as Re points out, in *Bernstein* v. *Van Heyghen Frères S.A.* [2]), which case was rather disturbing. In this case the rule was consistently applied and the result was held not open to discussion by the court. This result though no more smarting than in earlier cases, presented a very disagreeable character indeed. "The decision forcefully demonstrates the injustice that may result from the application of the 'rule of decision' principle" [3]. The court, meanwhile, found that it might be possible that the prin-

[1] Mann, *L.Q.R.* 1943, 56; to the same effect e.g. Wolff, 534.

[2] *Ann. Dig.* 1947, 11, *Clunet* 1950, 228, *A.J.I.L.* 1948, 217; cf. Re, 146. Here the act of state doctrine was applied though the Nazi-régime was already defunct. To the same effect *Banco de España* v. *Federal Reserve Bank of New York*, *Ann. Dig.* 1938–1940, 12; cf. Seidl-Hohenveldern, 27.

[3] Re, 151.

ciple of non review was inapplicable if there had been a determination by the Executive to that effect: "... our own Executive which is the authority to which we must look for the final word in such matters...". A letter, dated April 13, 1949, from the Acting Legal Adviser of the State Department [1] contained the important passage: "The policy of the Executive ... is to relieve American courts from any restraint upon the exercise of their jurisdiction to pass upon the validity of the acts of Nazi officials". This letter came too late to be taken into account in the action in question. Re sees no way to get rid of the act of state doctrine, in the Anglo-American sphere at least: "the principle is firmly entrenched in the law" [2]. Though he prefers to shake off the principle ("... the 'rule of decision' principle has earned a well-deserved rest" [3]), Re, as things are, hopes for the best from an "energetic Judiciary and a cooperative Executive" [4]. Van Panhuys, too, though holding the principle in itself most elegant and rational [5], stands for cooperation with the Executive. On the whole he believes that an international convention regarding the limitations of the jurisdiction of the courts in these matters would be very desirable [6]. This would mean a step forward for the Anglo-American courts which must but rest on their precedents.

So some trends indicate a tendency not to adopt the consequences of the "amoral principle".

f. Our Own Opinion further Developed

In our conception the rule is entirely thrown overboard; and judges can make free approaches. It is not necessary, then, that the Executive influences the decisions by giving instructions. This is not unusual in the Anglo-American sphere indeed, but we hold it undesirable on the whole: it interferes with the independence of the court; besides the risk of political decisions becomes obvious.

It is of importance to develop our view somewhat further. Al-

[1] *Dept. of State Bull.* 1949, 592.

[2] Re, 169.

[3] Re, 170.

[4] Under these circumstances diplomatic channels must be resorted to for a remedy; Re, 75.

[5] Van Panhuys, 222.

[6] Van Panhuys, 227.

though allowing public policy to come into it, this does not mean that public policy is always applicable [1].

Influence of Nationality

It might be possible to take account of nationality and of *bona* or *mala fides* of the person who acquired the confiscated property. We think that it is incorrect to take account of nationality, as was the case in a French decision [2]. Courts of a certain country have to see justice done. Though the law of their country may have a national colour, it can hardly be seen as law and justice exclusively to their citizens and as "am I my brother's keeper" to aliens.

Influence of Bona Fides

An inquiry into the existence of the *bona fides* [3] of a person who acquired the confiscated goods will become of more importance. Supposing a Dutch court would take our stand and consequently would have scope to invoke public policy, then two important points would be open to the court: First, it would have to decide whether the consequences of the confiscation in the subject-matter were of a nature to exclude in fact the foreign law, ordinarily applicable. This in itself would be a very difficult decision. Secondly, the court would have to find the rule which did apply. In the Netherlands no doubt section 2014 of the Civil Code would govern the situation with respect to movables. This would mean that for three years after the confiscation the decision has to be in favour of the original owner, unless the opponent would have acquired the confiscated goods in market overt. In the latter case the original owner would recover his property only on

[1] To invoke public policy is sometimes considere dundesirable since such use might impede commercial intercourse, cf. Seidl-Hohenveldern, 19, 52. This argument, however, is not a strong one, for it should be put in the reverse: if every court did apply the principle of public policy, such application would lead to less confiscations. Cf. also Jansma, 35.

[2] *In re Comp. Mexican Eagle, Cour d'Appel* of Rouen 27-7-1943, *S. Table Quinq.* 1941–1945, 214 (Cf. Niboyet, *Traité*, IV, 437). Seidl-Hohenveldern, 36, 37, suggests that such consideration played a part both in the French *Ropit*-cases (cf. *supra*, 59) and in the litigations *in re Potasas Ibericas* (cf. *supra*, 61), since the major part of the actions of the corporations involved was in French hands. To the same effect *A.G.* Waiblingen 26-6-1948, *Z.A.I.P.* 1949, 139; *L.G.* Kassel 20-7-1948, *Z.A.I.P.* 1949, 138; *A.G.* Dingolfing 7-12-1948, *Z.A.I.P.* 1949, 141. Jansma, 35, agrees with our opinion.

[3] Cf. Wolff, 527.

payment of the value. If the action of the original owner is brought three years after the confiscation, the *bona-fide* purchaser is protected (unless the contract of sale presents a void *causa*), but not so the *mala-fide* purchaser. This is based upon the following propositions. Confiscation is put on a level with involuntary loss of possession as pointed out in section 2014[1]. Besides, a person in possession is held to be *mala-fide* when he knows that his goods came from confiscation. In general it is a question of bad faith if the person who acquires property knows that he obtains this from an illegal possessor. Here the problem of the vicious circle may arise. The state which executes a confiscation owing to its own law cannot be said to possess in bad faith under that law. According to the same law the state's assignee is not *mala-fide*. It is obvious, however, that once the consequences of the foreign confiscatory law are excluded by virtue of public policy, then the law of the *forum* must state whether there is bad faith or not.

g. Particular Features of Confiscation of Debts

As already observed, it will be an extremely difficult decision for a judge to apply the principle of public policy, in particular when confiscation of debts (for convenience the term confiscation of debts is used though as a matter of fact confiscation implies a creditor's rights *vis-à-vis* a debtor) is at issue, which will often take place on nationalization of corporations. Both a creditor and a debtor will always figure; the property is based upon the *vinculum juris* between two persons.

Life Insurance

The following example illustrates this.

In a given country the branch of a foreign life insurance company is nationalized. The man who took out a policy with this branch, payable as a rule at the branch-office [2] — the law of the confiscating state is to be held the proper law of the contract — will not be able to claim his rights before the courts of the confiscating state. In fact both the branch and the policy-holder are affected by the confiscation. Now, the policy-holder

---

[1] This can be held possible in view of the wide interpretation given to this notion in Dutch case law.

[2] E.g. *Dougherty* v. *Equitable Life Assurance Society*, *Ann. Dig.* 1933–1934, 67.

will as yet try to claim performance either at the head-office, or at a branch-office elsewhere. Various factors are to be borne in mind in this respect. First, the branch, though not being a separate corporation, is usually considered one [1]. This is so in accordance with the insurance law of many countries ordering a deposit of the premium-reserve of the contracts taken out by the branch. This mere circumstance prescribes caution. Moreover the policy will as a rule contain the term: payable at the branch-office. Consequently the court would be obliged to alter the contract on this point, if it would give judgment for the policy-holder. This has occurred indeed [2], but it is going quite far. Besides, the point at issue must be well borne in mind. By the nationalization of the branch the policy-holder with a branch-policy is automatically affected. The "capital" of the branch is (except for the free reserves) no property in the proper sense of the word: it is the counter-value of the liabilities of the branch. So the curious fact arises that nationalizing the branch of a life insurance company will not primarily affect the branch, but other persons. If the claim of the policy-holder, directed against the head-office, is rejected, the confiscation continues as regards the policy-holder; to the company this means only loss of a part of the "earning capacity" and, if any, of the real property. This may be of importance but in itself is less serious. Not until judgment is given in favour of the policy-holder is the company considerably affected; then confiscation as regards for the policy-holder has disappeared. Here judges are between *Scylla* and *Charybdis*: whether they will reject the claim or give judgment for the claimant: a confiscation in fact takes place in both cases. In such a situation application of the principle of public policy is unsuitable, even undesirable. Public policy in this case will result in making the other person a victim of the confiscation; in the light of this a positive indication urging the use of public policy is lacking. If the case is settled by the rule normally applicable the result will surely be harsh. But once public policy is invoked the result is no less harsh. Moreover the use of public policy means a deviation from the normal rule. And it may be asked whether

[1] Cf. Prölss, *Z.A.I.P.* 1951, 203; this argument will sometimes do in the case of banks as well; cf. Seidl-Hohenveldern, 96.

[2] *Bürger* v. *New York Life Assurance Cy*, 43 T.L.R. 601; however cf. *infra*, 144

justice and morality speak so strongly in favour of deviation from the rule normally applicable . We think not [1].

A similar case may occur in a somewhat different form. In Germany the Nazi-régime confiscated life-insurance-policies of Jews. This amounted to the confiscation of the sums insured or the surrender values. The companies were forced to pay off. It was therefore not a matter of confiscation of the company, chiefly ending in loss of "earning capacity" with the automatic consequence of confiscation of the property of a policy-holder, but just the reverse: confiscation directly of an insurance with the consequence of loss of some "earning capacity". Now Jewish policy-holders started proceedings against another branch, viz. in the U.S.A., but their claim was dismissed [2]. Smarting though this result may be to the persons insured, there was no reason to affect the American branch. Here too, a positive indication to the use of public policy was lacking.

It is imaginable, meanwhile, that the branch-policy is not clear respecting the place of performance; or that the branch is established in a country not ordering deposition of the premium-reserve. Then which way the decision will go will depend on the circumstances. It is clear, however, that there must be serious grounds to deviate from the rule normally applicable.

Debts in General

This problem may arise in various forms; the life-insurance's case only covers a special aspect. To put it generally the matter at issue is how to adjudicate upon the confiscation of debts. If the property of the creditor is confiscated, including the debt, then a decision elsewhere, giving judgment in favour of this creditor, will always present confiscation *vis-à-vis* the debtor. We reject such a decision. In these cases it is of particular importance to ascertain the actual execution of the domestic confiscation [3]. Only in that case will judgment in favour of the

[1] To the same effect *Perry* v. *Equitable Life Assurance Society of the U.S.A.*, 45 T.L.R. 468.

[2] *Kleve* v. *Basler Lebensversicherungs-Gesellschaft*, *Ann. Dig.* 1943–1945, 4; *Bloch* v. *Basler Lebensversicherungs-Gesellschaft*, 73 N.Y.S. (2 d) 523, extract in *A.J.I.L.* 1948, 502. Similar case Supreme Court of Switzerland 12-4-1946, *R.O.* 72 III 52 (1946).

[3] As a matter of fact by execution must be understood execution by the confiscating state. If the debtor voluntarily payed his debt to the confiscating state, with the latter being unable to exert factual coercion, then such payment need not release

creditor make the other a victim. The confiscation being only a paper measure without effective seizure has in fact not taken place [1]. Then it is thinkable that judgment may be given for the creditor elsewhere; he will not need to base his claim on public policy since he will plead that the debtor is not released from his debt. It is not, as a matter of fact, a wholly hypothetical risk that the confiscating state will as yet collect the debt. Courts elsewhere, however, can hardly impose such a risk on the creditor. They can take account neither of a confiscation which may be executed perhaps in the future, nor of the possibility that a claim might be yet brought before another *forum* [2].

It is quite obvious, meanwhile, that a decision on the question whether or not a debt may be collected will often be very difficult. The creditor will have to prove that the contract permits the *forum* as a place of performance. In this respect a *situs*-conception is often used, which we do not consider wholly correct. In Chapter II [3] we pointed out that the *situs*-problem regarding confiscation is in fact rather simple: the matter at issue is to ascertain whether the confiscating state is able to execute a confiscatory measure with its own means of power, i.e. without another state's assistance. Such being the case, then territorial confiscation is at issue. Moreover, courts of the foreign *forum* need only assume a confiscation if the measure has in fact been

---

the debtor: *Reichsgericht* Germany 13-6-1934, *J.W.* 1934, 2537, Seidl-Hohenveldern, 151. In our opinion this case is not a case of territorial confiscation, cf. *supra*, 54 ff. However, we cannot approve the decision *Wolff* v. *Oxholm* (1817) 6 M & S, 92, Pitt Cobbett II, 59; here the debtor payed under coercion. This case is ranked with the German decision by Seidl-Hohenveldern, 151, but we consider this to be wrong. Neither appears the case cited by the author to be analogous with *Williams* v. *Bruffy*, 96 U.S. 176 (1877); for in the latter case the decision was based upon the fact that the measure of an unrecognized government, whose "whole fabric of its government (was) broken in pieces", was to be considered a nullity.

[1] This should be a general rule to any confiscation, cf. *infra*, 157.

[2] To the same effect *Sedgwick, Collins & Co Ltd.* v. *Rossia Insurance Cy of Petrograd* (*Employers Liability Assurance Corp. Ltd., Garnishees*) [1926] 1 K.B. 1, [1927] A.C. 95; in some other decisions, however, the risk of double payment was considered; in these cases the claim of the creditor was rejected: *Russian Reinsurance Co. and Paul Rasor* v. *Francis R. Stoddard and the Bankers Trust Cy*, decision App. Div., *Clunet* 1925, 451, Court of Appeals, *Ann. Dig.* 1925–1926, 54, *Clunet* 1925, 1070; to the same effect the decisions in first instance in *Petrogradsky Bank* v. *National City Bank, Ann. Dig.* 1929–1930, 38; by the Court of Appeals, however, the plea of double payment was rejected. Besides rightly it was put in the case *Sedgwick, Collins & Co Ltd.* that the risk of double payment could not be so great, since other states should take account of this decision.

[3] *Supra*, 54 ff.

executed [1]. In that case the court has to decide first whether it will take account of the confiscation; if the confiscation is not taken into account the court must decide from the contract whether the *forum* might be permitted as a place of performance. If the confiscation has not been executed, or if an extra-territorial confiscation which can not be executed by the confiscating state itself is at issue, then the court need take no account of the measure. In such a case the court may perhaps somewhat easier take the *forum* as a place of performance. In Seidl-Hohenveldern's views given to the *situs*-problem [2] two sides of the question are somewhat confused, viz. the question whether a territorial or an extra-territorial confiscation is at issue, and the question, left to the court of a given country, how to decide in the case of debts. The first question is an actual one [3] in that it has to be ascertained whether the confiscation has been executed by the confiscating state; the second question relates to the interpretation of the contract [4]. It may be demonstrated indeed in view of the interpretation of the contract that the confiscating state acted wrongly strictly speaking. However, with the confiscation once executed, this would be pointless.

The reverse of the problem may also come in issue: viz. when no property of the creditor, but property of the debtor is confiscated. In this case, too, it is painful to the debtor to be forced to perform the contract elsewhere. However, the debtor having suffered a certain loss, this can hardly influence his indebtedness [5]. To decide whether the claim may be granted will be a separate question [6]. It is clear that confiscation of debts has a

---

[1] Cf. *supra*, 144, 145, *infra*, 157.

[2] Seidl-Hohenveldern, 83.

[3] The latter question plays a major role e.g. in the English decisions from the War of Independence, cited by Seidl-Hohenveldern, 90; cf. also McNair, *Legal effects* ..., 348; the fact that here acts by the colonies of North America, while in a state of rebellion against His Majesty, were at issue, took an important part in these cases. Cf. *infra* note 6.

[4] It goes without saying that this will often be decided on grounds of equity in view of the extremely difficult situation; cf. Seidl-Hohenveldern, 102.

[5] *Yosselevitch* c. *Terestchenko, Cour d'Appel* of Paris 23-4-1931, *Clunet* 1931, 1117. Obviously it will be a different case if the debtor has to deliver a particular object which has been confiscated. Here it becomes impossible to perform: *Marchak* v. *Rabinerson, Cour d'Appel* of Paris 15-2-1933, *Clunet* 1933, 959; *Frumier/de Boylesve* c. *Jordaan & Cie, Cour d'Appel* of Paris 8-2-1927, *Clunet* 1927, 650.

[6] In the case *Crédit National Industriel* c. *Crédit Lyonnais, Trib. comm. de la Seine* 25-5-1925, *Clunet* 1926, 376 and *Cour d'Appel* of Paris 18-2-1926, *Clunet* 1927, 1061, a

somewhat particular character. And so it is understandable that Erades [1] thinks that such cases ought to be classified as a separate category. This appears unnecessary because territorial confiscations as we defined them, are equally at issue. However, as we remarked earlier, confiscations of debts deserve special treatment since in such cases the above mentioned risk of *Scylla* and *Charybdis* is always there.

6. *Confiscations in Occupied Countries; Conflict with the Law of Nations*

a. Occupation

A particular aspect is presented by confiscations in occupied countries. They might be regarded as territorial confiscations, since the occupying force is able to execute such measures with its own means of power without foreign assistance [2]. Yet they fall within a special category. The occupant has no sovereignty in the proper sense of the word but only has limited administrative authority over the occupied territory. Certain border-lines have been drawn by the Hague Regulations respecting the Laws and Customs of War on Land. A twofold objection can be raised against the validity of a "territorial" confiscation by an occupant: such confiscation indeed emanates from an authority, but certainly cannot be ranked with a governmental act; moreover, such a measure is contrary to the written rule of the law of nations. Both objections may result in the rejection of the validity of such a confiscatory measure. In several cases its validity was not recognized, both by the courts of the occupied country [3] and by the

---

deposit of the claimant at the Russian branch-office of the defendant was at stake. Judgment was given for the claimant, but we think it is possible for the court to decide otherwise, if the branch would have taken a completely independent position; cf. *supra* 143. Supreme Court Denmark 21-1-1925, *Z.A.I.P.* 1928, 866; continued several liability of Danish debtors whose affairs in Russia are confiscated.

[1] Cf. *supra*, 12.

[2] Cf. *supra*, 54.

[3] Such decisions are to be found both during and after the occupation.

During the occupation e.g.:

Austria: *O.G.H.* 27-10-1947, *Ö.J.Z. Ev. Bl.* No. 22/1948; *O.L.G.* of Vienna 17-9-1948, *Ö.J.Z. Ev. Bl.* No. 843/1948; cf. Seidl-Hohenveldern, 32 (Allied occupation).

Norway: *Øverland's* Case, District Court Aker 25-8-1943, *Ann. Dig.* 1943–1945, 446 (German occupation).

After the occupation e.g.:

Poland: *Siuta* v. *Guzkowski*, Supreme Court 15-2-1921, *Ann. Dig.* 1919–1922, 480 (horse spoliated by Ukrainian forces).

Belgium: *Laurent* c. *Le Jeune, Cour de Cassation* 3-3-1921, *Ann. Dig.* 1919–1922, 481 courts of the occupant itself [1], [2].

It is of importance to trace whether the rejection of its validity rests on the fact that no governmental act is at issue, or on the conflict with the law of nations. Seidl-Hohenveldern [3] regards this conflict with the law of nations as immaterial, since other confiscations, which might also be considered contrary to the law of nations (viz. confiscation of the property of aliens apart from occupation), are sometimes held to be effective [4]. This view, however, appears to be open to debate. The occupant does have certain powers though no sovereignty. And so the validity of certain acts may surely be claimed elsewhere. It might have been an extremely difficult question to state which acts should or should not be accorded such validity, if the law of nations would not have laid down written rules on the subject. But the law of nations has and so the lines have been drawn by international law. Both objections to the validity of confiscation by an occupant, viz. first that the act is not a real governmental act and secondly that the measure is contrary to the law of nations, are very closely connected. The international law feature, however, plays the leading part [5].

(German occupation); *Delville* c. *Servais*, *Cour d'Appel* of Liège 19-10-1945, *Ann. Dig.* 1943–1945, 448.

France: *Secret* c. *Loizel*, *Trib. civil* of Peronne 18-1-1945, *Ann. Dig.* 1948, 457 (German occupation); *Mortier* c. *Lauret*, *Cour d'Appel* of Rouen 17-5-1947, *Ann. Dig.* 1947, 274 (German occupation).

[1] U.S.A.: *Mc Leod* v. *U.S.*, 229 U.S. 416 (1913), concerning the validity of decrees of the U.S. army as the occupant of the Philippines.

[2] Decisions refusing validity were also given by foreign states. In Switzerland the wellknown "*Raubgutbeschlusz*" was enacted; cf. Seeliger, 150; cf. *Rosenberg* v. *Fischer*, Supreme Court Switzerland, 3-6-1948, *Ann. Dig.* 1948, 467. In the Dutch case *Papadopoulos* v. *N.V. Kon. Ned. Stoomboot-Maatschappij* an act of the occupant was at issue as well, viz. the seizure of tobacco by the British military occupant of Constantinopel. The Amsterdam District Court, 17-4-1925, *N.J.* 1925, 861, *Ann. Dig.* 1925–1926, 27, took the view that this act was not open to review by the court; the Court of Appeal of Amsterdam, 13-3-1928, *W.* 11816, *Ann. Dig.* 1927–1928, 34, however, held that it was possible to examine the validity of the act. There was no inquiry into the question whether the act was in accordance with the law of nations. The decision of the District Court was upheld under the regulations of the Treaty of Lausanne. In *Réprésentation comm. de l'U.R.S.S.* c. *Soc. franç. industr. et comm. des Pétroles (groupe Malapolska)*, *Trib. civil de la Seine* 12-1-1940, *Ann. Dig.* 1938–1940, 245, it was held that interference with property in occupied territory could not be recognized; the sovereignty of a state is only exercised within the limits of its frontiers; reversed on formal grounds, *Cour d'Appel* of Paris 12-2-1941, *Ann. Dig. Suppl. Vol.*, 145.

[3] Seidl-Hohenveldern, 33.

[4] E.g. *Ricaud* v. *American Metal Company*, 246 U.S. 304 (1918).

[5] This is in our opinion the ground of the well-known Allied Declaration of London, 5-1-1943, *Cmd.* 6418, which contained the warning that confiscations by the occupant would be held to be a nullity; a different view is held by Seidl-Hohenveldern, 33.

b. Conflict with the Law of Nations apart from Occupation

The foregoing is of great importance as this conflict with the law of nations may also occur in "normal" confiscations. However, since the rule that confiscation of the property of aliens is illegal, is controversial, the problem in such cases is somewhat more complicated. This conflict with international law may be put in two ways, viz. as a conflict with the law of nations as incorporated in the law of the *forum* [1], and as a conflict with the law of nations as such. In the former case it must be ascertained whether the law of nations holds such a rule; since international law is considered to form part of the domestic law, the validity of territorial confiscations might also be rejected on the grounds of public policy [2]. However, this does not hold in countries where the act of state doctrine governs the question. In the latter case, too, it is to be ascertained whether the law of nations contains a rule forbidding confiscation of the property of aliens. If the court takes the existence of such a rule for granted, the next question will be whether the validity of confiscation can be rejected on this account. It has been noted [3] that it is difficult to act in such a way, since the rule does not involve void confiscation but only a right to compensation. Such compensation had to be obtained through diplomatic channels. In this way, however, the rule would lose a substantial part of its effectiveness and often become illusory. Consequently to take the existence of the rule as a rule of the law of nations ought to render the confiscation a nullity [4]. In this case a certain protection must also be granted to the *bona-fide* purchaser. The act of state doctrine emanates from international law; this doctrine is based upon the law of nations. If the rule that confiscation of the property of aliens is illegal, is also considered a rule of international law, then there will be every occasion to have the latter rule prevail, since no doubt this latter rule is of more recent date [5].

---

[1] In this way it was put in *Anglo-Iranian Oil Co* v. *Jaffrate et al.* (*the Rose-Mary*), *A.J.I.L.* 1953, 325; cf. *supra*, 63.

[2] Both arguments were used in the *Rose-Mary* case.

[3] Seidl-Hohenveldern, 36; W. Lewald, 418.

[4] We fully agree with the interesting observations of Mann in *L.Q.R.* 1954, 181; his opinion is illustrated by the decisions, cited *supra*, 147, 149. Cf. also Wortley *Transactions* 1948, 30 and Raape, 429.

[5] Cf. Erades, 7; also Mann, *L.Q.R.* 1954, 198, states that the act of state doctrine should not lead to "legalisation of an international wrong."

It should also be possible to test a confiscation on the latter rule of international law as regards countries which invoke public policy regarding confiscations. Meanwhile a conflict with this rule will usually amount to a conflict with the nationally coloured public policy [1].

III. EXTRA – TERRITORIAL CONFISCATIONS

1. *Solutions of the Problem in Various Countries*

In discussing the validity of territorial confiscations mainly two conceptions proved to be at issue: the one view accepting its validity, the other rejecting it. More unanimity appears as regards the validity of extra-territorial confiscations: apart from some exceptions, which present a particular ground in all cases, the validity of extra-territorial confiscations though based on different arguments, is refused. Here, too, two main views are at issue but they yield the same result. The two conceptions have a different structure: in the one extra-territorial validity is considered contrary to public policy; rejection therefore is based on the principles of the jurisdiction of the *forum* [2]. In the other rejection of the validity is founded on the character of the measure, which by nature cannot be applied extra-territorially [3].

We will have to review both conceptions. Some remarks, however, will first have to be made regarding the exceptions allowing for validity of extra-territorial confiscations.

2. *Enforcement of Extra-territorial Confiscations*

a. Isolated Cases

Only in a few isolated cases was extra-territorial operation enforced. In the Netherlands there are two decisions accepting extra-territorial effect [4]. They are in the minority and have emanated from the lowest instance. In both cases extra-territorial powers were granted to a *Kommissarische Verwalter*. The decisions may

---

[1] Cf. Niederer, *Festschrift Hans Lewald*, 554.
[2] Cf. *supra*, 81 ff.
[3] Cf. *supra*, 84 ff.
[4] *Supra*, 78, 89.

be excused by the subtle design of the German anti-Jewish measures which did not use the formal term confiscation. The Italian decision [1] granting extra-territorial powers in a similar case may be explained by the political situation [2]. The judgment of the Tunesian court concerning the Carthusian liqueur [3] and the decision of the People's Court of Batoum regarding some Russian ships [4] rank with the Italian case. It may even be wondered whether in the Tunesian and Batoum cases a substantial extra-territorial confiscation was at stake in view of the constutional relationship.

b. Eastern European Countries

Cases adjudicated on the basis of a treaty are more extensive. The treaties of Soviet Russia with some Eastern European states [5] and the Litvinov Assignment [6] produced decisions which accepted the extra-territoriality.

The treaties of the Eastern European countries with Soviet Russia are generally considered as aiming at an extra-territorial effect of the Russian confiscations. However, such an interpretation is very doubtful. The treaty with Poland [7] contained no express term on this point, nor did the treaty with Esthonia [8]. Perhaps the treaties with Latvia [9] and Lithuania [10] gave rise to the notion of extra-territoriality. As for Latvia, however, further regulations based on the treaty appeared not to start from extra-territorial operation [11]. Only in a Lithuanian decision [12] was extra-territoriality based on the treaty with Russia.

c. Litvinov Assignment

Although the American case law resulting from the Litvinov

---

[1] *Supra*, 78, 89.

[2] Verzijl remarked on this point: "*Pourquoi pas? Pourquoi ne pourrait-elle* (viz. confiscation) *pas s'étendre au delà des frontières entre Etats qui professent la même foi spoliatrice?*", *Annuaire* 1950, I, 106.

[3] *Supra*, 45, 78, 89.

[4] *Supra*, 54, 78, 89.

[5] *Supra*, 90.

[6] *Supra*, 91 ff.

[7] *Supra*, 90.

[8] *Supra*, 90.

[9] *Supra*, 90.

[10] *Supra*, 90.

[11] *Supra*, 116, 124.

[12] *Supra*, 78, 91.

Assignment granted extra-territoriality in the end, it can hardly be maintained that the context of the assignment contains such extra-territoriality. Soviet Russia assigned to the United States certain rights. Very properly it has been observed [1] that Soviet Russia was unable to assign more rights than she had. Consequently the decisions stating that the U.S.A. was entitled to the assets of the branches of the nationalized Russian corporations point out that Soviet Russia automatically held the title to the assets before the Litvinov Assignment. This was the basis of the decisions. It is noteworthy that nevertheless the decisions could not be supported by the very context of the assignment. In fact no other inference can be drawn from it except that Soviet Russia assigned such rights as she had. The decisions did not refer to any particular terms of the context. They appealed to the "policy" of the assignment, which together with the recognition of the Soviet Government was to be regarded as one and the same transaction: "The effect ... was to validate ... all acts of the Soviet Government here involved from the commencement of its existence" [2]. The argumentation, meanwhile, was not only weak, but was extremely dangerous. Reference was made for example to cases recognizing territorial confiscations, such as *Underhill* v. *Hernandez* [3]. The courts quoted the well-known passage on: "... acts of the government of another (country) done within its own territory," and, by doing so, ran the risk of being forced to recognize every act of a foreign government on American territory. Indeed Mann [4] takes the view that the act of state doctrine involves such consequences. Moreover the intention of the Soviet Russian decrees to operate extra-territorially was held to be of decisive importance. Such intention was taken for granted owing to a statement of the Russian People's Commissar of Justice [5]. It will be the real consequence of this argument that every confiscation with the intention to operate extra-territorially has to be recognized. For "the United States acquired, under the Litvinov Assignment, only such

---

[1] *U.S.* v. *Pink*, 315 U.S. 203 (1942).
[2] Quoted from *U.S.* v. *Pink*, 315 U.S. 203 (1942).
[3] 168 U.S. 250 (1897).
[4] *L.Q.R.* 1943, 170, 171.
[5] Statement of the People's Commissar of Justice, dated November 28, 1937, see *U.S.* v. *Pink*, 315 U.S. 203 (1942); cf. *supra*, 95.

rights as Russia had". Russia was supposed to have the rights to the assets of the American branches of nationalized corporations; this was assumed by virtue of the interpretation of the decrees. It is stated that extra-territoriality was recognized only on the strength of the Litvinov Assignment, but this is untenable; in fact, reference was made to the extra-territorial operation intended by Russia; the Litvinov Assignment was referred to only because to refuse validity would mean; "a rejection of a part of the policy underlying recognition by this nation of Soviet Russia" [1]. The argument that the Litvinov Assignment was to decide the matter was put in the forefront. However, this does not alter the fact that the courts were to state that the confiscatory decrees had extra-territorial effect apart from the assignment.

Fortunately, case law was sufficiently inconsistent as not to take the decisions referred to as binding precedents [2].

3. Public Policy as a Ground for Non-enforcement of Extra-territorial Confiscations

As noted above [3] the inconsistency of a foreign confiscatory measure with the public policy of the *forum* is often appealed to. This argument in support of non-enforcement, though conceivable, is usually both illogical and superfluous [4].

The argument is indeed conceivable, since the application of public policy means in general that the fundamental principles of the law of the *forum* are at stake. It is also conceivable since it presents a method easy to employ: it prevents many questions and works as a reservoir for motives of rejection.

a. Application of Public Policy Illogical

In most cases, however, the use of public policy will be illogical. When is public policy to be taken as a last resource? This will only be the case if without this remedy the law of the confiscating state would govern the question. Only then, logically, should

---

[1] *U.S.* v. *Pink*, 315 U.S. 203 (1942).

[2] Cf. *supra*, 96.

[3] *Supra*, 81 ff.

[4] Cf. the Danish decision *Banska a Hutni Spolecnost* v. *Hahn*, Court of Western Denmark 12-5-1952, *Clunet* 1954, 480.

public policy be employed. Application of the principle of public policy consequently implies the conception of the confiscatory measure having also effect in principle on property outside the territory of the confiscating state. The latter view, however, is not held as such [1] and does not precede application of public policy in any decision on this point. It is suggested, however, by Herzfeld [2], that the confiscatory element of the nationalization of a corporation as personal law does in principle apply outside the territory, analogous to the transmission of property left by a deceased person. Quite rightly by stating this he elicits the effusion from Wolff [3] (*pectus est quod disertum facit!*): "This inference ... is, however, out of place, since under no legal system is the murderer allowed to succeed to the property of his victim". Even apart from this eloquent passage the view of Herzfeld is incorrect: the law of the *forum* is yet applicable to normal liquidations, let alone to a liquidation emanating from the confiscating state.

b. Application of Public Policy Superfluous

To apply public policy is not only usually illogical, but is also superfluous. If the law of the confiscating state can be established as not being applicable under the choice of law rules, the confiscatory law need not further be excluded by means of public policy. Indeed the application of public policy is conceivable, since it points out quite clearly that the court of the *forum* wants to disapprove of the confiscation. But it may in a very few cases make sense. This will only be the case if it is not wholly clear whether a territorial or an extra-territorial confiscation is at issue [4]. In the Belgian decision *Eismann* c. *Melzer* [5] the principle of public policy was employed as an alternative ground to excluding the extra-territoriality: only in case the law of the confiscating state (Germany) should be held applicable under the *rei sitae* rule. The Swiss decision *Böhmische Unionbank* g. *Heynau* [6]

[1] Cf. the exceptions *supra*, 89 ff.
[2] At p. 9.
[3] Wolff, 307.
[4] Cf. Seidl-Hohenveldern, 62.
[5] *Trib. comm.* of Brussels 9-6-1938, *J. des Trib.* 54, 3558, *Belg. Jud.* 1938, 563; cf. Van Hecke, *Revue de dr. int. et de dr. c.*, 1950, *No. spécial*, 58, 59.
[6] Supreme Court 22-12-1942, *R.O.* 68 II 377.

even takes this point without difficulty: *"Ob die Zwangsverwaltung auch die in Frage stehende Forderung erfaszte, ... braucht nicht untersucht zu werden ... weil die staatliche Anordnung, auf der die Zwangsverwaltung beruht, dem schweizerischen ordre public zuwider läuft"*. It is obvious that this view can hardly be shared by countries adhering to the act of state doctrine regarding territorial confiscations.

4. *Nature and Intention of the Confiscatory Measure as a Ground for Non-enforcement: Penal Law*

If extra-territorial effect of a confiscation is rejected on the strength of its inconsistency with public policy, the ground for such rejection is exclusively to be found in the law of the *forum.* If a court holds the view that a confiscatory measure by nature has no extra-territorial operation or is not intended to have this effect, it need not look to public policy. The basis of some of the arguments used here is sometimes rather narrow. If a confiscatory measure is considered to have no extra-territorial effect since the measure is regarded penal, the merits of the confiscation as such are appreciated. To appreciate the measure in this way ranks nearly with the application of public policy. This is obvious from Dicey's General Principle No. 2: "English courts will not enforce a right otherwise acquired under the law of a foreign country *which is ordinarily applicable* in virtue of English rules of the conflict of laws: (A) Where the enforcement of such right involves the enforcement of foreign penal, or confiscatory legislation or a foreign revenue law"; sub (B) the inconsistency with public policy is mentioned [1]. The reason why penal or confiscatory legislation is rejected is not that such legislation is not applicable under the English rules of the conflict of laws; on the contrary, it does apply in principle, but cannot be enforced since the conceptions of English courts do not permit such application. And so it is not too bold to say that the terms "penal law" and "confiscatory law" are used here only for the reason

[1] Dicey, 17, 18; to the same effect Cheshire 131; Wolff, 171, however, takes another stand; Raape, 424, holds the view that both the inconsistency of confiscation with the principle of the *lex rei sitae* and the principle of public policy plays a part: "*Hätte Bartolus schon der Begriff des ordre public gekannt, hätte er wohl das privilegium odiosum dazu gerechnet*" (427).

that the principle of public policy is resorted to very unwillingly, public policy being the "unruly horse", of which it was said: "once you get astride of it, you never know where it will carry you" [1]. Nuszbaum states that the rule rejecting enforcement of foreign revenue law and foreign penal law has its roots in public policy [2]. For the rest the term penal law is also rarely used; Anglo-American courts only apply very reluctantly the argument of public policy or of penal law. It is quite understandable that other arguments are in demand. Consequently some courts examined the question whether or not a given measure only intended to have purely territorial effect. This argument could readily be accepted regarding the Soviet Russian decrees since the question of intention was leaved undecided in the contexts [3]. The method, however, became quite apparent in the *Tallina*-cases [4] where an Esthonian confiscation was at issue. The decree in question showed an intention of having extra-territorial effect, so that the interpretation of the context would amount to nothing. Only another argument could be taken and so the conception of "penal law" was used. Adherence to the argument of the intent to have only territorial effect may even become dangerous if held too strongly. This was apparent from *U.S.* v. *Pink* [5], in which case the intention was considered to be of decisive importance. Since an official Russian statement pointed out the intention to have extra-territorial effect, giving it such effect became unevitable. This danger will always be at stake if the intention of the confiscatory measure is too much in view.

5. *The Author's View*

We found that denial of extra-territorial effect of confiscations based on the intention to operate purely territorially was danger-

[1] Judge Burrough in *Richardson* v. *Mellish*, 2 Bing. 229, 252, 130, Eng. Rep. 294 (1824) cited by Nuszbaum, 113.

[2] Nuszbaum, 125.

[3] Cf. *supra*, 60, 87.

[4] Cf. *supra*, 85.

[5] 315 U.S. 203 (1942); cf *supra*, 94 ff; a remarkable standpoint was taken in this respect by the United States Supreme Court in *Ingenohl* v. *Olsen and Company, Inc.*, 273 U.S. 41 (1927), *Ann. Dig. Suppl. Vol.*, 106, where the court held that "if the Alien Property Custodian purported to convey rights in English territory .... he exceeded the powers that were or could be given to him by the United States". In the Austrian case *O.G.H.* 10-3-1948, *J.Bl.* 1949, 70, *Z.A.I.P.* 1949–1950, 479, *re National-Sozialistische Lehrerbund* a similar decision was made. In both cases a confiscatory measure of the own government was held not to have any extra-territorial effect.

ous. For that reason this argument proves to be less desirable. The latter risk will not arise if the principle of non-applicability of the measure as "penal law" or a similar principle is used. These arguments do not appear to be sharp for all that; this is obvious from practice, where the conception of "penal law" is often applied very broadly.

We think that it is possible to arrive at the same result, viz. rejecting enforcement of extra-territorial effect of confiscations by a slightly different way. Thus a self-supporting rule can be framed on this point, so that it would not be necessary to apply conceptions such as penal law, *odiosa* and such-like, though several confiscatory measures may have a penal character or may be considered *odiosa*.

Again we must return to the essence of a confiscation. A confiscation is a governmental interference, an act emanating from public law, an act which has its consequences in the law of property. Three important aspects are to be distinguished here.

First there is the governmental interference as such. A confiscation which intends to have extra-territorial effect cannot in general be effected on the territory of another state [1]. It lacks power to effect the measure. It may even be put that a confiscatory measure intending to have extra-territorial effect will in itself never be able to achieve confiscation, because effecting the measure is a *conditio sine qua non* to the conception of confiscation [2]. Usually this view is also recognized in respect of territorial confiscations. This point, laid down in the Resolutions on the 3rd International Congress of Comparative Law (London, 1950) [3], is indeed of decisive importance if extra-territorial effect is claimed.

---

[1] Cf. 11 ff.

[2] To the same effect *Ware v. Hylton*, 3 Dall. 199 (U.S. 1796), cited by Re, 43; *Frenkel & Co* v. *L'Urbaine Fire Insurance Co. of Paris*, 65 A.L.R. 1490 (1930): ... "confiscation is not consummated by mere declaration. The debt does not automatically become vested in the government"; Re, 43; Seidl-Hohenveldern, 38; Foster, 109; this will apply to expropriation as well, *The Laurent Meeus, Ann. Dig.* 1941–1942, 141. Different view Wolff, 527; to the same effect Supreme Court of Moscow 9-6-1928, *Z.f.O.* 1929, 136.

[3] *Revue int. de dr. comp.* 1950, 530; *Revue Hellénique de Droit International* 1950, 285; *Z.A.I.P.* 1951, 491, cf. *supra*, 145; in respect of territorial confiscation it may often happen that a proprietor succeeds in rapidly exporting the goods after the enactment of a confiscatory decree. If in such a case judgment would be given for the confiscating state before a foreign court, this would amount to extra-territorial effect in practice.

It can be considered an added aspect of the question that a consequential interference with the law of property is here at issue. In this field the *lex rei sitae* rule always plays an important role, both regarding movables and immovables. There is not the slightest reason to make exceptions here, as e.g. in the law of matrimonial property or the law of succession. The consequences of confiscation interfere with the law of property; to compare such interference with the succession on death which was suggested for the confiscatory part of nationalization of corporations [1] does not fit. In virtue of this point the extra-territoriality cannot but fail.

The question presents still a third aspect. With regard to the intention of confiscation to operate extra-territorially not only is the interference of the confiscating state in itself at issue; here this state has to cross its frontiers and so has to try to realize its purposes on the territory of another state. So one state tries to execute its own purely nationally coloured measures, which indeed by sovereignty can be executed on its own territory, on the territory of another. It is obvious that such exercise of authority will conflict with the sovereignty of the other state. If state A has not the right e.g. to levy taxes on the territory of state B, than state A certainly has not the right to confiscate properties on the territory of B. [2]

These three conjoint aspects contribute in framing a self-supporting rule with respect to the review of extra-territorial confiscation. In fact every one of the three aspects will suffice to justify the rejection of extra-territorial effect. Only conjoined, however, do they present the full picture on which the rule may be worded: confiscation by a state has no effect with regard to property which can only in fact be seized by this state crossing its frontiers.

In exposing the roots of this rule it is clear that the rule certainly does not run concurrent with the argument that extra-territoriality conflicts with public policy. That the *lex rei sitae* is of importance here has nothing to do with public policy. The fact

---

[1] Cf. *supra*, 154.

[2] Cf. Wolff, 171; (American) *Restatement* § 610: "No action can be maintained on a right created by the law of a foreign state as a method of furthering its own governmental interests."

that state A in general will not be allowed to exercise acts of merely public interest on the territory of state B, holds good apart from the principle of public policy, and is based rather upon public international law. The rule formulated by us is to be considered a self-supporting rule of private international law, fed by several sources. Perhaps in the national conception of the conflict of laws this rule will be accepted less easily than in the supernational conception; but in both views the rule is preferable to the use of public policy. Decisions which refuse to grant extra-territorial effect to confiscations without comment, may be regarded as an indication that the rule is beginning to penetrate.

6. *Nationalization of Corporations*

A few words must be said about nationalization of corporations. On this point extinction and confiscation are to be distinguished. It is generally accepted that the personal law of a corporation is decisive respecting formation and dissolution. With the exception of a few cases the extinction by nationalization is recognized elsewhere as well [1]. There would indeed be little sense in not acting in such a way, because to act otherwise would present no way out. This is only to be expected from a just and efficient liquidation.

Meanwhile the picture of the liquidation of the branches of corporations nationalized elsewhere is not a nice one. In some countries there are statutory regulations, but in most countries there are none. The distribution of the assets is not uniform; a great number of questions are decided apparently without due rules of conduct. In one country a given creditor may take part in the distribution; in another country a similar creditor may not. This situation is far from satisfactory.

If nationalization of a corporation is held to extinguish the existence of that corporation, so that the branches elsewhere can be considered only for liquidation, then in practice the liquidation will easily tend to emphasize national interests.

Hence we make a suggestion: why not rather a single liquidation of the conjoint pieces? Perhaps this may be reached with

---

[1] Cf. *supra*, 112.

international co-operation. Great interests are involved here. Unity of the rules to be framed and legal security will thus be realized in a field on which more difficulties may arise than are outlined in this study, given the present situation of the world.

IV. ALLIED TOPICS

The conception of confiscation, as we viewed it in different forms, is allied to some other measures. Expropriation for public utility is far less radical, since compensation is involved; measures of foreign exchange control and such-like on the contrary, may often have a confiscatory trend and so become painful as well. It is interesting to make a comparison here with the rules of confiscation. In practice it may often be difficult for courts to state whether an expropriation or a confiscation is at issue.

1. *Expropriation for Public Utility*

With respect to expropriation for public utility a distinction may be made between territorial and extra-territorial effect, just as in the case of confiscation.

a. Territorial

The validity of territorial expropriation must no doubt be recognized under the act of state doctrine. The same result will generally be obtained by the other view which considers a territorial confiscatory measure to be governing law in principle. Though it is possible to apply public policy, this will not readily be used [1].

b. Extra-territorial

The extra-territorial effect will be less painful respecting extra-territorial expropriation than respecting confiscation. In this respect nevertheless, we take it that expropriations must

[1] *Etat Espagnol et Banque d'Espagne* c. *Banco de Bilbao* (ship *Mydol*), *Cour d'Appel* of Rouen 7-12-1937, *Ann. Dig.* 1935–1937, 229; moreover in this case immunity was invoked successfully. The French case law also considered the recognition of the expropriating government as a *conditio sine qua non* to expropriations: a protective measure by the so-called Bask-Government was held to be a nullity: *Rousse et Maber* c. *Banque d'Espagne, Cour d'Appel* of Poitiers 26-7-1937, *Clunet* 1938, 52, *Ann. Dig.* 1935–1937, 189.

not have extra-territorial effect as well. On this point, however, a development has taken place which deviates from this rule. This deviation is explicable from the political situation. It was connected with requisitions [1] in World War II; the fact that the *forum* strongly sympathized with the requisitioning state played an important part.

As early as the eve of World War II requisition of ships in foreign ports was held valid in a few cases. Often, however, the notion of the ship as a "floating portion of the flagstate" [2] played a role here; in some cases jurisdictional immunity could be invoked [3].

Measures of Governments - in - exile in World War II

In World War II, however, the question was put more clearly. The well-known cases *Lorentzen* v. *Lydden* [4] and *Anderson* v. *N.V. Transandine Handelmaatschappij* [5] meant a marked turn in English and American case law.

In the former case an Order in Council of the Norwegian Government-in-exile was at issue; here compensation was provided for. In the latter case the Dutch decree A 1 which expropriated, but met the restoration of the expropriated properties, played a part. The decree A 1 was apparently intended to operate protectively. In *Lorentzen* v. *Lydden* it was considered that no confiscatory legislation was at stake and that "England and Norway are engaged together in a desperate war for their existence". The conclusion was finally reached that English public policy was bound to apply the decree, since such application was in conformity with the *comitas gentium* and since the decree intended to have extra-territorial effect. Here the principle of public policy is not, as customary, used as a barrier, but rather as "an accelerator" [6].

The same result regarding the A 1 decree can be seen in *O/Y*

---

[1] Cf. Lourie & Meyer: Domke, *Trading with the enemy in World War II*, 345; Domke, *The Control of Alien Property*, 216; Mc Nair, *Legal Effects*..., 368; Belinfante, 25.

[2] Cf. *Col. L.R.* 1940, 504.

[3] Cf. *supra*, 36 ff.

[4] [1942] 2 K.B. 202.

[5] *Ann. Dig.* 1941–1942, 10, *A.J.I.L.* 1942, 701.

[6] Lourie & Meyer, 45.

Wasa Steamship Co. v. *Newspaper Pulp and Wood Export Ltd* [1]. From *Bank voor Handel en Scheepvaart* v. *Slatford* [2], however, a different opinion emerged. There the distinction between a confiscatory and an expropriatory decree was held to be quite immaterial; only the *lex rei sitae* was to govern the question, unless an express provision of the law would state the opposite failing which to regard the principle of public policy as an "accelerator" and consequently to attribute "positive" action to it would mean an abuse of the principle. The view of Wolff [3] stating that *Lorentzen* v. *Lydden* established a new rule of private international law, viz. that expropriation has extra-territorial effect if such effect is intended by the measure and is consistent with English public policy, is substantially weakened by the case *Bank voor Handel en Scheepvaart* v. *Slatford.* The Swedish *Rigmor*-case [4] also had to face the Norwegian Order in Council. The (Norwegian ship) Rigmor was in Swedish territorial waters at the time the decree was enacted; the transfer of property was registered on the ship's papers with the master's permission. Later the ship was taken over by the British Government. This government could successfully invoke immunity before the court. Besides, the court decided that no objections could be found to the operation of the decree on Swedish territory if the action was made with permission of the master and there was no inconsistency with Swedish public policy.

American courts had to face the Dutch decree A 1 repeatedly. *Anderson* v. *N.V. Transandine Handelmaatschappij* [5] was the first occasion. Here a line was taken in accordance with the English *Lorentzen*-case. Justice Shientag held: "The Decree is a measure of protection, not of expropriation. Its purpose is to conserve [6], not to confiscate; to protect the rights of the individual, not to destroy them". Therefore the policy of the decree was

---

[1] (1949) 82 Ll.L.L.R. 936.

[2] [1953] 1 Q.B. 248.

[3] Wolff, 528, 529; cf. Dicey, 157 and Cheshire, 139.

[4] Supreme Court of Sweden 17-3-1942, *Ann. Dig.* 1941–1942, 240; also *The Solgry*, Supreme Court of Sweden 16-6-1942, *Ann. Dig. Suppl. Vol.*, 153.

[5] *Ann. Dig.* 1941–1942, 10, *A.J.I.L.* 1942, 701.

[6] The protective character is regarded of material importance; this is apparent from e.g. the English decision *Royal Hellenic Government* v. *Vergottis* (1945) 78 Ll.L.L.R. 292; here the Greek Government claimed the insured sum after the destruction of a requisitioned ship; the claim was rejected since judgment in favour of the government would run close to confiscation.

held to be in accordance with the public policy of the *forum*; so its application was required by the *comitas gentium*. In this respect, meanwhile, a statement of the American Government is also of importance: "It is the policy of the United States that effect shall be given within the territory of the United States to that Decree insofar as it is intended to prevent any person from securing an interest in, or control over, assets of nationals of the Netherlands located in the United States in territory now at any time under the jurisdiction of the Netherlands government, for the benefit of persons who are not at the time of their assertion citizens or residents of the United States" [1]. By this statement the meaning of the *Anderson*-case was limited. This also became apparent from later decisions. In some cases the *Anderson*-case was followed [2]. In other cases, however, where residents of the *forum* did play a role, the effect of the Decree A 1 was rejected under the statement of the State Department [3, 4].

A general rule can hardly be elicited from the decisions granting extra-territorial effect to foreign expropriatory or protective decrees. Here the reference to "the interests of a foreign state allied in the great cause of resisting the common enemy and of invalidating the latter's measures of economic warfare" [5] was so evident, that it obviously was only the question of a limited exception.

2. *Other Measures*

Other measures which have a certain impairment of property in

---

[1] In Brazil the Decree A 1 was officially recognized by a presidential decree on the same grounds, see e.g. W. de Jager, *Ned. Recht in Oorlogstijd*, 52.

[2] *Birnbaum* v. *Irving Trust and Amsterdamsche Liquidatiekas*, N.Y.L.J. 14-8-1943, 315, col. 2 (cit. Belinfante, 27); *Grünbaum* v. *N.V. Oxyde Maatschappij voor Ertsen en Metalen*, N.Y.L.J. 27-8-1941, 439, col. 7; *Düstervald* v. *Lädwig*, N.Y.L.J. 15-1-1942, 215, col. 2 (cited in *A.J.I.L.* 1942, 282); *In re Van Dam's Estate*, 43 N.Y.S. 2d (1943), *Ann. Dig.* 1943–1945, 346; *In re Blak's Estate*, 65 Cal. App. 2d 232, 150 Pac. 2d 567 (1944); *Grünbaum* v. *Lissauer*, 57 N.Y.S. 2d 137 (1945), affirmed 61 N.Y.S. 2d 372 (1946) (cited by Domke, *Neth. Int. L.R.* 1954, 366); *State of the Netherlands* v. *Federal Reserve Bank of New York and Archimedes*, 79 F. Supp. 966 (1948), 99 F. Supp. 655 (1951), 201 F. 2d 455 (1953), see Domke in *Neth. Int. L.R.* 1954, 365.

[3] *In re Kahn's Estate*, 38 N.Y.S. 2d (1942) and *Transandine Handelmaatschappij* v. *Massachusetts Bonding*, N.Y.L.J. 3-3-1943, 9. 848, Col. 7 (cited by Belinfante, 27).

[4] Under the Decree A 1 the Dutch government never obtained a decision purporting to delivery of certain goods; in the case *Matter of Breitung*, N.Y.L.J. 15-3-1943, 1029, col. 3 (Belinfante, 28) such decision only was reached after a statement of guarantee was made by the Dutch government.

[5] Domke, *Neth. Int. L.R.* 1954, 373.

common with confiscation can be put besides those intending expropriation or requisition with compensation. Taxation, foreign exchange control and suchlike, however, differ basically from confiscation, since they have a different aim. In taxation levying of money is at issue to allow the state to carry out its task properly. There is no intention here to hit any particular individuals. Nor can this be said as regards measures of foreign exchange control. The penal character is lacking here, whereas such character will often be present in the case of confiscation. Moreover, complete confiscation can hardly be spoken of. The extra-territorial effect of taxation or foreign exchange control, however, must be rejected. The circumstances leading to refusal of extra-territorial effect of confiscations also play their part here [1].

[1] Cf. Dicey, 17, 152; Cheshire, 131; Wolff, 171; Schnitzer, 680; Seidl-Hohenveldern, 154.

EPILOGUE

In our study we have attempted to trace the standards applied by the courts to questions of confiscation. We have weighed the pros and cons of these standards. Some decisions proved to have confined themselves to the case at issue; in others, however, more general principles were laid down. Since legislation on this point is lacking in most countries we framed some rules which should be regarded as self-supporting rules of private international law. Several decisions rendered valuable support to our opinion.

At the close of our study, however, a final remark must be made. We cannot but consider confiscation an injustice. When such injustice disappears our study becomes valueless, but unfortunately the presentday situation shows another trend. If in the Western World, too, prominent jurists assist in undermining the inviolability of private property, the situation will become worse rather than better. Lauterpacht [1] states somewhere that "the rule is clearly established that a State is bound to respect the property of aliens". When this authorative jurist, however, completely deprives his statement of its power by holding it inapplicable to "cases in which fundamental changes in the political system and economic structure of the state or far-reaching social reforms entail interference, on a large scale, with private property", it is not to be wondered at that such opinion might become common property. And if the rule of the law of nations becomes uncertain, it is easy to understand that a rule which is concerned not only with aliens but also with citizens may even less count on adherence. The sessions of the *Institut de Droit International*, devoted to this subject [2], demonstrated quite obviously how things stand for the time being. The voice of Verzijl (and Wehberg) was of one crying in the wilderness.

---

[1] Oppenheim-Lauterpacht, I, 318.

[2] *Annuaire* 1950 (Bath) I, 42; 1952 (Siena) II, 251.

There is the more reason to emphasize this view [1]. Against the increasing practice to idealize confiscations and to use a varnish of nice terms, the answer of Verzijl shows the fact that "... *des méthodes de spoliation qu'une classe sociale pratique envers d'autres*"[2] are at issue. The possibility to expropriate should not depend on what the state wants, but on the contrary it should be limited by the possibility of payment by the state. We should strive energetically to make the rule of public international law an axiom; this rule ought to lose its controversial character. The same ought to apply to the protection of property in the municipal law systems in general. And although it may be remarked: "Law, like truth, is a feeble thing unless it is believed in", here the word of Philip Marshall Brown will fully account: "Scepticism concerning the existence and the value of international law when it is cynically violated is unpardonable. That is the moment for its friends to redouble their efforts in its defense" [3]. Here there is a chance to reach a real expression of international co-operation.

---

[1] An *argumentum a contrario* is not presented by the fact that after World War II several compensation-agreements came into force where compensation was not sufficient. Here the reasoning was rather that half a loaf was better than no bread; cf. also Kollewijn, *N.J.B.* 1954, 452.

[2] *Annuaire* 1950 (Bath) I, 102.

[3] Private versus public international law, *A.J.I.L.* 1942, 448.

BIBLIOGRAPHY

P. ABEL, Konfiskation und Expropriation vor englischen Gerichten, J.Bl. 1952, 8.

L. ALEXANDROFF et E. M. KLINE, Le développement de la jurisprudence de l'état de New York en droit international, Clunet 1940–1945, 309, 741.

CH. P. ANDERSON, Title to confiscated foreign property, A.J.I.L. 1926, 528.

CH. P. ANDERSON, Recognition of Russia, A.J.I.L. 1934, 90.

ARISTEIDES, The Chinese Aircraft in Hong Kong, I.L.Q. 1951, 159.

P. ARMINJON, Les lois politiques et le droit international privé, Revue Darras 1930, 385.

P. ARMINJON, Les lois politiques, fiscales, monétaires en droit international privé, Annuaire 1950 (Bath), II, 1, Annuaire 1954 (Aix en Provence), II, 228.

H. W. BAADE, Die Anerkennung im Ausland vollzogener Enteignungen, Jahrbuch für internationales Recht III, 132.

LYDIA BACH, Le droit et les institutions de la Russie Soviétique (Paris, 1923).

E. BARTIN, Principes de Droit International Privé (Paris 1930–1935).

T. BATY, "De Facto" States: Sovereign Immunity, A.J.I.L. 1951, 166.

G. BEITZKE, Probleme der Enteignung im Internationalprivatrecht, Festschrift für Leo Raape (Hamburg, 1948), 93.

N. BENTWICH, The Soviet Government and Russian Property in foreign Countries, Brit. Yearb. 1924, 78.

R. L. BINDSCHEDLER, Verstaatlichungsmasznahmen und Entschädigungspflicht nach Völkerrecht (Zürich, 1950).

W. W. BISHOP, New United States policy limiting sovereign immunity, A.J.I.L. 1953, 93.

O. BLUMENTHAL, Rubelversicherungen bei amerikanischen Lebensversicherungsgesellschaften, Ostrecht 1926, 157.

A. VON BOCHMANN, Regelung der Forderungen gegen die ehemaligen russischen Aktienbanken, Z.f.O. 1927, 1357.

S. BOLLA, Grundrisz des österreichischen Internationalen Privatrechtes (Wien, 1952).

E. M. BORCHARD, The Unrecognized Government in American Courts, A.J.I.L. 1932, 261.

E. M. BORCHARD, Confiscations: Extraterritorial and Domestic, A.J.I.L. 1937, 675.

E. M. BORCHARD, Extraterritorial Confiscations, A.J.I.L. 1942, 275.

M. BOS, Le premier procès de la République des Moluques du Sud contre la S. A. "Koninklijke Paketvaart Maatschappij", Clunet 1953, 286.

S. VAN BRAKEL, Grondslagen en Beginselen van Nederlandsch Internationaal Privaatrecht (Zwolle, 3rd ed.).

H. W. BRIGGS, Non-recognition in the Courts: The Ships of the Baltic Republics, A.J.I.L. 1943, 585.

PH. MARSHALL BROWN, Private versus public international law, A.J.I.L. 1942, 448.

J. P. BULLINGTON, Problems of international law in the Mexican Constitution of 1917, A.J.I.L. 1927, 685.

J. BUNYAN and H. H. FISHER, The Bolshevik Revolution (Stanford University, Calif., 1934).

J. CHAMPCOMMUNAL, La condition des Russes à l'étranger, spécialement en France, Revue Darras 1924, 321, 525.

E. E. CHEATHAM, Observations au sujet de la décision rendue par la Cour Suprème des Etats-Unis dans l'affaire United States c. Pink, Clunet 1940–1945, 48.

TI-CHIANG CHEN, The International Law of Recognition (New York, 1951).

G. C. CHESHIRE, Private International Law (4th ed. Oxford, 1952).

R. P. CLEVERINGA, Artikel 517^{d} W.v.K. (Leiden, 1947).

L. CONNICK, The Effect of Soviet Decrees in American Courts, Yale L. J. 1924/1925, 499.

L. F. CRANE, Le statut du Gouvernement soviétique en Angleterre et en Amérique, Clunet 1925, 344.

H. P. CRAWFORD, Expropriation of Petroleum Companies in Mexico, Comparative Law Series 1938, 105.

J. DELEHELLE, La situation juridique des Russes en France (Lille, 1926).

J. DELEHELLE, Conséquences juridiques de la Reconnaissance du Gouvernement des Soviets par la France, Revue Darras 1927, 193.

DICEY'S, Conflict of Laws, ed. J. H. C. Morris (6th ed., London, 1949).

E. D. DICKINSON, The Unrecognized Government or State in English and American Law, Michigan L.R. 1923, 29, 118.

E. D. DICKINSON, Recent Recognition Cases, A.J.I.L. 1925, 263.

E. D. DICKINSON, Recognition Cases 1925–1930, A. J.I.L.1931, 214.

E. D. DICKINSON, The Case of Salimoff & Co., A.J.I.L. 1933, 743.

N. R. DOMAN, Compensation for Nationalized Property in Postwar Europe, Intern. Bar Association, Sec. Confer. The Hague, 1948, vol. 9, I.L.Q. 1950, 323.

N. R. DOMAN, Postwar Nationalization of Foreign Property in Europe, Col. L. R. 1948, 1125.

M. DOMKE, Trading with the Enemy in World War II (New York, 1943).

M. DOMKE, The Control of Alien Property (New York, 1947).

M. DOMKE, On the extraterritorial effect of foreign expropriation decrees, The Western Political Quarterly 1951, 12.

U. DROBNIG, Extraterritoriale Reflexwirkungen Ostzonaler Enteignungen Z.A.I.P. 1953, 659.

P. N. DROST, Human Rights as Legal Rights (Leiden, 1951).

A. DRUCKER, The Nationalisation of United Nations Property in Europe, Transactions 1950 (36), 75.

A. EHRENZWEIG, Die ausländische verstaatlichte Gesellschaft, J. Bl. 1949, 425.

L. ERADES, Het Rechtseffect van Nationalisatie-maatregelen genomen door vreemde Staten, Mededelingen van de Nederl. Ver. voor Intern. Recht N^{r} 32, 1 (1954).

P. A. M. VAN DER ESCH, Prelude to War (The Hague, 1951).

A. P. FACHIRI, Expropriation and International Law, Brit. Yearb. 1925, 159.

A. P. FACHIRI, International Law and the property of aliens, Brit. Yearb. 1929, 32.

A. P. FACHIRI, Recognition of foreign Laws by Municipal Courts, Brit. Yearb. 1931, 95.

J. E. S. FAWCETT, Some Foreign Effects of Nationalization of Property, Brit. Yearb. 1950, 355.

P. FEDOZZI, De l'efficacité extraterritoriale des lois et des actes de droit public, Rec. des Cours 1929, II, 145.

R. H. FITZGIBBON, The Constitutions of the Americas (Chicago, 1948).

H. G. FICKER, Grundfragen des deutschen interlokalen Rechts (Berlin-Tübingen, 1952).

J. Fischer-Williams, International Law and the Property of Aliens, Brit. Yearb. 1928, 1.
M. Flory, Le statut international des gouvernements refugiés et le cas de la France libre (Paris, 1952).
J. Foster, La Théorie Anglaise du droit international privé, Rec. des Cours 1938, III, 399.
J. P. A. François, Handboek van het Volkenrecht (Sec. ed., Zwolle, 1949, 1950).
A. von Freytagh-Loringhoven, Die Gesetzgebung der russischen Revolution (Halle, 1920).
A. von Freytagh-Loringhoven, Die bolschewistische Rechtspflege, D.J.Z. 1921, 357.
H. Freund, La révolution bolchevique et le statut juridique des Russes: Le point de vue de la jurisprudence allemande, Clunet 1924, 51.
H. Freund, Les rapports des traités russo-allemands et l'application du droit soviétique en Allemagne, Clunet 1925, 331.
H. Freund, La jurisprudence allemande dans les affaires russes, Clunet 1934, 529.
H. A. Frey, The Swiss Financial and Property Control Measures after the War, Intern. Bar Association, Sec. Confer. The Hague, 1948, vol. 13.
W. Friede, Der neue Mexikanische Erdölstreit, Bruns Z. 1939–1940, 31.
S. Friedman, Expropriation in International Law (London, 1953).
R. Fuchs, Die Grundsätze des Versailler Vertrags (Berlin, 1927).
L. le Fur, La guerre d'Espagne et le Droit, Revue dr. int. 1937, II, 347, 1938, I, 53.
A. Garcia Robles, La question des matières premières au Mexique et le droit des gens, Revue dr. int. 1939, 514.
J. W. Garner, International Law and the World War (London, 1920).
J. A. Gathings, International Law and American Treatment of alien enemy property (Washington, 1940).
S. Gemma, Les Gouvernements de Fait, Rec. des Cours 1924, III, 297.
T. Gihl, Lois politiques et droit international privé, Rec. des Cours 1953, II, 167.
E. A. Gmür, Zur Frage der gerichtlichen Immunität fremder Staaten und Staats-unternehmungen, Schweiz. Jahrb. für intern. R. 1950 (VII), 9.
E. Goeldlin de Tiefenau, L'existence à l'étranger des sociétés russes (Paris, 1928).
A. Grouber et P. Tager, La révolution bolchevique et le statut juridique des Russes: Le point de vue de la jurisprudence française, Clunet 1924, 8.
A. Grouber et P. Tager, La condition des étrangers dans l'Union des Républiques Soviétiques, Clunet 1925, 307.
J. Gutteridge, Expropriation and Nationalisation in Hungary, Bulgaria and Roumania, I.L.Q. 1952, 14.
M. Habicht, The Application of Soviet Laws and the Exception of Public Order, A.J.I.L. 1927, 238.
W. Hahn und A. von Lilienfeld-Toal, Regelung des Handels und Verkehr in Ruszland (Jena, 1921).
C. J. Hamson, Immunity of Foreign States: The Practice of the French Courts, Brit. Yearb. 1950, 293.
G. van Hecke, Confiscation, Expropriation and the Conflict of Laws, I.L. Q. 1951, 345.
G. van Hecke, Les effets des mesures de confiscation, d'expropriation et de réquisition émanant d'une autorité étrangère, Revue de dr. int. et de dr. c. 1950, N° spécial, 57.
J. Hémard, Théorie et Pratique des Nullités de Sociétés et des Sociétés de Fait (Paris, 1926).

H. HENRICH, Die russischen Enteignungsdekrete und ihre Rechtswirkung im Ausland (Hamburg, 1933).
J. HERZ, Expropriation of Foreign Property, A.J.I.L. 1941, 243.
W. HERZFELD, Nationalization of Foreign Corporations-Effect on Local Assets, Contemporary Law Pamphlets, Series 9, N° 1 (New York, 1943).
E. HOCHBERGER, Die rechtliche Beurteilung der entschädigungslosen Nationalisierung von Vermögen im Ausland durch die inländischen Gerichte, J. Bl. 1946, 436.
W. S. HOLDSWORTH, The History of Act of State in English Law, Col. L. R. 1941, 1313.
E. DE HOFMANNSTHAL and R. BERGER, International Protection of Axis Victims and Revindication of their Property Rights, Contemporary Law Pamphlets, Series 5, N° 5 (New York, 1942).
B. HOLLANDER, Confiscation, Aggression and Foreign-Funds Control in American Law (New York, 1942).
C. C. HYDE, International Law, chiefly as interpreted and applied by the United States (Boston, 1947).
C. C. HYDE, Confiscatory Expropriation, A.J.I.L. 1938, 759.
V. R. IDELSON, La révolution bolchevique et le statut juridique des Russes: Le point de vue de la jurisprudence anglaise, Clunet 1924, 28.
S. JÄGERSKIÖLD, The immunity of State-owned vessels in Swedish judicial practice during World War II, A.J.I.L. 1948, 602.
JAENICKE, Die Frage der Immunität in der Rechtsprechung zum spanischen Bürgerkrieg, Bruns Z. 1939–1940, 354.
K. JANSMA, Het standpunt van onze rechtspraak inzake het rechtseffect van Nationalisatie-maatregelen genomen door vreemde staten, Meded. van de Ned. Ver. voor Intern. Recht, N° 32, 24 (1954).
PH. C. JESSUP, The Litvinoff-Assignment and the Belmont-case, A.J.I.L. 1937, 481.
PH. C. JESSUP, The Litvinoff-Assignment and the Pink-case, A.J.I.L. 1942, 282.
F. M. JOSEPH, International Aspects of Nationalization, Intern. Bar Association, Fifth Confer. Monaco, 1954.
C. KATZAROV, Nouveaux aspects de l'immunité judiciaire de l'état, Revue int. de dr. comp. 1951, 429.
KLIBANSKI, Eheschliessung und Ehescheidung russischen Staatsangehörigen in Deutschland, J. W. 1920, 606.
A. KING, Sitting in judgment on the acts of another government, A.J.I.L. 1948, 811.
J. L. KUNZ, Two "causes célèbres", The Hungarian Quarterly 1939, 42.
J. L. KUNZ, The Mexican Expropriations, Contemporary Law Pamphlets, Series 5, N° 1 (New York, 1940).
R. LABRY, Une législation Communiste (Paris, 1920).
E. LAGARDE, La reconnaissance du gouvernement des Soviets (Paris, 1924)
B. LANDAU, La reconnaissance du gouvernement des Soviets par les tribunaux américains, Clunet 1934, 564.
M. A. DE LA PRADELLE, Les effets internationaux des nationalisations, Annuaire 1950 (Bath) I, 42.
H. LAUTERPACHT, The Cristina, note in L.Q.R. 1938, 339.
H. LAUTERPACHT, Recognition in international Law (Cambridge, 1947).
H. LAUTERPACHT, The Problem of Jurisdictional Immunities of Foreign States, Brit. Yearb. 1952, 220.
R. LEMKIN, Axis Rule in Occupied Europe (Washington, 1944).
G. LEPOINTE et D. PETCHORINE, L'évolution de la jurisprudence anglaise concernant les sociétés russes naticnalisées, Clunet 1932, 853.
H. LEWALD, Zur one man's company als Mittel der Nationalisierung von Aktiengesellschaften im internationalen Privatrecht, J.Bl. 1952, 238.

W. Lewald, Wirkungen der Enteignung durch einen fremden Staat, Deutsche Landesreferate zum III. internationalen Kongresz für Rechtsvergleichung in London 1950 (Berlin-Tübingen, 1950) 416.
K. Lipstein, Recognition of governments and the application of Foreign Laws, Transactions (35) 1949, 157.
E. Loewenfeld, Der Schutz wohlerworbener Rechte von Ausländern im Völkerrecht und in den Friedensverträgen, Z.f.O. 1927, 1347.
E. Loewenfeld, Some legal aspects of the immunity of State property, Transactions (34) 1948, 111.
E. H. Loewenfeld, The Doctrine of Sovereign Immunity, Report of the 44th Conference of the International Law Association, Copenhagen, 1950, 204.
S. A. Lourie and Max Meyer, Governments-in-exile and the effect of their expropriatory decrees, Chicago L.R. 1943, 26.
Y. Loussouarn, Les conflicts de lois en matière de sociétés (Paris, 1949).
A. D. McNair, The Law Relating to the Civil War in Spain, L.Q.R. 1937, 471.
A. D. McNair, Legal Effects of War (Cambridge, 1948).
W. Magerstein, Zum Problem der exterritorialen Wirkung von Konfiskationsgesetzen, J.Bl. 1950, 349.
W. Magerstein, Nochmals zum Problem ..., J.Bl. 1950, 454.
W. Magerstein, Hoheitsakte fremder Staaten und ordre public mit besonderer Berücksichtigung der Frage der Anerkennung ausländischer Konfiskationen, J.Bl. 1954, 424.
A. N. Makarow, Précis de Droit International Privé d'après la Législation et la Doctrine Russes (Paris, 1932).
A. N. Makarow, Französische Rechtsprechung in russischen Sachen, Z.f.O. 1933, 427.
A. N. Makarow, Übersicht der Judikatur ausländischer Gerichte in russischen Sachen, Z.f.O. 1935–1936, 563.
A. N. Makarow, Die Nationalisierungsmasznahmen und die Entschädigung der durch sie betroffenen Ausländer in der internationalen Praxis der letzten Jahre, Um Recht und Gerechtigkeit, Festgabe für Erich Kaufmann (Stuttgart-Köln, 1950), 249.
F. A. Mann, Immunity of Sovereign States, Modern L.R. 1938–1939, 57.
F. A. Mann, Extra-territorial Effect of Confiscatory Legislation, Modern L. R. 1941–1942, 262.
F. A. Mann, The Sacrosanctity of the Foreign Act of State, L.Q.R. 1943, 42, 155.
F. A. Mann, International Delinquencies before Municipal Courts, L.Q.R. 1954, 181.
M. Mann, The dissolved foreign corporation, Modern L.R. 1955, 8.
M. J. Marks, Protective Expropriatory Decrees of the Governments in Exile: Their Application in the United States, Col. L.R. 1941, 1072.
P. A. Massouridis, The effects of confiscation, expropriation and requisition by a foreign authority, Revue Hellénique de droit international 1950, 62.
G. Melchior, Die Grundlagen des deutschen internationalen Privatrechts (Berlin-Leipzig, 1932).
W. Michaeli, Internationales Privatrecht (Stockholm, 1948).
B. Mirkine-Guetzévitch, Les Constitutions Européennes (Paris, 1951).
R. Monsarrat, Le Companies Act 1929 et les sociétés étrangères, Clunet 1930, 82.
F. Morgenstern, Judicial practice and the supremacy of international law, Brit. Yearb. 1950, 42.
F. Morgenstern, Recognition and enforcement of foreign legislative, administrative and judicial acts which are contrary to international law, I.L.Q. 1951, 326.

F. MORGENSTERN, Jurisdiction in seizures effected in violation of international law, Brit. Yearb. 1952, 265.
A. C. J. MULDER, Inleiding tot het Nederlandsch Internationaal Privaatrecht (Arnhem, 1947).
G. NEBOLSINE, The recovery of the foreign assets of nationalised Russian Corporations, Yale L. J. 1929–1930, 1130.
J. P. NIBOYET, De l'effet, en pays neutre, des mesures de guerres, Revue Darras 1920, 248.
J. P. NIBOYET, Traité de Droit International Privé Français (Paris, 1944–1951).
W. NIEDERER, Der völkerrechtliche Schutz des Privat-eigentums, Festschrift Hans Lewald (Basel, 1953), 547.
NOËL-HENRY, Les Gouvernements de Fait devant le Juge (Paris, 1927).
B. NOLDE, Les mesures soviétiques d'expropriation devant les tribunaux étrangers, Revue dr. int. 1929, 201.
F. S. NOORDHOFF, De Mexicaanse Petroleumindustrie in Staatsbezit overgegaan, Economisch-Statistische Berichten 1950, 453.
R. DE NOVA, Völkerrechtliche Betrachtungen über Konfiskation und Enteignung, Die Friedenswarte 1954, 116.
A. NUSZBAUM, Principles of Private International Law (New York, 1943).
D. P. O'CONNELL, A Critique of the Iranian Oil Litigation, I.C.L.Q. 1955, 267.
L. W. F. H. OMTA, Immuniteit van staatsschepen en -ladingen en van staatsluchtvaartuigen (Amsterdam, 1938).
OPPENHEIM-LAUTERPACHT, International Law (7th ed., London).
N. J. PADELFORD, International Law and the Spanish Civil War, A.J.I.L. 1937, 226.
N. J. PADELFORD, Foreign Shipping during the Spanish Civil War, A.J.I.L. 1938, 264.
N. J. PADELFORD, International Law and Diplomacy in the Spanish Civil Strife (New York, 1939).
H. F. VAN PANHUYS, De Beoordeling door de nationale Rechter in rechtsgedingen tussen particulieren van handelingen van vreemde staten, R. M. Themis 1953, 127.
H. PERRET, La Liquidation des "Sociétés Russes" (Paris, 1937).
B. PERRIN, L'Anschlusz et la confiscation des valeurs mobilières appartenant aux émigrés, Nouv. Rev. de dr. i.pr. 1938, 527.
D. PETCHORINE, Condition des Russes en France et celle des Etrangers (spécialement les Français) en U.R.S.S. (Paris, 1929).
M. PHILONENKO, L'expropriation des biens des particuliers par les Soviets devant la justice allemand, Clunet 1929, 13.
M. PHILONENKO, Les atteintes à la propriété privée et l'ordre public international, J. des Trib. 1949, 193.
M. PHILONENKO, Une des affaires de l'Anglo-Iranian (à propos d'un Jugement de la Cour d'Aden), Clunet 1954, 380.
L. VAN PRAAG, L'immunité de juridiction des états étrangers et l'examen de leurs actes de puissance publique par les tribunaux internes, Revue de dr. int. et de lég. comp. 1923, 436.
L. VAN PRAAG, La question de l'immunité de juridiction des états étrangers et celle de la possibilité de l'exécution des jugements qui les condamnent, Revue de dr. int. et de lèg. comp. 1934, 652.
L. PREUSS, State immunity and the requisition of ships during the Spanish civil war, A.J.I.L. 1941, 263, 1942, 37.
E. R. PRÖLSS, Das Statut der Zweigniederlassung im Internationalen Versicherungsrecht, Z.A.I.P. 1951, 203.
ANDRÉ-PRUD'HOMME, La reconnaissance en France du Gouvernement des Soviets et ses conséquences juridiques, Clunet 1925, 318.
ANDRÉ-PRUD'HOMME, L'ordre public français et la Révolution Espagnole, Clunet 1937, 488.

L. Raape, Internationales Privatrecht (Berlin, 1950).
E. Rabel, The Conflict of Laws (Chicago, 1945–1950).
J. M. Rabinowitsch, Die Anwendung der russischen Sovetdekrete in Deutschland,D.J.Z. 1921, 402.
J. M. Rabinowitsch, Das ausländische Vermögen der in Sovetruszland nationalisierten Unternehmungen, Ostrecht 1926, 1168.
J. M. Rabinowitsch, Die Aufhebung des alten russischen Rechts, Z.f. Osteur. Recht 1927, 18.
J. M. Rabinowitsch, Die Nationalisierung der russischen Aktiengesellschaften durch die Sovetregierung im Spiegel der internationalen Praxis, Z.f.O. 1929, 1109.
A. R. Rado, Czechoslovak Nationalisation Decrees: Some International Aspects, A.J.I.L. 1947, 795.
E. D. Re, Foreign Confiscations in Anglo-American Law (New York, 1951)
W. A. Robson c.s., Problems of Nationalized Industry (London, 1952).
A. H. Roth, The Minimum Standard of International Law applied to Aliens (Leiden, 1949).
J. H. van Royen, De rechtspositie en de volkenrechtelijke erkenning van nieuwe staten en de facto-regeeringen (The Hague, 1929).
S. Rundstein, Zweigniederlassungen russischer Aktien-gesellschaften in Polen, Ostrecht 1925, 330.
R. Sarraute et P. Tager, Les effets en France des nationalisations étrangères, Clunet 1952, 496, 1138.
G. Sauser-Hall, Les Traités de Paix et les Droits Privés des Neutres (Lausanne, 1924).
G. Sauser-Hall, L'occupation de guerre et les droits privés, Schweiz. Jahrb. für intern. R. 1944, 58.
R. Savatier, La liquidation des sociétés russes en France, Travaux 1934, 130, 1935, 11.
R. Savatier, Le sort des biens des anciennes sociétés Russes en France, R.C.D.I.P. 1935, 663.
R. Savatier, Les nationalisations en droit international privé, Travaux 1946/47 et 1947/48, 47.
G. Scelle, La guerre civile espagnole et le droit des gens, Revue générale de droit international public 1938, 265.
H. E. Scheffer, Het Mexicaansche Petroleum-Conflict, De volkenbond 1938/39, 10.
J. Scheftel, Des effects des décrets de nationalisation sur les sociétés russes ayant conservé des biens à l'étranger, Clunet 1931, 565, 953.
J. Scheftel, La reconnaissance internationale du Gouvernement Soviétique et ses répercussions sur la jurisprudence américaine, Clunet 1938, 453.
K. Schilling, Die Behandlung vorrevolutionärer russischer Rechtsverhältnisse vor deutschen Gerichten, Z.f. intern. R. 1932, 342.
D. Schindler, Besitzen konfiskatorische Gesetze auszerterritoriale Wirkung, Schweiz. Jahrb. für intern. R. 1946, 65.
C. M. Schmitthoff, A Textbook of the English Conflict of Laws (2nd ed. London, 1948).
A. F. Schnitzer, Handbuch des internationalen Privatrechts (3rd ed. Basel, 1950).
Dr Schöndorf, Was ist heute unter "russischem" Rechts zu verstehen?, D.J.Z. 1920, 305.
K. G. Seeliger, Das ausländische Privateigentum in der Schweiz (Munich, 1949).
I. Seidl-Hohenveldern, Extra-territorial Effects of Confiscations and Expropriations, Intern. Bar Association, Sec. Confer. The Hague, 1948, vol. 21.
I. Seidl-Hohenveldern, Zur Abwehr ausländischer Konfiskationsmasz-

nahmen gegen das Inlandsvermögen ausländischer Gesellschaften, J.Bl. 1949, 515.
I. SEIDL-HOHENVELDERN, Extra-territorial Effects of Confiscations and Expropriations, Modern L. R. 1950, 69.
I. SEIDL-HOHENVELDERN, Extra-territorial Effects of Confiscations and Expropriations, 49 Michigan L.R. (1950–1951), 851.
I. SEIDL-HOHENVELDERN, Getarnte extra-territoriale Konfiskationsansprüche, J.Bl. 1952, 410.
I. SEIDL-HOHENVELDERN, Internationales Konfiskations- und Enteignungsrecht (Berlin-Tübingen, 1952).
I. SEIDL-HOHENVELDERN, Völkerrechtswidrige staatliche Eigentumseingriffe und deren Folgen, Die Friedenswarte 1955, 1.
R. SERICK, Zur Enteignung juristischer Personen in der Sowjetischen Besatzungszone Deutschlands, Z.A.I.P. 1955, 86.
B. E. SHATZKY, La défense des intèrêts privés russes devant les tribunaux américains, Clunet 1929, 951.
H. SHAWCROSS, Some Problems of Nationalisation in International Law, Intern. Bar Association, Fifth Confer. Monaco, 1954.
P. SHEPARD, Sovereignty and State-owned commercial entities (New York, 1951).
A. SOLLOGOUB, La nationalisation des banques en Russie et ses effets à l'étranger (Paris, 1939).
J. SPIROPOULOS, Die de facto-Regierung im Völkerrecht (Kiel, 1926).
H. H. STENEKER, Activa van buitenlandse rechtspersonen in de staat New York, N.J.B. 1949, 864.
P. STIERLIN, Die Rechtsstellung der nichtanerkannten Regierung im Völkerrecht (Zürich, 1940).
H. E. STILLE, Die Rechtsstellung der de fakto-Regierung in der englischen und amerikanischen Rechtsprechung (Berlin, 1932).
P. STOFFELS, Vijandelijk Vermogen en Volkenrecht, N.J.B. 1949, 377, 393.
P. TAGER, Die französische Rechtsprechung in russischen Angelegenheiten Z.f.O. 1933, 395.
B. TRACHTENBERG, La situation légale des sociétés russes en France, Clunet 1926, 572.
B. TRACHTENBERG, Les biens des sociétés russes en France, Revue Darras 1927, 561.
R. D. ULRICH, Refugee Government Property Conservation Decrees in the Courts of the United States, Michigan L. R. 1942/43, 706.
A. VERDROSZ, Zur Konfiskation ausländischen Privateigentums nach Friedensvölkerrecht, Z.f. öff. R. 1925, 321.
CH. DE VISSCHER, Les gouvernements étrangers en justice. Reconnaissance internationale et immunités, Revue de dr. int. et de lég. comp. 1922, 149, 300.
H. DE WEINDEL, Histoire des Soviets (Paris, 1922).
A. WEISZ-TESBACH, Zur extra-territorialen Wirkung von ausländischen Verstaatlichungsmasznahmen, J.Bl. 1948, 352.
S. WIERZBOWSKI, Die Liquidation des in Polen befindlichen Vermögens der ehemaligen russischen juristischen Personen, Z.f.O. 1928, 1097.
P. WOHL, Die Nationalisierung der Bankaktiengesellschaften in Sovetruszland und ihre Rechtswirkung im Ausland, Ostrecht 1925, 26.
P. WOHL, Das rechtliche Schicksal der Aktiengesellschaften alten russischen Rechts im Ausland, Zeitschrift f. intern. R. 1928, 244.
M. M. WOLFF, Die neueste Wendung der englischen Gerichtspraxis in der Frage der nationalisierten russischen Banken, Z.f.O. 1933, 411.
M. M. WOLFF, Probleme der Liquidierung russischer Aktiengesellschaften in England, Z.f.O. 1933, 723.
M. WOLFF, Private International Law (2nd ed. Oxford, 1950).
M. WOLFF, Das internationale Privatrecht Deutschlands (Berlin-Göttingen-Heidelberg, 1954).

L. H. WOOLSEY, The Expropriation of oil properties by Mexico, A. J. I.L. 1938, 519.
L. H. WOOLSEY, Nazi Laws in United States Courts, A.J.I.L. 1950, 129.
B. A. WORTLEY, The Dissolution of Foreign Corporations, Brit. Yearb. 1933, 1.
B. A. WORTLEY, Problèmes soulevés en droit international privé par la législation sur l'expropriation, Rec. des Cours 1939, I, 345.
B. A. WORTLEY, Expropriation in International Law, Transactions 1947, 25.
B. A. WORTLEY, The general principles of private international law from the English standpoint, Rec. des Cours 1947, II, 5.
L. ZAITZEFF, Die Rechtswirkung im Auslande der unentgeltlichen Nationalisierung von Handelsgesellschaften in Sovetruszland, Europabuch der Rechtsanwälte und Notare 1926, 821 (Summary in Clunet 1927, 262).
A. ZEEGERS, Socialisatie (Amsterdam, 1948).
K. ZWEIGERT, Französische Urteile zu Ergnissen des Spanien-Krieges, Z.A.I.P. 1937, 939.

* * *

Mexico: Expropriation of Foreign-owned Oil Properties (ed. Standard Oil, 1938).
Nederlandsch Recht in Oorlogstijd (London, 1945).
De Rechtsgedingen tussen de Ambonnezen en de K.P.M., Part I (The Hague, 1951), opinions of A. J. P. Tammes, J. H. W. Verzijl and G. H. J. van der Molen.
Russische Verträge im englischen Recht, Z.f.O. 1929, 1160.
Should Judicial Respect be accorded to Nazi Acts of State?, note Col. L. R. 1947, 1061.
Effects of Soviet Recognition upon Russian Confiscatory Decrees, note Yale L. J. 1941/42, 848.
"Act of State" Immunity, note Yale L.J. 1947/48, 108.

TABLE OF CASES

Page numbers are printed in italics

ADEN

ARGENTINA

AUSTRIA

BELGIUM

GEORGIA

GERMANY

GREAT BRITAIN

IRELAND

ITALY

JAPAN

LITHUANIA

THE NETHERLANDS

NORWAY

POLAND

RUMANIA

RUSSIA

SWEDEN

SWITZERLAND

TUNIS

Rey c. Lecouturier, Trib. civil of Tunis 11-5-1907, S. 1908.2.115 (*45, 78, 89*)

U.S.A.

Ambrose Light, The, (1885) 25 F. 408, Hudson, 132 (*31*)
American Banana Co. v. United Fruit Co., 213 U.S. 347 (1909) (*65, 129, 131, 137*)
Amstelbank N.V. v. Guaranty Trust Cy. of New York, Ann. Dig. 1941–1942, 584 (*80*)
Anderson v. N.V. Transandine Handelmaatschappij, Ann. Dig. 1941–1942, 10 (*161, 162*)
Anninger v. Hohenberg, Ann. Dig. 1938–1940, 19 (*88*)
Augstein v. Banska a Hutni Akciova Spolecnost, A.J.I.L. 1954, 513 (*88*)
Baglin v. Cusenier, Circuit Court of New York, Revue Darras 1907, 972, Supreme Court 221 U.S. 580 (1911) (*45, 86*)
Baldy v. Hunter, 171 U.S. 388 (1897) (*31*)
Banco de España v. Federal Reserve Bank, Ann. Dig. 1938–1940, 12 (*68, 131, 139*)
Banque de France v. Equitable Trust Co. of New York, Banque de France v. Chase National Bank, Ann. Dig. 1929–1930, 43 (*32, 68*)
Bernstein v. Ned.-Amerikaanse Stoomvaart My, Ann. Dig. 1948, 20 (*69*)
Bernstein v. Van Heyghen Frères S.A., Ann. Dig. 1947, 11 (*68, 133, 139*)
Birnbaum v. Irving Trust and Amsterdamsche Liquidatiekas, N.Y.L.J. 14-8-1943, 315, col. 2 (*163*)
Blak's Estate, *In Re*, 65 Cal. app. 2d 232, 150 Pac. 2d 567 (1944) (*163*)
Bloch v. Basler Lebensversicherungs-Gesellschaft, 73 N.Y.S. (2d) 523, extract in A.J.I.L. 1948, 502 (*49, 144*)
Bollack v. Société Générale ..., Ann. Dig. 1941–1942, 147 (*84, 89, 96*)
Boris N. Sokoloff v. National City Bank of New York, Supreme Court of New York, Clunet 1925, 443, New York Court of Appeals, Ann. Dig. 1923–1924, 44, 37 A.L.R. 712 (*31, 80, 112*)
Cia Minera Ygnacio Rodriguez Ramos S.A. v. Bartlesville Zinc Co. et al., Ann. Dig. 1925–1926, 67 (*67, 130*)
Clark v. United States, (1811) 3 Wash. C.C. 101 (*30*)
Consul of Spain v. La Conception, (1819) Fed. Cas. No. 3137, 2 Wheel. Cr. Case (1819), 597 (*31*)
Denny, The, Ann. Dig. 1941–1942, 80 (*32*)
Dougherty v. Equitable Life Assurance Society, Ann. Dig. 1933–1934, 67 (*49, 142*)
Düstervald v. Lädwig, N.Y.L.J. 15-1-1942, 215, col. 2 (*163*)
Eastern States Petroleum Co. v. Asiatic Petroleum Corp. et Al., 139 A.L.R. 1211, Ann. Dig. 1938–1940, 90 (*68, 131*)
Ervin v. Quintanilla, Ann. Dig. 1938–1940, 219 (*40*)
Fields v. Predionica I Tkanica, Ann. Dig. 1941–1942, 204, 208 (*40*)
Fred. S. James & Co. v. Rossia Insurance Cy. of America, Clunet 1928, 789 (*80, 112, 119*)
Fred. S. James & Co v. Second Russian Insurance Cy, Ann. Dig. 1925–1926, 57 (*32, 80, 112*)
Frenkel & Co v. L'Urbaine Fire Insurance Co. of Paris, 65 A.L.R. 1490 (*157*)
Gelston v. Hoyt, (1818) 3 Wheat. 246 (*30*)
Grünbaum v. Lissauer, 57 N.Y.S. 2d 137 (1945), affirmed 61 N.Y.S. 2d 372 (1946) (*163*)
Grünbaum v. N.V. Oxyde Maatschappij voor Ertsen en Metalen, N.Y.L.J. 27-8-1941, 439, Col. 7 (*163*)

INDEX

STELLINGEN

I.

Confiscatie is te beschouwen als territoriaal, indien de confisquerende staat de confiscatie met eigen middelen op eigen territoir uitvoert; als extra-territoriale confiscatie is te beschouwen de confiscatie die een staat beoogt uit te strekken over eigendom, dat niet met eigen middelen op eigen territoir, doch slechts met behulp van een vreemd staatsapparaat in de macht van de confisquerende staat is te brengen.

II.

Afwijzing van het met een elders verrichte territoriale confiscatie beoogde gevolg, nl. eigendomsovergang aan de confisquerende staat, behoort in beginsel met een beroep op de openbare orde mogelijk te zijn.

III.

Pretenties van extra-territoriale confiscatiemaatregelen behoren te worden afgewezen, echter niet op grond van de openbare orde.

IV.

Het arrest van de Hoge Raad van 7 Februari 1941 (Ned. Jurisprudentie 1941, No. 923) inzake El Aguila tegen Petroservice, waarbij de Hoge Raad enerzijds overwoog, dat een eventuele dwaling van de lagere rechter in de toepassing van ongeschreven beginselen van volkenrecht niet tot cassatie kan leiden, doch anderzijds uitsprak, dat in de gegeven omstandigheden geen beroep op de Nederlandse openbare orde kon worden gedaan, hinkt op twee gedachten.

V.

Indien op grond van het in een staat geldende internationaal privaatrecht een bepaalde casus verwijst naar het recht van een vreemde staat, behoort het antwoord op de vraag of het recht van die vreemde staat toepassing kan vinden te worden gegeven onafhankelijk van het feit, dat de vreemde staat of zijn regering eventueel niet erkend is door eerstgenoemde staat.

VI.

Van beschikken over het wettelijk erfdeel in de zin van artikel 960 Burgerlijk Wetboek is geen sprake, indien een erflater heeft bepaald, dat dit erfdeel zal vallen buiten de algehele gemeenschap van goederen waarin de legitimaris gehuwd is.

VII.

Voor de stelling, dat het Nederlandse recht de schuldoverneming kent — zoals aangegeven b.v. door Prof. Mr. A. Pitlo, Het verbintenissenrecht naar het Nederlandse Burgerlijk Wetboek, 4e druk, blz. 289 e.v. — kan geen beroep worden gedaan op de artikelen 34 en volgende van de Wet op het Levensverzekeringbedrijf (1922, S. 716).

VIII.

De overeenkomst van levensverzekering is een eenzijdige overeenkomst, die het vereiste van belang noch dat van schade als essentiale kent.

IX.

Het in overeenkomsten van levensverzekering gebruikelijk beding, dat bij overlijden tengevolge van zelfmoord binnen b.v. twee jaren na het tot stand komen der overeenkomst gepleegd, geen uitkering van het verzekerde bedrag verschuldigd is, verdient uit een oogpunt van bedrijfsbeleid geen aanbeveling.

X.

Terecht verklaart het ontwerp Wet op stichtingen zijn bepalingen niet van toepassing op zg. overheidsstichtingen; het is echter gewenst, dat omtrent deze lichamen afzonderlijke regelen worden gesteld, die onder meer dienen te bepalen dat de naam van zodanig lichaam niet het woord stichting bevat.

XI.

Voor het optreden als rechtspersoon van een vereniging, resp. een naamloze vennootschap behoort niet de eis te worden gesteld van Koninklijke goedkeuring, resp. Ministeriële verklaring van geen bezwaar; wordt deze eis niettemin gehandhaafd, dan dient bij weigering de mogelijkheid van beroep te bestaan.

XII.

De ten gunste van de doodstraf aangevoerde argumenten, met name ook die ontleend aan de Bijbel, zijn niet overtuigend.

XIII.

De mogelijkheid tot een veilige vlucht doet een beroep op noodweer vervallen.

XIV.

Schenking van een lijfrente heeft geen heffing van inkomstenbelasting ten laste van de schenker ten gevolge.

XV.

De regeling van artikel 84 iuncto artikel 86 der Successiewet, op grond waarvan de in algehele gemeenschap van goederen gehuwde vrouw die ten gevolge van het overlijden van haar echtgenoot een bedrag uit levensverzekering verkrijgt, successierecht verschuldigd is over de waarde van het verkregene verminderd met de helft van de som der premiën betaald tijdens het bestaan der gemeenschap, is onbillijk en onlogisch.

XVI.

De Wet Assurantiebemiddeling miskent de aard en het wezen van de functie van tussenpersoon, althans ten aanzien van hem die bemiddelt op het gebied van levensverzekeringen.

XVII.

Het behoud van Amsterdams oude stadskern dient met kracht te worden bevorderd.

GPSR Compliance

The European Union's (EU) General Product Safety Regulation (GPSR) is a set of rules that requires consumer products to be safe and our obligations to ensure this.

If you have any concerns about our products, you can contact us on ProductSafety@springernature.com

In case Publisher is established outside the EU, the EU authorized representative is:

Springer Nature Customer Service Center GmbH
Europaplatz 3
69115 Heidelberg, Germany

Batch number: 10830943

Printed by Printforce, the Netherlands